ACTAS

DEL II CONGRESO INTERNACIONAL SOBRE MACROCRIMINALIDAD

«EL DESASTRE "LENTO" DE LA EXPOSICIÓN AL AMIANTO DE LAS PERSONAS Y EL MEDIOAMBIENTE»

---

7 Y 8 DE MAYO DE 2024
UNIVERSIDAD PABLO DE OLAVIDE

GI³CRIM
Grupo Interuniversitario e Interdisciplinario de Investigaciones sobre la Criminalidad (PAIDI SEJ678)

mc macro crimes
Centro studi giuridici europei sulla grande criminalità
Dipartimento di Giurisprudenza Università degli Studi di Ferrara

UNIVERSIDAD PABLO DE OLAVIDE SEVILLA

© Editorial Colex, S.L.
Calle Costa Rica, número 5, 3.º B (local comercial)
A Coruña, C.P. 15004
info@colex.es
www.colex.es

I.S.B.N.: 978-84-1194-822-7
Depósito legal: C 1954-2024

ACTAS
DEL II CONGRESO INTERNACIONAL SOBRE MACROCRIMINALIDAD

«EL DESASTRE "LENTO" DE LA EXPOSICIÓN AL AMIANTO DE LAS PERSONAS Y EL MEDIOAMBIENTE»

DIRECCIÓN ACADÉMICA

Pastora García Álvarez
GI³CRIM, Universidad Pablo de Olavide.

Donato Castronuovo
Centro Macrocrimes, Università di Ferrara.

COORDINACIÓN ACADÉMICA

Víctor M. Macías Caro
GI³CRIM, Universidad Pablo de Olavide.

COORDINACIÓN DE ORGANIZACIÓN

Marta Rodríguez Ramos
GI³CRIM, Universidad Pablo de Olavide.

Carmen Fernández Nicasio
GI³CRIM, Universidad Pablo de Olavide.

COLEX 2024

Sumario

PRESENTACIÓN

Antonia Jiménez Rodríguez
Vicerrectora de Investigación,
Transferencia y Doctorado.
Universidad Pablo de Olavide

Buenos días.

Es un honor dar la bienvenida al Congreso Internacional sobre Macrocriminalidad «El desastre lento de la exposición al amianto de las personas y el medio ambiente». Es un placer para mí estar aquí hoy y compartir mesa con don CÉSAR HORNERO, compañero, amigo y, además, decano de la Facultad de Derecho, y con la investigadora de nuestra Universidad PASTORA GARCÍA ÁLVAREZ, organizadora de este Congreso junto a DONATO CASTRONUOVO, investigador de la Universidad de Ferrara, y a otras personas más a las que también quiero agradecer que hoy estemos aquí sentados, como son VÍCTOR M. MACÍAS CARO, MARTA RODRÍGUEZ y CARMEN FERNÁNDEZ, que nos reúnen para abordar uno de los desafíos más apremiantes y complejos de nuestra sociedad contemporánea: el de la macrocriminalidad relacionada, en este caso, con la exposición al amianto.

Me gusta que en el título catalogáis este desastre como «lento», porque nos recuerda que la criminalidad puede manifestarse de manera sutil, extendiéndose a lo largo del tiempo e incluso a lo largo de las generaciones, con lo cual me parece que es un Congreso muy importante y una temática que había que abordar. Para comenzar con esta inauguración quiero pasar la palabra, en primer lugar, a don CÉSAR HONERO, decano de la Facultad de Derecho, para que nos introduzca un poco en esta temática.

César Hornero Méndez
Decano de la Facultad de Derecho.
Universidad Pablo de Olavide

Buenos días. Muchas gracias a la vicerrectora, querida Antonia.

Yo me dedico al Derecho civil, no me ocupo precisamente de estas materias, pero lo primero que tengo que hacer es felicitarlos a los organizadores porque es una cuestión que incide indudablemente sobre la realidad. Vivimos en un mundo del riesgo y de peligros sordos que parece que nos acechan y por eso, como decía muy bien la vicerrectora, está muy bien elegido el título de este Congreso. Además, trata una materia que no hace mucho tiempo afectó a una zona relativamente cercana, una fábrica muy conocida en Sevilla en la que se utilizaba indiscriminadamente la uralita como material de construcción. Por tanto, felicitar a los a los organizadores: nuestra compañera, la profesora García Álvarez; también al profesor Macías Caro, que me consta que ha hecho una labor importante en la organización de este Congreso; y al profesor Castronuovo, al que damos la bienvenida y, en su nombre, a todos los profesores que vienen de fuera y que conforman este programa tan interesante y atractivo. Por supuesto, a las coordinadoras, que llevan también el trabajo que hay detrás de un Congreso como este, con muchas horas de trabajo y con la implicación de muchas personas. Solamente el haberlo organizado es un éxito; a partir de aquí, lo único que hay que recoger son más éxitos.

Los felicito y, también, les agradezco que se celebre en nuestra Universidad y en nuestra Facultad. Desde esta última hemos contribuido, como no podía ser de otro modo, a la realización de un Congreso de estas características que, además, tiene la virtualidad de afrontar, como decía al principio, una cuestión que es real. Con esto hago una reivindicación del trabajo que hacemos en la Universidad porque, muchas veces, se nos acusa de estar en el cielo de los conceptos, como decía el clásico, y dedicándonos a cuestiones cuya proyección en la realidad y cuya materialización es, a veces, discutible. Soy de los convencidos de que en la Universidad estamos para estudiar muchas cosas que parecen inútiles (el conocimiento puede parecer inútil, no corren buenos tiempos para este planteamiento), pero desde luego donde eso no se puede reprochar nunca es en una cuestión como esto que, además, incide sobre esos peligros que acechan al hombre contemporáneo. Muchas veces no sabemos que vivimos rodeados del mundo, pensamos que hemos alcanzado cierta perfección tecnológica, pero vivimos rodeados de peligros como este del amianto.

No quiero cansarlos más. Solo darles la bienvenida a la ciudad, que la disfruten, aunque el programa, por lo que veo, es bastante intenso. Me imagino que los organizadores, ya que han preparado tan bien el evento, habrán previsto también esos momentos que les van a permitir disfrutar de Sevilla. Nada más, les deseo un buen Congreso, que sea de provecho, como estoy seguro de que así será, y nos tienen a su disposición en la Facultad. Muchas gracias.

Pastora García Álvarez
Codirectora del Congreso.
Universidad Pablo de Olavide, GI³CRIM

Buenos días a todos.

En primer lugar, quiero agradecer a la señora Vicerrectora de Investigación, Transferencia y Doctorado, así como al señor Decano de la Facultad de Derecho, su presencia en este acto de inauguración y sus amables palabras.

En segundo lugar, agradecer a todas las entidades que han hecho posible la celebración de este Congreso. A la Universidad Pablo de Olavide, por su «Ayuda al desarrollo de una línea de investigación propia»; a la Facultad de Derecho, por su Ayuda a la organización de actividades académicas; así como al Grupo Interuniversitario e Interdisciplinario de Investigaciones sobre la Criminalidad (GI³CRIM) de la Universidad Pablo de Olavide; al Centro de Estudios Jurídicos Europeos sobre Macrocrímenes de la Universidad de Ferrara; al Departamento de Derecho de esta misma Universidad; a la Universidad de Milán-Bicocca y a la Universidad de Brescia. Gracias a ellas ha sido posible la organización de este evento, continuando la línea que nos marcamos algunos de los presentes (el profesor DONATO, codirector de este Congreso, VÍCTOR M. MACÍAS CARO y otros compañeros del Grupo de Investigación del que soy responsable) con la Fundación de la Disaster & Criminality Network como punto de encuentro para poner en marcha proyectos en común.

Este II Congreso sobre Macrocriminalidad se centra específicamente en el desastre lento que la exposición al amianto supone tanto para la salud de las personas como para el medio ambiente. El amianto, o asbesto, es el nombre que recibe un grupo de minerales metamórficos fibrosos compuestos por silicatos (de magnesio, cobre o hierro). Su característica principal es la presencia de fibras largas y perdurables, lo que lo convierte en un material suficientemente flexible como para poder ser trabajado con comodidad y lo bastante resistente para soportar altas temperaturas. Estas cualidades lo convirtieron, en la segunda mitad del siglo XX, en el material estrella en el campo de la construcción, en la fabricación de tuberías, de tubos de extracción de humos y depósitos de agua. El problema es que no era una sustancia inocua y, aunque había sospechas con anterioridad, no sería hasta 1977 cuando la OMS, tras los pertinentes análisis, procedió, por fin, a catalogarlo como producto cancerígeno. Un par de años más tarde, el Parlamento Europeo acordó que debía prohibirse su uso en todos los países de la entonces Comunidad Económica Europea. Sin embargo y a pesar de ello, todavía en el año 2019 dos terceras partes de la humanidad seguía estando sometida al amianto. De hecho, podemos encontrar datos estadísticos que afirmaban en 2021 que en Europa morían al año más de 80.000 personas por la exposición a este material. Es más, su inhalación o ingestión supone un riesgo no solo para las personas, sino también para los animales, el agua y el medio ambiente, por lo que la retirada de este material —que también ha de realizarse de una determinada manera— resulta fundamental. La gravedad e importancia de esta problemática es, pues, evidente.

Durante los dos días de duración de este Congreso esta temática va a ser abordada desde un punto de vista interdisciplinar e internacional. La internacionalidad es máxima: esta tarde, la conferencia invitada será impartida por BARRY CASTLEMAN, consultor ambientalista que ha intervenido en importantes casos de contaminación por amianto; y toda la mañana del miércoles estará dedicada a la experiencia italiana sobre la problemática generada por este material. Por supuesto, abordaremos también la realidad en nuestro país, todo ello desde un punto de vista multidisciplinar: medioambiental, penal, criminológico, laboral..., sin olvidar, por supuesto, a los afectados. Tendremos así dos sesiones en las que se abordará la perspectiva de las víctimas, para lo que contamos con la presencia del presidente de la Federación Española de Asociaciones y Colectivos de Víctimas del Amianto.

Con esta breve panorámica sobre la temática y la forma en la que va a ser abordada, termino mi presentación, agradeciendo una vez más a las autoridades, a los especialistas en las distintas materias, a mis compañeros del Grupo Interuniversitario e Interdisciplinario de Investigaciones sobre Criminalidad, muy especialmente a VÍCTOR M. MACÍAS CARO, auténtico promotor de esta iniciativa, que la ha hecho posible con su trabajo y tesón. Asimismo, trasladar mi agradecimiento al Centro de Estudios Jurídicos Europeos sobre Macrocriminalidad de la Universidad de Ferrara, y a su director, el profesor DONATO CASTRONUOVO. Por último, a todos los asistentes, los verdaderos protagonistas en cuanto que a ellos va dirigido, en última instancia, este Congreso. Muchas gracias a todos. Cedo la palabra al profesor Donato.

Donato Castronuovo
Codirector del Congreso.
Università degli Studi di Ferrara

Muchas gracias. Solo quiero traer el saludo del Centro Macrocrimes y agradecer la perseverancia de los amigos de la Universidad Pablo de Olavide, en particular, de la profesora PASTORA GARCÍA y del profesor VÍCTOR M. MACÍAS CARO.

Hemos llegado a las segundas jornadas, tras las del año pasado sobre los desastres en general, celebradas también aquí en la UPO, coorganizadas por el Grupo Interuniversitario e Interdisciplinario de Investigaciones sobre la Criminalidad y por Macrocrimes en el marco de esta red espontánea de investigación en torno a los desastres, constituida gracias al impulso decisivo del mismo Víctor. Una vez más conseguimos dotar el encuentro de su necesario doble carácter; es decir, multidisciplinar e internacional, como sin duda requieren estos temas. El Congreso está magníficamente introducido por las palabras de Pastora. Nada más, solo un buen Congreso a todos.

Antonia Jiménez Rodríguez
Vicerrectora de Investigación, Transferencia y Doctorado.
Universidad Pablo de Olavide

Muchísimas gracias.

Como antes apuntaba Pastora, este Congreso deriva de la investigación que hace el Grupo Interuniversitario e Interdisciplinario de Investigaciones sobre la Criminalidad aquí en nuestra Universidad. En este caso, este grupo aborda desde la perspectiva del Derecho penal y se enfrenta a la pregunta de cómo responsabilizar aquello que, por acción u omisión, pueda haber contribuido a este desastre ambiental y haya puesto en peligro la salud y la vida de las personas. Pero este Congreso, como también apuntaba antes el compañero, no solo se centra en el ámbito del Derecho penal, sino que busca explorar la intersección de esta problemática con otras disciplinas, porque la exposición al amianto no solo plantea desafíos legales, sino que también tiene implicaciones, por ejemplo, en el área de la salud pública y la medicina, la ingeniería, y en un aspecto que me parece muy interesante: la política ambiental y la justicia social.

La medicina y la salud pública son la parte en la que se investiga y se identifican los contaminantes químicos y los contaminantes ambientales a los que estamos expuestos en continuo (hoy en día casi nadie lleva productos naturales, casi todos vamos vestidos de petróleo, fundamentalmente). Estos grupos estudian cómo llegan estos compuestos al organismo y cómo se pueden evitar o mitigar estos impactos. Por su parte, la ingeniería busca desarrollar alternativas seguras, en este caso, al amianto y mejorar los métodos para remediar los daños ambientales y minimizar su propagación. Pero, como comentaba, lo que me parece fundamental es la aplicación de políticas ambientales sólidas para proteger a las comunidades de futuros desastres y para abordar las desigualdades sociales que, a menudo, hacen que ciertos grupos sean más vulnerables que otros a la exposición de tóxicos y, en este caso concreto, a la exposición del amianto.

En este sentido, más allá de la aplicación de la ley debemos considerar cómo prevenir futuros casos de macrocriminalidad. A finales del año 2023 se publicó en prensa una investigación del doctor Nicolás Olea, director científico del Instituto de Investigación Biosanitarias de Granada y catedrático de Radiología, mostrando datos que apuntan a que, por ejemplo, el bisfenol, que recubre el interior plástico de las latas de conserva, es cancerígeno y provoca enfermedades coronarias. El doctor ha pedido que se elimine ese tóxico porque hay muchas personas que lo consumen a diario sin darse cuenta. También estaba en los biberones de los niños, donde se dejó de utilizar, pero en este caso la Unión Europea ha decidido pensárselo y dar un tiempo de margen para ampliar este uso. Como este ejemplo podríamos poner muchísimos otros.

Creo que este Congreso representa un esfuerzo multidisciplinario para comprender y abordar la macrocriminalidad asociada con la exposición al amianto desde diversas perspectivas, y estoy segura de que las discusiones y colaboraciones que surjan aquí van a ayudar a avanzar hacia soluciones efectivas y justas para esta crisis global. Por lo tanto, bienvenidos a este importante evento, que queda inaugurado, y, a todas las personas que no conocéis Sevilla, que disfrutéis de una ciudad que es bastante bonita ahora a pesar de que se acerca el verano y aumentan rápidamente las temperaturas. Muchísimas gracias.

CONFERENCIA INAUGURAL

"ASBESTOS: FORCES AND COUNTERFORCES"

Yvonne Waterman
European Asbestos Forum

Welcome everyone. It's an honour to be invited to give the inaugural presentation. I would like to thank the organisation very much, also Victor, for being such a pleasant correspondent and a kind host. I'm just loving this, to be honest.

I'm very happy, in particular, to see many students here. All of you are important because in your careers you will be confronted with asbestos time and time again; you'll be making the policy; you'll be seeing that the policy is properly executed; you'll be saving people from horrible diseases. That is a crude way of putting it, but that is really what it comes down to. Your futures are going to be a future for other people, so I am absolutely delighted that all of you are interested in this. And I would like to invite you to connect with me on LinkedIn and then we can message each other. You are always welcome anytime, as often as you like, to ask me any questions on asbestos. I am well informed, that is quite true, but I do not profess to know everything, and I have an exceedingly large global asbestos network, so If I can't answer your question myself, I'll be sure to know somebody who will and connect because it takes all of us.

Asbestos is a hugely wide, diverse topic. It pervades all aspects of society, and it really is a much bigger problem in many ways than people realise.

I will tell you a little anecdote when I was a student back in the 90s. That was the first time that asbestos became a topic in the Netherlands and my professor at the time, the national professor for liability issues, he reprimanded me for my interest in asbestos. He said something that at the time I found very crude and to this day I still find very crude, but I will quote him exactly because his words are seared in my memory, he said: "Yvonne, your interest in asbestos is misplaced. Those people will die. That is very sad. And then where will you be?" I just thought: "How can you be the top professor in liability law and not understand the size of this problem?", and I asked, and this grasp qualified me as a difficult student, regretfully: "But, professor, those ceiling plates above there [this was an old building], there is asbestos isolation there? If you look out the window, you see the bicycle shed, all of that is asbestos. If you look around your window, the putting that is keeping it to the wall, there is asbestos there. If you walk to the hallway to the kitchen, there's a fire door, there's asbestos in that. If you go to the kitchen and you see the linoleum floor, that is classic asbestos flooring. We are surrounded by asbestos and I'm just a student. I'm probably missing 9 out of 10 applications, but I can tell you that in this building alone, on this floor, there is asbestos everywhere. We are being exposed to it as workers. When it will be removed, there will be asbestos removal workers being exposed to it. When it is transported, there will be a problem. When the building will eventually be demolished, all the dust everywhere. And the remains, the asbestos will likely be brought to landfill or thrown into a ditch and be a problem there. Even if it's crossed to landfill, it will be a problem for the environment forever because asbestos doesn't decay. This is not going away, and this is everywhere. I've been looking at factories with entirely new eyes and seeing all these pipes transporting hot temperature and chemicals, you name it, all of them are isolated with asbestos. If you look at a regular factory, there's asbestos everywhere. The boilers in this room, downstairs, they contain asbestos." But he said: "Yeah, well, we're about to ban it or we had just banned it, so the problem is gone."

No, no, no. The ban is as best just the start. It's a legacy. It's still all around us. And until it is removed, people will be exposed, and this will go on and on and on. There is not one group that will eventually die out. And he still didn't understand it, and at that point, I thought: "I've given it my best." And yeah, the relationship was never the same after that.

But cutting back to the presentation itself, I have been asked to give you basically a sort of 101 course on asbestos and explain to you the very basics that you need to know for your future and to explain to your families and colleagues, and I would encourage you to share what you learn here at the conference. So basically, to set you up for the whole conference. What is it asbestos?

Basically, I wear two hats. In everyday life I am Waterman legal consultancy. It's a one woman legal firm that specialises on asbestos, particularly from the tort aspect. Any kind of liability, be it direct liability, or product liability, or criminal liability, or personal injury liability, when it comes to asbestos then I'm very interested in this, and the amazing thing is nobody seems to share this. It's only reasonably that other law firms are thinking, hey, he's on to something. But I have the global playing field, honestly. In the course of this year alone, I'll probably go to about, well, I think just over a dozen different asbestos conferences from Philadelphia to Australia and from Oslo to possibly South America, now Colombia. So that's what I do in everyday life.

I also have a European Asbestos Forum Foundation. I'm the proud founder of that, I have to say. The reason for founding it is that I saw that there were very many conferences everywhere that I had attended. For instance, for victims by victims, for insurers by insurers, for asbestos removers by asbestos removers, and so on. And, basically, they were just finishing the budget every single year in order to have the money to do exactly the same the next year. And I thought this is a crying shame because I hear at every conference: "Oh, we have a problem. We are looking for solutions."

And, having been to very many different conferences all over the world, I thought I've been telling them they need to call him and I'll introduce you to someone, so I have to formalise this and teach people that they need to network because there are solutions out there. Everybody all over the world has the same problem with the asbestos legacy. So that is indeed why I'm encouraging you, particularly youth connect with me and I'll hook you up with whoever you like and that is a problem that is solid 20-30 years from now. It's specifically for asbestos professionals, but I also always include asbestos victims and asbestos victim organisations and this year we will have our 7th global conference, 12th and 13th of December, in Brussels. Last year, there were 26 countries represented there from six continents, and I hope for some more.

So talking about asbestos and you can see there, it's a mineral silica base very common, it's found in many countries all over the world, Scandinavian countries, Greece, Italy, Turkey, India, Indonesia, Canada, United States, Australia, Brazil, Colombia, you name it, it's actually a fairly normal mineral. It's usually divided into two types: the curly fibres which are called Serpentine, and that's just one type of classified asbestos fibre. It's called chrysotile. Chrysotile is also called just commonly light asbestos. Please be aware chrysotile is not actually light. There is nothing white and wonderful and clean about it. It's Just a name. Then we have the other group, the empty balls. They are somewhat more beta fibres. The European Union has recognised five of these, being the five that are the most commercially used. And these are crocidolite, amosite, apophyllite, tremolite and actinolite.

Usually in many products where asbestos is incorporated, it's a mix of various kinds of asbestos. Even if you are being told: "oh, this is only chrysotile", I'll bet you anything that if you go to a proper certified experienced laboratory they will be able to find other kinds of asbestos in there as well.

The difference between chrysotile which is approximately 90% of what was used on the markets and the other ones is merely the speed with which they kill you. Brown and blue asbestos, for instance, can kill you in a matter of 15-20 years; chrysotile will take a bit longer. Please don't think that chrysotile is less dangerous than the other ones. That is only what the asbestos industry is trying to convince you of. All of these are seriously carcinogenic.

So, what is asbestos? That is actually a really difficult question. Only a matter of weeks ago, I was at a conference in Philadelphia with a whole group of specialists, geologists, mineralogists, chemical experts, doctors, lawyers, producers of different kinds of sand and natural materials and all of them were debating: "Can we find a common definition for asbestos?" And they couldn't. And the reason for that, of course, is either you include new things and then new producers have a problem or you exclude things and then you can say from a legal perspective that is not asbestos, but it still kills you. Please be aware that the EU recognises these

6 minerals commonly together as asbestos because they were the six most used commercially, but there are dozens and dozens of other minerals which we call asbestiform and they are just as carcinogenic.

So, do please be aware you have asbestos, the legal type and the not so legal type, but basically in every aspect the same effects.

Asbestos fibres are so small, they are invisible to the human eye and it actually takes about 100,000 fibres put lengthwise together to achieve the width of one human hair. That is why it is able to float around in the air. How many of you have heard that one asbestos fibre can kill you? Actually, that is a theory that is derived from International Association for Research on Cancer (IARC). In the 60s, they wrote a monograph on asbestos and said there is no safety limit for asbestos. So, in theory, one fibre could kill you. In actual daily life, that is not the case. I can tell you from what we know scientifically from the Dutch air: 1 cubic metre of Dutch air will typically contain about 30 asbestos fibres, which is rather low, much lower than has been in previous decades because we are removing asbestos roofs, a big source of asbestos, and that is reflected in the amount of fibres that we find in the air.

So here and now, where we are in this whole way, undoubtedly in this room, there will be asbestos. We are all of us, every living breath that we take, inhaling asbestos, to an amount that usually doesn't kill us.

Having said that, the asbestos industry will say: "Oh, you are only at risk at really heavy exceptional long-term exposure." And then I have to say: "Actually no, we know from the 60s already that one single exposure, for instance, demolishing a chicken coop for instance, something like that, could lead 30-35-40-45 years later to asbestos diseases.

So, while it is common in the air and it doesn't kill your average person, it is really something that you need to avoid when you can because it is a staggered risk. The more you are exposed, the bigger your chance of eventually getting a disease. And then on the other hand, nobody knows why one person will get an asbestos disease and the other ones not. Perhaps it has to do with smoking and if you want to take one message away from this event then I would say. apart from sharing. Always: The combination of asbestos and tobacco is really very hazardous. If you are working with people who work professionally with asbestos, please tell them stop smoking and that will really decrease your risk of getting ill.

So, the very basics: Carcinogenic, especially dangerous when disturbed, because then, the fibres are more released than otherwise. You can inhale them, which is the way that people always think about asbestos and actually over the past 15-20 years we are realising that there is a second way of getting asbestos diseases, because if they're in the air and on your tongue and you swallow them, then they go through the whole digestive tracts and cause problems there.

It has, I have to admit, beautiful qualities all combined in one mineral. It's perfectly isolating for heaps, for water, which is why we have it in our ropes. It's very sound isolating. It's acid resistant. It's particularly helpful in enforcing cement for all kinds of practical purposes and it's cheap. I mean, apart from the little thing that it can be fatal, what's not to like? I say this, of course, in a sarcastic way.

Asbestos diseases are fatal. All of them, and they cause unnecessary deaths. Remove the asbestos exposure and you will remove people dying from it. When you see this man here, cutting through asbestos roof. The amount of fibres will be in the millions in the 10s of millions. If he does this, even for a day, he might wake up 40 years later and think: "ah, I still have about 8-9 – 10 months to live." This is extremely dangerous, not just for himself, but for everybody around him as well.

So, the big six, as they are called, and these are the ones that are recognised legally by the European Union, and again, there are actually many more kinds of asbestiform minerals. We have Chrysler tile, which is 90% of what is used everywhere. Actinolite, crocidolite, the blue one. And you can really see that it is actually a matrix of rock with a vein of a fibrous material there. Strange thing is that asbestos and talc are mineralogically very closely associated, which is why, for instance, there are now scandals going on about asbestos and talc products, because if you have talc mine, then there will be events of asbestos running through that as well. And then it will get mixed up in the consumer products.

But you can see this is very easy to treat, to weave, to do all kinds of things with it. And now we have the other three, amosite, tremolite, and anthophyllite. Now, if you want to see more photos, then you should go to the website *asbestorama*, which is owned by my good friend Tony Rich. Every year he gives a beautiful photo exhibition at the EAF conference. And you are welcome to use those photos, but please at least give him his copyrights. If you want to use them for publications and the like, then just contact me and we'll arrange something. But *asbestorama* is a beautiful website for raising awareness and that's what it's there for. There is a natural beauty to asbestos. It's strange to say, but it can be beautiful as a mineral, as so many other minerals are.

So how do you get sick? While the common way as we think of it is inhalation. Basically, there is asbestos in the air, for instance because it is disturbed, you inhale it and you can get tongue cancer from it, mouth cancer, laryngeal cancer and all the way down into your lungs. The most common kind of asbestos disease is called mesothelioma. And that's basically refers to the outside lining of the lungs, and that gives the lungs a structure, hold them in place. And what happens is that the fibres that you inhale gets stuck into the individual lung cells, damaging them, causing infection that the person concerned really won't notice at all. Certainly, if he is a smoker and coughing sometimes anyway, he won't notice a difference at all. In the time of decades and, on average, the median average it's about 40 years, can be a bit shorter, can be a bit longer, but on average 40 years, this infection will turn into a tumour that will harden the outsides of the mesothelioma affects of the lungs. And it will really harden it to such an extent that a surgeon will need a cement saw to saw through it. Imagine that trying to breathe with lungs that have become so hard on the outside. And here you can see that there is a very big tumour here and, of course, they don't breathe at all. So, this person is already feeling very ill and commonly, once you are diagnosed with the most common asbestos diseases, particularly mesothelioma and asbestos related lung cancer, then you have a life expectancy of about 10 to 12 months.

So, more exposure means more risk and, remove asbestos, which I hope you will be doing in the future, will be removing the risk. Being aware of this is essential. Never ignore asbestos. There's also the other way of getting asbestos inside your body, and that is ingesting it, consumption. Eating something, swallowing it and it goes through the whole intestinal tract. And then people you know will say:

"Oh, I have intestinal cancer, I have colon cancer. Where did that come from do?" And you think: "what kind of work did you do 30 years ago, or 40 years ago?" "Oh, I was a labourer. I built houses." You were cutting through asbestos pipes and asbestos roofing and doing all that kind of work, and now you have colon cancer.

So, there is a list of asbestos related diseases and as our scientific understanding of it increases globally, there are continually more diseases added to this list. So, you have asbestosis, many people will say, "oh, well, that's harmless". Well, actually no. It's scarring of the lungs and eventually, it will kill you. You have mesothelioma, the big one. Asbestos related lung cancer. Always forgotten, but please, bear in mind, we think that for every mesothelioma victim caused by asbestos, there are 6 to 8 asbestos related lung cancers out there and they receive very little attention in society. They never go to court. People say, oh, there can be so many reasons why you get lung cancer, or you were a smoker, or your parents were smokers at home, and the like. Asbestos related lung cancer is a very real thing. We always talk about mesothelioma victims, but there are actually many more asbestos related lung cancers out there. Laryngeal cancer, ovarian cancer, typically, when women use talc products, for instance, from Johnson & Johnson with asbestos in it. Colorectal, stomach cancer. These scientists are 99% sure of, it's not absolutely shut tight, but we are pretty certain that these diseases are caused by asbestos as well. And again, there is a very strong relationship between asbestos and tobacco. People who work with asbestos and smoke, according to epidemiologic rates have an increased chance of 80 to 120 times more lung cancer risk than if they wouldn't be smoking.

Just stopping smoking when somebody works with asbestos and has been exposed to asbestos is a very real thing to diminish your chances of getting such an illness. And I say this very carefully, an illness. Because it's difficult to confront that all of these diseases are absolutely horrible, basically untreatable, and inevitably fatal. These are horrible ways to die. We can't go about every day talking about asbestos saying, oh, it's a horrible way to die, but please bear that in mind that's what I'm talking about. We call them diseases and that's just a bit easier to stomach.

So, where do you find asbestos? Well, just think of your home. The kitchen floor, the roof, the isolation material, all kinds of products that you might have bought on the Internet and imported from India, for instance. I had a bit of a sore discussion with the son of my neighbours because he bought brakes for his mopeds. I took one look at them, put them in my pocket and said: "I'm giving these to an asbestos removal company and I'll pay you to buy new brakes, but these contain asbestos and you were about to put them into your mopeds". But I did promise to repay him so that he could buy a new asbestos-free brakes.

In the workplace, universities, hospitals, swimming pools, garages... Any kind of place you can think of that was basically built before the mid 90s is likely to contain asbestos and with likely I mean, at least 90% of all the buildings built before the mid 90s are likely to contain asbestos. Be aware of that, also in your own homes when you are doing do-it-yourself work. First, ask yourself, could this possibly be asbestos? If the answer is in any way yes, then let it be a surveyed by a professional and removed by a professional. Whatever you do, don't do it yourself and then hoover the dust away with your own private hoover, and then use said hoover all over your house again, because then you're spreading the asbestos everywhere and that is going to bankrupt you to clean.

Roads, bridges, tunnels, water pipes. Many, many water pipes, late in the 50's, the 60s and 70's, the 80s contained asbestos of cement, which means that the water running through them may contain asbestos and well. This is a whole new field of science, what is the risk of drinking water that has been transported through those water pipes? And the reason that it is so late in the day that we are researching this, is that before, basically, nobody wanted to know the answer, so it wasn't research. Ships, absolutely, old cars, trains, everyday objects, like your grandma's iron or hair dryers, linoleum, still in many homes, heaters, makeup based on talc, there's a chance it could be asbestos in that. Toys, there are approximately 40,000 applications of asbestos.

I once thought: "Well, how much asbestos has been basically produced or imported in Europe?" And it was such a huge amount that I couldn't really imagine what it meant. A hundred million tonnes of asbestos in Europe alone and approximately the same in the rest of the world. Well, just for Europe alone, what does that mean? So, I asked my dad, I'm a jurist, I'm good with words, but my dad was an engineer, he's good with figures. And he did a few calculations, and he said: "Yvonne, if you have big trucks filled to the brim with asbestos and you put them bumper to bumper, they would go 2 1/2 times around the world, and that's the amount of asbestos in Europe alone."

So, I looked up some figures. And they said, well, in Spain alone we have about 5000 fatal victims every year, since the early 90s, at least. So, 5000 victims. Over the past decades you are just talking about 200,000 victims in the past decades and this is not going to go away. So this will be tens of thousands of victims in the future as well. As long as there is asbestos in our society, this is going to go on. Now people say, "oh, but asbestos is banned, therefore it's not a problem anymore." Again, not true. I said it before. I'll say it again. It's everywhere around us, and as long as it's everywhere around us, people are being exposed, as long as it's in landfill, it's an environmental problem. It's a legacy. Asbestos is a legacy problem, and that's the title of this year's Conference. It has been banned all over Europe and several other countries as well. At present, it stands at about 70 countries, meaning that there are, approximately, something like 200 to 220 countries in the world where it's not banned. And indeed, there are countries out there, and I visit them, where they say: "You really pay people to remove asbestos?." And I'll show you at the end of my presentation why they think so.

So, if there is one article that you particularly would like to read on asbestos, that really says it all and is one of the main reference points in recent asbestos literature, just google "the global asbestos disaster". There are some very famous names there within the authors. Basically, what this article advocates is that the occupational exposure level should be reduced to a thousand fibres per cubic metre. Last year, the European Commission decided that it should be two thousand fibres per cubic metre because there were several companies who complained that they couldn't reach that, and then they'd go bankrupt, and you think that would be wonderful if those companies went bankrupt. Why the European Commission took their sides rather than that of the victims, I cannot explain to you. But let's go on.

In this article, Professor Yokota Ocala, of the International Commission on Occupational Health, he recently stepped down as president, says this: "However, when applying the value of statistical life of €4,000,000 per cancer death, any kind of cancer death, as used by the Euro Commission, we would arrive at a much higher cost, while the human suffering and loss of life is impossible to quantify". Basically, every asbestos victim cost society one way or another, approximately €4,000,000, but this does not include the cost for pain and suffering, loss of life, devaluation of buildings, costs for remediation of buildings and soil, cost of the Labour inspectorate, cost of the judiciary, cost of the landfill, cost of eventually cleaning up the landfill, I hope. Asbestos is not only a horrible menace on human lives, but it is also a very heavy financial toll or society, whichever way you look at it. Imagine if the monetary value of 1's life was put towards raising asbestos awareness and prevention in Spain, just for one person, €4,000,000 for the asbestos awareness campaign. How much would that? That would be a huge difference. But you have approximately 5000 victims every year and by victims, I mean unnecessary deaths. So, is there someone who can tell me quickly how much 4,000,000 times 5,000 victims is?

20,000 million. That's one year. 20,000 million for one year. Imagine if you go back until the 80s. All those victims, if you look forward into the victim's future, all those victims, and you add the cost per year. Do you have any idea how big a thing this is? How much work there is to remove asbestos, to raise awareness? To clean the environment, how difficult that is, how much we are challenged by the need for innovation and so many fronts.

So, the EU Commission has these climate goals, they say we need to accelerate the energy renovations of buildings and give people better homes, safer homes, warmer homes. This means more renovation and demolition, and therefore also more exposure. So, this is really contradictory. On the one hand, we wish to decrease the number of asbestos victims and, on the other hand, we are creating the perfect storm for more asbestos victims in the future. People are telling me, even now, "oh, Yvonne, your work eventually will go away (remember that professor in the 90s) and then where will you be?" And I think: "Really? Forty years from now, we will have more expensive victims than ever before.

I want to talk to you about a few legal aspects. One thing that you want to know about liability is this question: When did they know of the dangers? That is the defining point of if somebody is liable. Can they be blamed? Because if they can honestly hold up their hands and say "we really didn't know and we couldn't have known about it", then there is no blame, no fault, no liability, no duty to pay compensation.

Pliny the Elder wrote: "Don't buy slaves who works at asbestos mines because they're always coughing and hacking away and dying soon. And that's the waste of your good money."

Then, 1858, the big American asbestos company Johns Manville was founded. Basically, the big asbestos industry started around that time. The first Eternit factory was established in Brussels these days called ETEX. It is established all over the world in dozens and dozens of countries. At present, Eternit, I should say, is fighting like mad at the Brazilian courts trying to keep their asbestos mine in Brazil open. The government is trying to shut it down and Eternit is trying to keep it open.

1918. The American insurers were very interested, as they always are, in statistics, and they decided that it wasn't good policy to insure asbestos workers in asbestos factories like these ladies here because of the health hazards, since they died fairly soon and then they had to pay up.

1925. Asbestosis as a long-term fatal disease. While science was progressing, the asbestos industry was very aware of this and they colluded together and created all kinds of associations between themselves to keep up and coordinate their PR campaigns, their long-term strategies of dealing with public awareness of asbestos risks. The funny thing is, these companies have the same PR, as advisors, as the tobacco industry, and that really tells you a lot right there. So, they were very much interested in all the medical literature, all asbestos diseases, particularly if finding ways to contradict that, to stop that, to hinder that, even to the point of getting scientists fired from their universities.

The asbestos industry has always been very, very aware of the risks that they caused, not only for their workers, but also for society, because of their products. 1950s. Asbestos causes lung cancer. A very famous epidemiologist. 1964. Dr Salikhov publishes his numbers. Appalling death numbers. Conferences on the dangers of asbestos and, at the same time, the asbestos industry was growing. Very much. It was a marvellous industry and, for instance in Belgium, they were seen as industrial royalty. Imagine that. It was used tremendously in the homes, in the environment, in industry, in schools, you name it, and, at the same time. The awareness was increasing that it was really, highly dangerous and still governmental authorities would say, "put asbestos into your home, into your farms, we insist that you do."

The 80s. Still, advertisements going on by the asbestos industry. And what do they say? "The bigger the building, the more important fire proofing becomes. That's why today's buildings have asbestos cement walls and even floor containing asbestos", "Asbestos, we couldn't live the way we do without it." There are unmeasurable amounts of asbestos in the Twin Towers. Of course, when it was wrecked and destroyed by the terrorist attacks, all of that asbestos was spread all over Manhattan, and everybody who inhaled that in huge quantities is still becoming ill, this is still ongoing.

In the 1990s. Many asbestos lawsuits started and more and more countries started to ban asbestos, and again bear in mind banning is just a word, the situation is still the same. It doesn't remove anything.

1995. Doctor Peto published on mesothelioma and it really shows that this is a very big disease. And again, asbestos-related lung cancers are many more times than usual mesothelioma.

1999. Very late in the day. The EU bans asbestos.

So, the general conclusion is asbestos health hazards are well documented from the early 60s, and at the same time the use of asbestos exploded. That is absolutely bizarre.

The asbestos industry strives to contain public debates on asbestos and they said, for instance, even in 2008, "well, recent scientific data clearly demonstrates that chrysotile, as used today, presents no measurable risk to human health." A blatant lie, founded on absolutely no data whatsoever, simply to prevent countries, like Indonesia, from instigating their own asbestos ban.

There's even been one Asian country that tried to instigate an asbestos ban and then the Russian ambassador came along and said, "if you do that, then we won't buy your tea anymore", and they dropped the whole idea right there and then.

What they would also say is that properly controls and in absence of amphiboles, chrysotile does not present a health risk of any significance to the workers and the general public. These Eternit factories were horrific. The people who used to work there would be covered in asbestos within the hour and would only be recognisable to their colleagues by their outline. They would philtre the air and spread it all over the vicinity, exposing the people who lives in the area and in the wind's direction. The people who worked there would take their filthy clothes back home and expose their families that way. There is no properly controlled way of using asbestos.

So, the asbestos industry has been trying to control the narrative. They say, "well, it hasn't been conclusively proven yet that it's dangerous, so we need more research", which is basically stalling for time, and they managed to do so for decades. They tried to lobby with governmental organisations and said "well, if you want to create asbestos legislation, then of course you need to have specialists to inform you correctly on asbestos, so let us sit in your governmental commissions and will provide the expert knowledge that you need as legislators on asbestos."

They would say: "Well, it's been encapsulated in cement, so therefore it cannot be released and it does no harm". But think about all those asbestos cement roofs that are deteriorating. The cement deteriorates, the asbestos never. That's how it gets released into the air. Controlled use. If they export it to third world countries where people are illiterate, especially in a foreign language, how is there controlled use? There is no controlled used. There was even a very big court case where controlled use was the main argument between Canada and France and WHO, and Canada was not able to prove that there is such a thing as controlled use.

"Chrysotile is innocent, it's the other ones, 10%, that are dangerous." Also, ridiculous.

So, I thank you for your very kind attention. I apologise for possibly having gone over the time limits. If you want to contact me at any time, feel free to do so. Connect with me on LinkedIn. Asbestos is such a global massive problem. It really takes all of us. I hope that all of you will take notes of wherever you see asbestos. And remember this, and in particular share what you have learned: that we need much more awareness.

MESA I

CUESTIONES INTRODUCTORIAS

«ACERCAMIENTO A LA PROBLEMÁTICA DEL AMIANTO COMO CONTAMINANTE EN EL MEDIO AMBIENTE, EN ESPECIAL AGUAS Y SUELOS. EVOLUCIÓN Y SITUACIÓN ACTUAL»

Marga Zango-Pascual
Universidad Pablo de Olavide

Muchas gracias a la anterior participante, ha sido muy interesante. Espero resolver alguna de las cuestiones que se han ido planteando relativas, por ejemplo, a los residuos. Veo muchísimos estudiantes, os agradezco mucho que estéis aquí.

Bueno, no quiero repetir cosas que ya han explicado perfectamente quienes me anteceden, pero os voy a presentar al culpable del problema que se ha presentado: una serpentinita, una de las rocas de las que obtenemos los minerales que llamamos comúnmente asbesto o amianto. Simplemente voy a hablar sobre algunos conceptos básicos, centrándome en la parte que tiene que ver con la contaminación en aguas y suelos.

Primero, aclarar que simplemente por el hecho de que existe determinada configuración de la tierra existe una mínima contaminación natural, pero no estamos hablando de esta sino de la contaminación que se va a producir, generalmente y, sobre todo, con el desmantelamiento del amianto. Ya ha quedado claro que es peligroso, que es cancerígeno y que existe legislación suficiente a lo largo de los años que obliga a desmantelar cualquier resto de amianto que podamos tener en tuberías, fachadas, etc. Pero ¿qué ocurre con todo eso? ¿Qué hacemos con ello?

Una de las problemáticas ambientales más grandes que hemos tenido durante mucho tiempo es que, cuando esto se ha desmantelado sin los controles adecuados, ha producido contaminación en otros lugares y, si contamina el suelo y el agua, puede darse la situación de que acabemos inhalando o ingiriendo estas fibras; por tanto, es muy importante tener los suelos descontaminados. ¿Cuál es la legislación que tenemos en Europa y en España a este respecto?

Centrándonos en España, el asbesto procede de un tipo de minerales presentes en las rocas metamórficas que se localizan en afloramientos muy concretos. ¿Por qué los encontramos en unos lugares y no en otros? Esto se debe a la contaminación natural, de la cual ahora os mostraré un mapa a continuación: si estamos en una zona granítica, donde es normal que haya más radón que en otras, las casas se construyen con determinados sistemas para evitar que el radón se acumule en ellas (por ejemplo, si vives en Galicia puede ser que exista una mínima contaminación natural mayor de la que encontraríamos en otros lugares, pero no tan preocupante a nivel de salud como el tema que tenemos hoy sobre la mesa).

Pues bien, el asbesto se usa desde la Antigüedad, incluso se le presumían propiedades mágicas. Tiene propiedades ignífugas, lo que ha llevado a utilizarlo por entre otros usos, en trajes de bomberos; propiedades aislantes, etc. Su uso masivo en España se produjo en los años 60 y 80 del siglo pasado. Como tiene una vida útil de entre 30 y 50 años, ahora mismo es cuando se está deteriorando más. Existen muchos lugares donde ha habido tuberías de amianto, tejados de amianto, casas construidas con materiales derivados del mismo, etc., que se están deteriorando mucho en la actualidad y, por tanto, pueden emitir más fibras. Su manipulación provoca que las sucesivas divisiones de tamaño sean cada vez mayores, de manera que, si desmontamos un edificio que tiene amianto y no lo hacemos de la forma correcta (manteniendo las necesarias medidas sanitarias legalmente obligatorias), los trabajadores pueden ingerirlas o inhalarlas y, con ello, acabar sufriendo enfermedades de las que ya se ha hablado, lo que, desgraciadamente, está ocurriendo en la práctica.

Aprovechando que hay muchos alumnos de Ciencias Ambientales, os dejo aquí las fórmulas químicas de cada uno de los grupos de los minerales y unas fotos tomadas de una de las muchas guías que las comunidades autónomas están elaborando ya, porque es obligatorio por ley, ahora os diré a partir de cuál. Esta, por ejemplo, procede de *Ihobe*, que es una equivalente a una sociedad de Medio Ambiente del País Vasco muy competente, y muestra precisamente suelos contaminados por amianto. Aquí veis los grupos de minerales. Recordad, una roca es una agrupación de minerales, y unos más perjudiciales que otros.

¿Por qué os pongo este mapa? Simplemente para que veáis que los minerales de los que estamos hablando son de metamorfismo bastante elevado, pero sobre todo que tiene mucha presión. No los vamos a encontrar en cualquier lugar del mundo sino en lo que entendemos como cicatrices de colisiones de una antigua orogenia, lo que sucede en una parte del territorio de Galicia, como podéis observar, y en otras partes de España.

¿Cómo ha ido evolucionando el concepto de cómo nos protegemos en el suelo, en el medio ambiente y en el agua con respecto al amianto? Tenemos una situación bastante curiosa que afortunadamente ha ido evolucionando. En un primer momento, la primera Directiva importante que se hizo sobre este tema, que es del año 83, ya prevé una prohibición extensa del empleo de la crocidolita, también llamada «amianto azul», que exigía sustituirla por otros materiales. El artículo 3.1 de esta Directiva anuncia que la protección sanitaria de la población es el objeto central de la misma; «en último análisis, el riesgo que corre el hombre es infinitamente mayor que el que corre el medio ambiente». Por supuesto, estamos de acuerdo, pero si estos residuos los llevamos a sitios donde no los vamos a gestionar adecuadamente, se convierten en un nuevo riesgo para el ser humano, no solo para las especies, las aguas y los suelos.

Ya en el año 2006 se elabora un reglamento que recoge todas las sustancias químicas peligrosas. Entre ellas se incluye el amianto, al que se dedica un apartado concreto. En el año 2007 surge la Ley de Responsabilidad Medioambiental en el ámbito contencioso-administrativo para prevenir los daños al medio ambiente cuando no hay intención de causarlos. Surge a partir del año de la rotura de Aznalcóllar y del caso de un petrolero que se hundió en la costa de Francia, el Erika. Estas dos legislaciones ya empiezan a considerar conjuntamente que tenemos que proteger los suelos y las aguas, el problema es saber dónde están las aguas y los suelos a proteger.

Esta cuestión puede resolverse fácilmente en la actualidad ya que contamos con visores de uso público, elaborados con fuentes públicas, sobre todo tipo de materias. El visor nos dice qué tipo de aguas subterráneas tenemos en unos lugares o en otros. Como cualquier roca no es susceptible de contener agua, si se trata de una zona muy rocosa en la que no tenemos suelo, este no se podrá contaminar y podremos eliminar con mucha más facilidad los residuos procedentes del amianto (serán retirados en una cápsula y llevados a un vertedero específico). Hay muchas zonas en las que no existen datos, otras zonas en las que tenemos terrenos permeables detríticos, otras con terrenos impermeables volcánicos o metamórficos, y otros terrenos sin interés. La peor situación que podemos tener para que se produzca una contaminación es una zona con un acuífero detrítico, que tendrá abundante agua y se facilitará la contaminación de aguas y suelos.

Esto ocurre, por ejemplo, en una terraza de río. En ella, cualquier depósito que se ponga encima penetra con facilidad y se extiende a una zona bastante amplia. Si el depósito en cuestión está contaminado con amianto, los manantiales que nazcan del agua del acuífero o los pozos que se llenen con esta agua van a absorber la contaminación. Si el acuífero es detrítico, peor aún, porque en él la comunicación es muchísimo mayor. El coste de la descontaminación de un acuífero es, además, muy elevado (mínimo 300.000 euros). Y en el caso del amianto existe el problema añadido del daño a la salud humana de quien trabaje cerca de las zonas en las que hay suelos contaminados.

¿Qué situación tenemos actualmente en Europa? Nuestro continente pretende ser una región libre de amianto en 2032. Otros países ya lo han hecho: Suecia, por ejemplo, en 15 años se ha librado de amianto; Australia empezó el proceso en 2009 y cuenta con una guía muy buena a este respecto. En cuanto a cifras, el 78 % de los cánceres conocidos en la Unión Europea podrían estar relacionados con el asbesto; y a fecha de 2019 había 70.000 trabajadores afectados.

¿Cuál es la situación en España? En la actualidad contamos con la Ley de Residuos y Suelos Contaminados para una Economía Circular, que sustituye y actualiza a la Ley de Residuos anterior, del año 2011. En la Ley hay una parte especialmente interesante que tiene relación con lo que tratamos hoy: la disposición adicional decimocuarta, sobre instalaciones y emplazamientos con amianto, que obliga a todos los ayuntamientos del país a que, en el plazo de un año desde la entrada en vigor de la Ley, elaboren un censo de todos los puntos de su municipio donde pueda haber amianto. Este tema es especialmente importante porque luego tiene que desarrollarse a nivel autonómico. Para llevar a cabo el proceso rige la norma UNE 171370-2:2021, que establece los requisitos y metodología necesarias para planificar y llevar a cabo una inspección en materiales con amianto con el objetivo de localizar y diagnosticar su presencia evaluando el riesgo potencial asociado a cada uno de ellos. Su finalidad es establecer prioridades de acción y tomar decisiones sobre las medidas adecuadas para gestionarlas de manera apropiada.

Ya hay bastantes empresas en España que se dedican expresamente a esto y que se ofrecen incluso a los ayuntamientos para que puedan elaborar sus censos, porque muchos de ellos no tienen capacidad de elaborarlos. A día de hoy, ha pasado un año desde que esta obligación tenía que estar en marcha y, sin embargo, no lo está en su totalidad. De hecho, esta noticia del 15 de marzo de 2023 informa de que el Defensor del Pueblo ha pedido explicaciones ya que hay muchos ayuntamientos que no han cumplido con esta obligación.

Muchas veces se imponen obligaciones legales que no son fáciles de llevar a cabo dada la falta de recursos humanos y técnicos en muchos de los ayuntamientos. Por eso es importante que volvamos a una ley que, aunque no es expresamente sobre amianto sino sobre prevención de contaminación en suelos y aguas, la Ley 7/2007, también sería un instrumento muy eficaz para poder aunar estos temas porque, obliga a cualquier operador, a cualquier actividad industrial que puede provocar un daño al medio ambiente, por contaminación a las aguas, a los suelos, la flora o la fauna, a hacer un análisis de riesgo, a mitigar al daños y a prever la posibilidad de que esto ocurra, de manera que tiene incluso que constituir una garantía financiera.

Como decía, la mayoría de las comunidades autónomas han elaborado sus propias guías para abordar este tipo de problemáticas. En el caso andaluz son del año 2015 (se tienen que actualizar con la nueva legislación, pero ya marcan la base) y están disponibles. Si alguien tiene curiosidad, que me las pida, porque cuento con ellas. Os pongo algunos ejemplos simplemente pues no tenemos mucho tiempo. Hay varias guías, algunas son, en general, sobre sustancias de todo tipo, pero también incluyen ejemplos de contaminaciones de aguas y suelos con los acuíferos, el nivel freático, etc., y, en concreto, tenemos una, la *Guía de evaluación de riesgos para salud humana en suelos potencialmente contaminados*, que es la que tiene más relación con el tema del amianto.

Con esto solo os quiero enseñar que esto es un mundo; o sea, cuando un suelo se declara contaminado no es porque alguien haya ido allí y simplemente haya visto que hay contaminación encima, sino que previamente hay todo un trabajo técnico científico con muestreos importantes que están recogidos en estas guías. Ello para normalizar el trabajo y que todo el mundo lo pueda hacer de la misma manera. Con esto termino. Me tenéis a vuestra disposición y solo deciros que, como ambientólogos, podéis trabajar perfectamente en este tipo de cuestiones. Muchísimas gracias.

«LA RESPUESTA DEL DERECHO PENAL AL FENÓMENO DE LA CONTAMINACIÓN HISTÓRICA Y LENTA»

Alejandro Luis de Pablo Serrano
Universidad de Valladolid

Muchas gracias, VÍCTOR. Buenos días a todos y a todas.

Antes de proceder a la presentación es imprescindible, porque lo hago, de verdad, con sinceridad y con corazón, agradecer a PASTORA, a VÍCTOR y a DONATO la organización de este evento internacional, que es muy difícil, y, además, en el que han conseguido congregar a expertos (no lo digo, en absoluto, por mí sino por la presentación fabulosa de IVONNE esta mañana). Sois increíblemente afortunados porque vuestros profesores consigan traer gente de cualquier rincón del mundo para que escuchéis a los mejores, así que agradecédselo y disfrutadlo. Por mi parte, sin duda es una alegría siempre que me invitan a venir a Sevilla. Yo fui profesor aquí durante dos años y esta ciudad me encanta, me tiene cautivado. Organizad más cosas porque yo quiero estar aquí continuamente, pues es para mí un placer y una alegría ver compañeros y amigos del departamento donde trabajé y me sentí tan bién acogido. Agradezco también, a los coordinadores y directores, pero también a CARMEN y a MARTA. No sé si estáis ahora aquí, pero sé que habéis trabajado muchísimo en este Congreso y os lo agradezco.

Pasando a la presentación, yo me acerqué a este tema por primera vez a raíz de un proyecto de investigación del que formé parte hace unos años y en el seno del cual escribí un pequeño capítulo, ni siquiera íntegramente porque lo hice con otros dos compañeros. Se trataba de un proyecto de investigación, también, de profesores italianos, lo que demuestra que Italia tiene una gran preocupación con este asunto. El proyecto se titulaba «La contaminación histórica. Respuestas penales y alternativas extrapenales desde una perspectiva interna, comparada y europea», y lo dirigían los profesores Francesco Centonze, Stefano Manacorda y Gabrio Forti. Nos pidieron a representantes de distintos países, todos del ámbito de la Criminología y del Derecho penal, que elaboráramos un informe (que, finalmente, en formato de capítulo, publicamos en un libro) sobre cómo se resolvían desde el Derecho penal o desde otras áreas estos problemas.

Los países invitados fueron España, Italia, Francia, Reino Unido y Estados Unidos. Se nos pidió a cada uno de los miembros representantes de estos países que intentáramos ofrecer un concepto de contaminación histórica, si ya existía contaminación lenta o histórica en nuestro país; si no, que intentáramos definir cuáles eran las pautas que la doctrina nacional manejaba sobre este concepto. Nosotros observamos que, aparte del caso de la utilización del amianto, también el caso de la contaminación de la ría de Huelva era representativo. Este último fue un supuesto trágico, aunque ha dejado un paraje ciertamente bello. Toda la minería que se produjo alrededor de la ría de Huelva en el momento del desarrollismo, sobre todo en el franquismo, provocó sin embargo la contaminación de toda esa zona con componentes muy tóxicos. En su momento, el franquismo lo vendió como un ejemplo de desarrollismo, de industrialización poderosa de puestos de trabajo, pero eso ha provocado una contaminación enorme: la zona quedó tan contaminada que incluso las administraciones decidieron que, ya que era, en cierto modo, un vertedero de contaminación, que podría seguir siendo un lugar de almacenaje de más y más contaminación.

Estos dos casos se podían corresponder con lo que luego vamos a definir como «contaminación histórica». Pues bien, se nos pidió que analizáramos cómo se podía afrontar ese problema desde una perspectiva amplia del Derecho, sobre todo del Derecho penal, pero ahora vamos a ver que la conclusión de casi todos los Estados fue que esta no era la vía idónea. En nuestro caso, lo que hicimos los españoles fue analizar qué se había dicho sobre contaminación histórica, y lo cierto es que, en primer lugar, ese concepto no existía como tal. En la doctrina de las Ciencias Ambientales sí que existían otros conceptos naturalmente similares, pero no eran válidos para lo que se buscaba en el proyecto. Les preocupaba el problema de actividades industriales propias de la economía del ser humano del siglo XX y XXI, la cual producía un impacto medioambiental que se ha conocido con el paso del tiempo. Se trataba de actividades que se habían realizado en condiciones de legalidad porque el ordenamiento jurídico vigente en la época (que era tremendamente flexible y generoso para la realización de esas actividades que generaban crecimiento económico y puestos de trabajo) lo permitía; sin embargo, con el avance de la ciencia se descubrió que sus efectos se producen tardíamente. ¿Cómo responder, entonces, ante ese problema?

Nosotros observamos que, desde luego, ya se manejaban en la doctrina penal conceptos cercanos como el de «contaminación difusa», «contaminación persistente», etc., pero ninguno se ajustaba a la realidad que queríamos afrontar. Ya existía en doctrina el término de «daño medioambiental», que era el daño que se producía sobre el medio ambiente en términos generales, y también los «daños derivados del daño medioambiental», es decir, los daños para las personas que se producían por impacto medioambiental, y ambos tipos, eran útiles. Por tanto, a ese primer nivel nos podíamos acercar, aunque no contáramos con un concepto.

En la doctrina española también se ha analizado la segunda parte de la preocupación de este problema: el resultado. En este caso, el problema del resultado era que somos conscientes del mismo, pero ocurre mucho más tarde de su producción. ¿Cómo podemos afrontarlo si cuando se originó era desconocido y, para colmo, era permitido por la legislación?

En nuestro país este problema ya se conocía en Derecho penal, sobre todo a raíz de las infecciones contra la salud como, por ejemplo, el SIDA. En este caso el padecimiento de la enfermedad se conoce mucho después de haber contraído el virus y, entre medias, ha pasado una distancia temporal que puede hacer romper por completo la conexión entre la acción y el resultado porque pueden haber interferido otras tantas infecciones.

En el caso del medio ambiente, otros tantos cursos naturales han podido influir en una contaminación. Este hecho es muy difícil de determinar y a los juristas nos interesa una *causalidad* que esté clara (una acción produjo el resultado), porque si tenemos dudas no podemos hacer responsable a quien hizo la acción de ese resultado. Por este motivo, el concepto de «resultado tardío» era válido.

Al final, llegamos a la conclusión de que el concepto que mejor nos permitía atribuir esta responsabilidad era el de «contaminación histórica», que ya fue homogéneo para todos los miembros del equipo de investigación. La definimos como aquella contaminación que resulta de actividades económicas industriales lícitas y neutrales (en cuanto a su impacto medioambiental y para la salud humana) al tiempo de su realización, que tuvieron lugar en el pasado y que han finalizado, pero cuyos efectos contaminantes se conocen con posterioridad y, por eso, son resultados tardíos.

Entonces se nos dice: ¿cómo afrontan ustedes esta situación? Los miembros del equipo español llegamos a algo tremendamente desesperanzador, ya que los mecanismos jurídicos no han sido suficientes para resolver este tipo de situaciones. Desde luego, si alguna rama ha sido mejor que otra en esta tarea, esta ha sido el derecho administrativo, y esta era una de las conclusiones de nuestro informe. Las normas administrativas han definido conceptos que deben ser protegidos y han establecido sus propias sanciones medioambientales.

Existe una ley que es, por así decirlo, de Derecho administrativo pero común a los entornos naturales que cada una de las normas anteriores protegen, la Ley de responsabilidad medioambiental, que es tremendamente útil porque establece el marco para sancionar y recuperar aquellas zonas medioambientales que se han visto contaminadas por actividades industriales. Prohíbe un gran elenco de actividades, tales como la elaboración, importación o adquisición de productos con sustancias peligrosas, la no realización de operaciones de limpieza o la mezcla de distintas categorías de residuos produciendo residuos peligrosos. En cuanto al tipo de sanción, en estas leyes administrativas medioambientales la sanción paradigmática es la multa, pero esta no debe ser la única ni mucho menos. También el cierre de instalaciones, la prohibición de realización de actividades en el tiempo o de acudir a determinadas licitaciones públicas, etc.

Finalmente, cuando estamos ante una contaminación medioambiental, la clave, tanto para el Derecho administrativo medioambiental como para el Derecho penal medioambiental, debería ser no solo prevenir que esto suceda en el futuro sino, respecto de esas zonas que han quedado contaminadas, repararlas o devolverlas a su posición original. La intervención del Derecho penal es siempre tardía y reactiva en el caso de los daños medioambientales; por eso, la gran preocupación tiene que ser, una vez sancionados penalmente a sus responsables, que se les imponga la obligación de recuperar esas zonas, porque seguimos necesitando el medio ambiente como medio de vida no solo para realizar nuestras actividades económicas sino para vivir. Y si no se puede detectar al responsable, ya que en algunos casos esto es muy difícil, debe recuperarlo el propio Estado (al final, somos todos los que vamos a recuperar esas zonas con nuestro dinero público que otros han contaminado para su beneficio económico).

La restitución y la indemnización deben hacerse conforme a la Ley 26/2007, de 23 de octubre, de Responsabilidad Medioambiental, cuyo artículo 20 introduce todo un elenco de procedimientos de recuperación o de limpieza verdaderamente interesantes y necesarios. ¿Por qué creemos que esta ley es mejor para afrontar estos problemas de contaminación histórica que el Código penal? Fundamentalmente, porque su artículo 4 establece un ámbito temporal mucho más extenso que la prescripción de los delitos medioambientales. Dice «esta ley no será de aplicación si han transcurrido más de treinta años desde que tuvo lugar la emisión, el suceso o el incidente que los causó»; sin embargo, la prescripción de los delitos ecológicos es de cinco años. Así, cuando estamos ante una contaminación histórica y lenta como a la que nos estamos refiriendo, su resultado tiene que ser conocido antes de que transcurran cinco años porque si no, desde el punto de vista penal, estas conductas habrían prescrito. Esto, en cierto modo, también es bastante lógico en el Derecho penal por razones de merecimiento de pena (porque la necesidad de la pena en la comunidad va disminuyendo a medida que va transcurriendo el tiempo y el delito se va olvidando) y porque no podemos utilizar los recursos materiales y humanos de la justicia eternamente a perseguir delitos.

Otra ventaja de la norma administrativa es que el ámbito de aplicación es bastante más extenso que el Derecho penal. Su preámbulo dice «la responsabilidad medioambiental es, por último, una responsabilidad de carácter objetivo en la que las obligaciones de actuación se imponen al operador al margen de cualquier culpa, dolo o negligencia que haya podido existir en su comportamiento». Este párrafo está reflejado en el artículo 3 de la Ley, que es el que incluye ese régimen amplio de responsabilidad objetiva, pero luego el artículo 14.2 introduce una limitación que va a dejar fuera casos de contaminación histórica. Este precepto dice: «el operador no estará obligado a sufragar el coste imputable a las medidas reparadoras cuando demuestre que no ha incurrido en culpa, dolo o negligencia y que concurre alguna de las siguientes circunstancias: a) Que la emisión o el hecho que sea causa directa del daño medioambiental constituya el objeto expreso y específico de una autorización administrativa otorgada de conformidad con la normativa aplicable a las actividades enumeradas en el anexo III; b) Que el operador pruebe que el daño medioambiental fue causado por una actividad, una emisión, o la utilización de un producto que, en el momento de realizarse o utilizarse, no eran considerados como potencialmente perjudiciales para el medio ambiente con arreglo al estado de los conocimientos científicos y técnicos existentes en aquel momento».

No es que la Ley se hiciera para resolver la contaminación histórica, pero nosotros, que necesitábamos buscar soluciones, encontramos este artículo 14. Efectivamente, los que impone siguen siendo unos límites enormes porque, de acuerdo con el precepto, en los casos de contaminación histórica el operador no responde de reparación, aunque el Estado sí tiene la obligación de hacerlo. Ahora bien, sí que incurriría en un delito en caso de que se le impongan medidas de reparación y no las cumpla, pero esto ya no es un delito propiamente medioambiental sino de desobediencia.

El Derecho administrativo, por tanto, era una vía más adecuada que el Derecho penal, aunque tiene un artículo de delito ecológico (que es el eje sobre el que pivota todo el Derecho medioambiental y que es una conducta verdaderamente amplia y está bien construido, aunque tendrá sus matices) a través del cual se podrían reconducir todos los casos de contaminación histórica que nosotros estábamos estudiando. Muy básicamente, este artículo castiga al que, «contraviniendo las leyes u otras disposiciones de carácter general protectoras del medio ambiente, provoque o realice directa o indirectamente emisiones, vertidos, radiaciones, extracciones o excavaciones, aterramientos, ruidos, vibraciones, inyecciones o depósitos, en la atmósfera, el suelo, el subsuelo o las aguas terrestres, subterráneas o marítimas, incluido el alta mar, con incidencia incluso en los espacios transfronterizos, así como las captaciones de aguas que, por sí mismos o conjuntamente con otros, cause o pueda causar daños sustanciales a la calidad del aire, del suelo o de las aguas, o a animales o plantas».

A pesar de las buenas intenciones que pudiera tener el legislador, el Derecho penal, tal y como está regulado y, sobre todo, con los principios básicos y garantías que conocéis y con los que se construye, resulta inoperante para afrontar estos problemas de contaminación histórica, fundamentalmente por dos problemas.

En primer lugar, si las consecuencias son tardías, no es nada fácil afirmar lo que en Derecho penal es clave, que es el nexo de causalidad entre acción y el resultado. No podemos afirmar con total rotundidad y seguridad que el resultado fue fruto de la acción, y, si esto falla, si hay quiebras o dudas en esa conexión causal, no podemos hacer responder por más que queramos a determinada empresa de esa contaminación porque desconocemos qué otras causas de la naturaleza han podido influir en el aumento de la contaminación que se ha producido en ese lugar y que, quizás, solo conoceremos en un futuro. En segundo lugar, porque puede que no solo ese agente empresarial o ciudadano haya influido en la contaminación en cuestión; por tanto, se rompe el nexo de causalidad.

Otro problema es el problema de la prescripción. Como hemos dicho, el Derecho administrativo es más útil para enfrentar esta problemática porque establece un plazo de prescripción de treinta años junto a un régimen de responsabilidad mucho más amplio. Si mantenemos los periodos de prescripción quc impone el Código penal, los casos de contaminación histórica quedan fuera. Una posible solución que ha dado la doctrina sería atenuar la pena para estos casos, pero ello supondría saltarnos ciertos principios y garantías clásicas, como el principio de legalidad y el principio de culpabilidad (si el sujeto actuó en ese momento desarrollando una actividad industrial y económica permitida conforme a la legalidad).

Al final, tanto los españoles como los miembros del proyecto representantes del resto de países considerábamos que nos enfrentábamos a situaciones similares. Por ejemplo, países como Francia o Alemania reconocían tener una normativa medioambiental administrativa muy extensa al efecto, pero desde el punto de vista del Derecho penal reconocían que sus instrumentos no eran adecuados para afrontar estos problemas, y consideraban que este solo es aplicable para la contaminación heredada (aquella contaminación cuyos efectos ya están cerrados y que era ilegal ya en el tiempo de su realización). Para los casos de contaminación histórica consideraban aplicables a los culpables condenas por omisión de limpieza o de contención, pero no por haber producido la contaminación sino por no haberla reparado o evitado en el futuro habiendo una resolución administrativa que obligaba a reparar esas zonas.

Los representantes de estos países decían, además, que los delitos para la protección de la salud y la vida humana tendrán poca relevancia en los casos medioambientales debido a la dificultad de probar la causalidad y la imposibilidad de imputar las consecuencias de la contaminación acumulativa a autores individuales.

Concluyo ya. Recapitulando, el Derecho penal medioambiental no es adecuado para responder a la contaminación histórica. La respuesta es tardía, primero, porque estos procesos tienden a ser tremendamente largos, y, segundo, porque el Estado y la sociedad se dan cuenta de estos problemas de manera, también, muy tardía porque el estado de la ciencia lo reconoce cuando se descubre. Pero es que, además, la concienciación medioambiental sobre estos problemas es todavía más lenta que la propia ciencia. Aunque las empresas hayan producido crecimiento económico, tenemos que preferir la protección medioambiental y sentirnos víctimas de esa contaminación a pesar de que hayan generado puestos de trabajo y riqueza en determinadas zonas, algo que no suele considerar la población en la práctica. Parece que los delitos medioambientales son delitos sin víctimas, pero esta denominación es tremendamente engañosa.

Por otro lado, ¿de qué sirven las sanciones penales a la hora reparar el medio ambiente, que sigue siendo el entorno en el que vivimos y que necesitamos para respirar? Debemos tener presente que es una respuesta muy problemática, porque supone flexibilizar o cerrar los ojos a garantías básicas. Es más útil el Derecho administrativo ambiental y, en todo caso, sigue siendo necesario porque el principio de «quien contamina paga» suena muy bien, pero se aplica regular. De hecho, ya hay versiones actuales que dicen que el principio, realmente, es «quien paga contamina», a quien tiene dinero para pagar las sanciones le permitimos contaminar porque actualmente tenemos los derechos de emisión de contaminación y los vendemos en el mercado de la Unión Europea a ciertas empresas. Esto es el colmo de la legalización de la contaminación, de modo que, pese al principio de «quien contamina paga», vamos a seguir teniendo que confiar y dotar debidamente fondos públicos estatales de reparación y conservación de estas zonas porque, al final, el medio ambiente necesita ser recuperado. Tendremos que hacerlo entre todos.

Muchas gracias. Estoy a vuestra disposición.

MESA II

LA EXPERIENCIA ESPAÑOLA

«LA CUESTIÓN DEL AMIANTO EN LA JURISPRUDENCIA ESPAÑOLA (NO SOLO) PENAL: UN BALANCE PROVISIONAL»

Víctor M. Macías Caro

Universidad Pablo de Olavide

Buenos días a todos y a todas.

Esta va a ser la primera intervención que realice sobre este tema. Pero bueno, espero que no sea la última, que sea, en el contexto de esta nueva línea de investigación común que estamos emprendiendo, el inicio de algo que se pueda ir completando poco a poco. Voy a intentar ser breve. En primer lugar, para dejar espacio a que, después de que nosotros intervengamos, que lo puedan hacer también los asistentes y el resto de ponentes que nos acompañan. Y, en segundo lugar, porque, como ya decía y como refleja el título de la intervención, el balance que voy a realizar es un balance provisional incompleto, básicamente, por tres razones.

Primero, porque se trata del resultado de una línea de investigación que aún está en curso. Por ahora consiste en un dibujo de las tendencias generales y en lanzar puentes de comparación con otros Ordenamientos jurídicos, sobre todo con el Ordenamiento jurídico penal italiano, pero también entre distintas ramas del mismo Ordenamiento jurídico, sobre todo entre el Derecho civil de daños y el Derecho penal. Segundo, porque la jurisprudencia no penal en esta materia es amplísima y, por lo tanto, debo seleccionar solo aquellas resoluciones que sean más importantes. De hecho, aunque para las consideraciones —sobre todo, las conclusiones— que haré al final de mi intervención he tenido en cuenta muchas otras, en la intervención como tal voy a exponer solo una de las sentencias no penales: la sentencia del caso Uralita de Cerdanyola del Vallés del 2021. He elegido esta resolución porque resuelve cuestiones centrales en esta materia, que son los criterios de imputación del resultado: tanto la causalidad (la imputación objetiva) como la imputación subjetiva. En tercer lugar, se trata de un balance provisional porque probablemente vamos a seguir hablando de amianto durante muchísimos años.

A pesar de que su comercialización y su uso están totalmente prohibidos, esta prohibición no hace desaparecer el amianto, ya que está instalado y seguirá presente en muchísimas edificaciones y en muchísimos otros elementos de la vida cotidiana a menos que sea removido. Pero esta política de desamiantización o desamiantado, que viene de Europa y que ha sido traspuesta al Derecho español, es necesaria desde un punto de vista técnico. La doctora WATERMAN, por ejemplo, ha defendido con ahínco esta mañana que, además, era económicamente rentable; es decir, que los costes de mantener el amianto son mucho mayores que los de la desamiantización. Pero desde un punto de vista criminológico ese proceso va a ser también un nuevo para que se puedan cometer nuevos delitos, y esto lo demuestra ya este balance provisional con alguna de las sentencias no penales de las que voy a hablar a lo largo de la intervención. Lo único que puedo hacer en este sentido es esperar que, al menos, algo hayamos aprendido y que dentro de tres décadas no nos encontremos con un nuevo desastre que haya estado afectado lentamente durante estos años a quienes ahora están trabajando en las labores de desamiantado, que dé la cara con una nueva ola de mesotelioma, etc., dentro de treinta o cuarenta años.

Bien, como decía, comienzo con el caso Uralita de Cerdanyola del Vallés[1]. Se trata de una de una de las fábricas que la empresa Uralita tenía en territorio español, y tomo esta sentencia como representación porque creo que, en cierta medida, viene a ser el destilado de muchas tendencias anteriores, sobre todo en la jurisdicción civil. No se trata de una sentencia dictada

1 Para el análisis de este caso, me baso en el completísimo análisis realizado por YZQUIERDO TOLSADA, Mariano, «Asbestosis: un compendio de aspectos nucleares y discutidos en la responsabilidad civil: Sentencia del Tribunal Supremo de 15 de marzo 2021 (141/2021)» en YZQUIERDO TOLSADA, Mariano (dir.), *Comentarios a las sentencias de unificación de doctrina: Civil y Mercantil*, vol. 13, 2021, pp. 265-292.

para resolver las acciones ejercitadas por las personas que, en su momento, estuvieron expuestas al polvo de amianto por convivir con los trabajadores, sino por los convivientes de los trabajadores ya fallecidos, o también por los vecinos que residían en las proximidades de la citada factoría.

En esta resolución, el Tribunal Supremo efectúa un estudio muy completo de varias cuestiones, pero me voy a centrar en los criterios para determinar la causalidad y la culpa porque son aquellos aspectos en los que se puede hacer una comparación con el Derecho penal. No me voy a ocupar de otras cuestiones a las que esta sentencia también les presta mucha atención como, por ejemplo, la compatibilidad entre el daño moral sufrido por los familiares en la transmisión hereditaria del crédito que correspondería a los perjudicados padecido por los trabajadores directamente afectados, ni tampoco de la valoración del daño. Pero no porque todo esto no sea importante, sino porque se trata de cuestiones que son más ajenas al penalista. Tampoco voy a desarrollar, aunque sea interesante, la muy debatida cuestión del deslinde entre la jurisdicción civil y la jurisdicción social o laboral en función de cada categoría de damnificado.

Empecemos hablando, por lo pronto, del resumen de los hechos. Entre 1907 y 1997, Uralita Sociedad Anónima desarrolla en Cerdanyola del Vallès (Barcelona) una actividad industrial que consiste en la fabricación de elementos para la construcción mediante el uso, básicamente, de amianto. Los demandantes, que eran 39 afectados en este caso entre familiares de trabajadores y vecinos de la fábrica, argumentaban que el hecho de cumplir las disposiciones legales y reglamentarias por parte de Uralita no elimina la responsabilidad civil. Se razonó por parte de los demandantes que concurría la relación de causalidad entre las actividades desarrolladas en la fábrica de Uralita y el daño sufrido; que esta relación de causalidad era conocida por Uralita desde, al menos, los años treinta del del siglo XX; que la incidencia que el amianto desencadena en la salud de las personas era algo conocido y que, por lo tanto, la empresa actuó con negligencia en la prevención y en la evitación del daño.

Esto llega al Juzgado de Primera Instancia número 96 de Madrid, que en sentencia de 30 de enero de 2015 entendió que la normativa contenida en la Orden Ministerial de 9 marzo del 71 prohibía que los equipos protectores de los trabajadores se sacasen de la fábrica, y en el acta levantada por la Inspección de Trabajo en el 77 se había advertido que los trabajadores de la fábrica no disponían de las dos taquillas de las que debían disponer, una para la ropa de trabajo y otra para la de la ropa de la calle, para evitar la contaminación cruzada. Además, la limpieza de la ropa de trabajo debía efectuarse regularmente por la propia empresa o, al menos, por una empresa de lavandería y la ropa sucia debía haberse introducido en sacos impermeables y cerrados, cuestión toda esta que no se cumplía. Por todo ello, el Juzgado argumentó que Uralita era responsable de las patologías sufridas por los familiares durante ese acotado período de tiempo (desde el 71 en el que entra en vigor la normativa, hasta el 77, año en el que existe la prueba en el acta de la Inspección de Trabajo), pero no de las posteriores. En cambio, se desestimó la demanda en relación con los pasivos ambientales porque, aunque se había infringido la normativa existente con respecto a la limpieza general de los locales, así como la normativa relativa a las dosis permitidas en exposición ambiental en el interior de la fábrica, no se podía, según esta primera sentencia, colegir que tales incumplimientos tuvieran repercusión en el exterior de la fábrica, con la correlativa contaminación.

Esta primera sentencia se apela por ambas partes y la Audiencia Provincial de Madrid dicta sentencia en apelación el 7 diciembre de 2017 revocando parcialmente la sentencia dictada por el Juzgado. En primer lugar, la Audiencia destaca una cuestión sobre la que ya he adelantado que no iba a entrar, la competencia de la jurisdicción civil, y se establece que existía una relación de causalidad entre las actividades desarrolladas por la demandada y las patologías constatadas por la exposición doméstica y la ambiental. Dice que se trata de un riesgo científicamente demostrado y que nada permitía deducir un origen diferente para las patologías que sufrían los vecinos. Esta es una primera novedad en la sentencia de apelación con respecto a la sentencia de primera instancia.

Además, en relación con los pasivos domésticos, la Audiencia considera que la demandada no había actuado con la diligencia debida según se iba contando con los conocimientos acerca de los efectos perniciosos y perjudiciales que producía el manejo de tales sustancias para la salud de las personas, lo que condujo a la Audiencia Provincial a la conclusión de que no se habían adoptado las medidas oportunas. Los trabajadores de la fábrica portaban adheridas a su ropa las partículas de amianto, que pasaban a ser inhaladas por quienes se ocupaban de su lavado, y esto era conocido por Uralita a pesar de que no existiese hasta 1971 una normativa específica al respecto. Por lo cual, según esta sentencia en apelación no corresponde limitar los daños indemnizables al periodo entre el 1971 y el 1977 sino que deberían alcanzar, también, los daños que pudieran ser imputados a un período anterior al 71.

En lo que se refiere a los pasivos ambientales, tras analizar el marco legal general en materia ambiental y el existente específicamente sobre contaminación producida por el amianto, la sentencia entendió que la doctrina del riesgo en la gestión de actividades especialmente peligrosas, si bien no elimina la necesaria concurrencia de una acción u omisión culposa, sí exige tener en cuenta que un riesgo mayor conlleva un deber de previsión de mayor intensidad por parte de quien crea dicho riego o quien lo aumenta, con la correlativa obligación de adoptar medidas necesarias para prevenirlo, máxime cuando puede estar en peligro la vida de las personas. Todo ello, como ya adelantaba hace unos minutos, con la nítida posibilidad de la inversión de la carga de la prueba. La actividad desarrollada por Uralita, esto lo dice así negro sobre blanco la sentencia, era peligrosa y era creadora de un riesgo superior al normal, y no era suficiente con el cumplimiento de las normas reglamentarias para excluir el reproche culpabilístico. De hecho, la sentencia entiende que Uralita, pese a conocer el peligro que conllevaba la inhalación de la fibra de amianto, no actuó con la de diligencia exigible al emitir sin el control adecuado dichas fibras al ambiente exterior, con independencia de que se cumpliesen o incumpliesen normativas específicas Téngase en cuenta que los demandantes, en este caso los pasivos ambientales, eran personas que vivían en las inmediaciones de la fábrica en un radio inferior a dos mil metros.

Esta sentencia en apelación es objeto de recurso y llegamos al Tribunal Supremo. Por un lado, Uralita alega en el terreno de la relación de causalidad y en el de la previsibilidad de los daños en los casos de exposición a las fibras de amianto de origen no laboral sino doméstico ambiental, y también en lo que respecta a la apreciación de la culpa o negligencia. En términos resumidos, aduce que la sentencia recurrida valora la culpa prescindiendo del elemento constitutivo de la previsibilidad, dando lugar a una conclusión según la cual Uralita sería responsable de todas las patologías o afecciones de personas que hubieran sido vecinos o trabajadores de los municipios afectados. Por su parte, los demandantes basan su recurso en cuestiones en las que no voy a entrar relacionadas con el cálculo de la cuantía indemnizatoria.

Finalmente, el Tribunal Supremo respondió reunido en pleno el 15 de marzo de 2021. Con respecto a la causalidad, la sentencia parte del hecho de que era perfectamente conocido, cuando menos en la década de los años 40 del siglo pasado, que la utilización del amianto en los procesos industriales y, especialmente, la inhalación del polvo que se desprendía de la fabricación de productos derivados conformaba un indiscutible riesgo para la salud. En definitiva, Uralita tenía, según la sentencia, perfecta constancia de los riesgos de toda índole no solo para los trabajadores sino, también, para terceros. De hecho, la propia Uralita en el proceso admitía la causalidad general existente entre la exposición al asbesto y determinadas enfermedades, pero lo que discutía era la exposición concreta a su fábrica de microcemento pues, en sus palabras, «existen una multitud de situaciones alternativas de exposición al amianto que pueden justificar las patologías sufridas». Es decir, no niega la causalidad general, pero alega que no existe una prueba de que no haya existido una explicación alternativa.

Pero esta genérica invocación no convence al Tribunal Supremo; de hecho, declara como hecho constatado «la muy superior incidencia de dichas patologías en la población donde se asienta la fábrica con respecto a otras localidades de la geografía española y la ausencia de otros focos alternativos de contaminación conocidos» (en el debate italiano, esto se traduciría como causalidad epidemiológica más ausencia de una explicación alternativa). El hilo lógico del Tribunal Supremo es el siguiente: en primer lugar, la toxicidad de la exposición al amianto se encontraba científicamente demostrada; en segundo lugar, el estudio llevado a cabo en la comarca del Vallés Occidental concluye que aquella fábrica suponía un factor de riesgo importante si se compara con otra zona próxima; en tercer lugar, examinadas las circunstancias de contacto con el foco contaminante en cada uno de los demandantes, así como sus respectivas actividades laborales, no cabía aducir una hipótesis alternativa de exposición contaminante de aquella naturaleza; y, en cuarto lugar, no cabe entender que exista un error manifiesto de la apreciación de la prueba por el hecho de que no haya en el caso una certeza absoluta, cuando lo que sí hay es una causalidad probable, pues, «si queremos aspirar a la racionalidad dentro del marco de la incertidumbre debemos conformarnos con la probabilidad suficiente que satisfaga el estándar probatorio». Quizás es este mismo paso el que podría distinguir estos pasos lógicos en una sentencia civil de una sentencia penal, pero sobre ello volveré al final de mi intervención.

A continuación, el Tribunal pretende dilucidar si hubo negligencia o si bien estamos ante una actividad anormalmente peligrosa que permita elevar el nivel de diligencia exigible, y si ello permite presumir la negligencia por inversión de la carga de la prueba de la culpa.

Con respecto a los pasivos ambientales, el Fundamento Cuarto de la sentencia da respuesta a este primer motivo del recurso. Uralita negaba su negligencia a la vista de que la factoría siempre había contado con los necesarios permisos y autorizaciones, nunca había sido objeto de expediente administrativo sancionador relacionado con su actividad industrial y, además, mientras la factoría estuvo operativa a lo largo del pasado siglo, no eran conocidos ni previsibles los riesgos para la salud de los vecinos. En suma, se achacaba a la sentencia recurrida haberse pronunciado en términos de responsabilidad puramente objetiva. Frente a estas alegaciones, como ya hemos adelantado, el Tribunal desarrolla el concepto de responsabilidad por culpa presunta como algo distinto a la responsabilidad objetiva o sin culpa. Los daños causados —y que, por lo tanto, no es del todo en mi opinión incompatible con un punto de vista penal— en actividades anormalmente peligrosas (esto es, que comportan un riesgo considerablemente elevado por su frecuencia, su alcance o su gravedad) se rigen por la regla de la culpa, pero, cuanto mayor sea el peligro, mayor deberá ser el nivel de diligencia exigible, y ello, a veces, conducirá a exigir una pericia extrema.

En el caso presente estamos ante una actividad que no se puede calificar como común o habitual sino como anormalmente peligrosa. Ello se conocía desde antes de 1940, y la contaminación ambiental al menos de los años 60. La factoría estaba integrada en el núcleo urbano e incluso había un centro escolar a doce metros, sin que pudiera servir como defensa al hecho de que la contaminación de quienes vivían en las proximidades era inevitable, máxime si, además, quedó probado que la evacuación del polvo de amianto mediante extractores y chimeneas se llevaba a efecto sin filtros ni dispositivos de retención y recogida. Todavía a finales de los años 70 se llevaban sacos de amianto en bolsas de yute, material muy poroso.

Con respecto a los pasivos domésticos (es decir, las personas que resultaron contaminadas por el contacto con las prendas de trabajo) se pronuncia el Fundamento de Derecho Quinto. En este sentido, Uralita negaba que hubiese existido negligencia por su parte dado que la factoría había comenzado a adoptar las medidas necesarias incluso antes de que fuera establecidas por la normativa. No obstante, la sentencia deja claro que no había que esperar a que la autoridad laboral impusiera de manera expresa la obligación de que el lavado de la ropa de trabajo se efectuase en las dependencias de la propia empresa o en una lavandería, ni menos aún había que esperar a que la Inspección de Trabajo ordenase la paralización de distintos sectores de la fábrica, haciendo mención a una cita literal de la sentencia: «cuando las garantías adoptadas conforme a las disposiciones legales para prever y evitar los daños previsibles y evitables no han ofrecido resultado positivo, revela ello la insuficiencia de las mismas y que faltaba algo por prevenir que no se hallaba completa la diligencia».

Paso a la jurisprudencia penal. Hay relativamente pocas resoluciones judiciales penales directamente relacionadas con la exposición al amianto de personas y de medio ambiente. En concreto, una búsqueda en el CENDOJ arroja una treintena de resoluciones entre sentencias y autos en los últimos 20 años. Básicamente, se pueden agrupar en tres categorías.

En primer lugar, sentencias que tienen que ver con delitos contra la seguridad higiene en el trabajo por violación de las normas de prevención de riesgos laborales relativos directamente a la exposición al amianto durante los trabajos en los que se tiene contacto con el amianto, más el riesgo la lesión para la vida o la salud (por lo tanto, homicidios o delitos de lesiones). Aquí voy a mencionar solo tres sentencias, todas absolutorias. La Sentencia del Juzgado de lo Penal de Alicante en el 2006, confirmada luego por la Audiencia Provincial de Alicante también en el 2006, absolvió a cuatro acusados, dos jefes de personal y dos médicos de la empresa Cimientos Sociedad Anónima, una empresa de fabricación de fibrocemento, debido a que se limita la exposición causal hasta 1982, fecha en la que ninguno de los acusados tenía todavía, o no se había probado, funciones concretas en materia de prevención de riesgos laborales. También absuelve en un auto de la Audiencia Provincial de Sevilla en el año 2011 al dueño de una finca incendiada y al responsable de obras de un delito contra la seguridad e higiene en el trabajo por no haber realizado un estudio previo sobre la posibilidad de existencia de amianto, que finalmente se encontró. Sin embargo, se absuelve debido, entre otras razones, a que el estado ruinoso del edificio impedía o dificultaba mucho haber hecho ese estudio previo. Por último, el auto también de la Audiencia Provincial de Oviedo, sección tercera, en el año 2019, que resuelve un recurso contra un auto del Juzgado de Instrucción Número 2 de Avilés. En ambas instancias se absuelve por no considerar probado que los acusados, en sus respectivos ámbitos de competencia, tuvieran conocimiento de la exposición a productos químicos de los trabajadores de la factoría, ni tampoco que, de conocerlo, tuvieran atribuciones para adoptar medidas para evitarlo, presupuestos inexcusables a fin de abordar la imprudencia grave puesta a su cargo en los términos exigidos por artículo 142 del Código Penal, sobre todo tras la reforma del 2015, que ha eliminado la punibilidad de la imprudencia leve. Por lo tanto, al menos a mí no me consta ahora mismo ninguna sentencia penal de condena por homicidio, lesiones o por delitos contra la seguridad e higiene en el trabajo que estén relacionadas con la exposición al amianto.

¿Qué es lo que está sucediendo en los últimos diez años? Está habiendo sentencias, no pocas, de condenas por delitos contra la seguridad e higiene en el trabajo relacionadas con caídas y con lesiones fruto de accidentes de trabajo en los trabajos de desamiantado. Por lo tanto, el amianto juega ahí un determinado papel: no estamos hablando de un daño por una exposición o un riesgo por una exposición, pero son casos que están de determinada manera relacionado con el amianto. Por ejemplo, la Audiencia Provincial de Coruña en el año 2016 estima una apelación contra una sentencia del Juzgado de lo Penal de Ferrol del 2014 en la que se condena por delito contra la seguridad e higiene en el trabajo por una caída durante trabajos de retirada de tejados y por manipulación indebida de los mismos sin medios de protección. Esto es lo más parecido a una condena por puesta en peligro por exposición al amianto, porque también está en los en los hechos probados que no solo el trabajador se cayó, sino que, también, manipuló los elementos de amianto sí medios de protección. De hecho, en concreto, se menciona que se limpiaban los tejados de uralita con agua a presión y se cortaban con una radial sin usar ningún tipo de protección. Además, se cortaban porque los trabajos consistían en coger los tejados de un aparcamiento para reutilizarlos en un edificio; entonces, como no cabían, había que cortar los tejados con una radial. Si el trabajador no se hubiese caído, probablemente no hubiera habido condena.

Me consta otra condena por homicidio por imprudencia y delito contra la seguridad en el trabajo en el caso de la muerte de un trabajador de 32 años mientras retiraba un tejado de amianto. Hay absoluciones y otras condenas, pero no voy a leer toda la lista de la jurisprudencia. Estas conforman el segundo grupo de sentencias.

La tercera categoría de sentencias penales está relacionada con los delitos contra el medio ambiente y contra la ordenación del territorio. Son sentencias muy recientes, estamos hablando del año 2021-2022. Condena, por ejemplo, por la construcción ilegal de una vivienda en la cual, además, se utilizaron tejados de fibrocemento. De nuevo aquí, en realidad, la condena no se basa en que se hayan utilizado tejados de fibrocemento sino en que se edificó en una finca que no tenía la extensión necesaria para poder edificar. Sí que hay una condena en un caso de acumulación de residuos peligrosos de todo tipo, también de residuos de amianto, en una planta de Chiloeches (Guadalajara) que terminó por incendiarse.

Termino con las conclusiones que he extraído como penalista. En España ha habido, tal y como hemos podido comprobar, muy pocos casos de afectación a bienes jurídicos por la exposición al amianto de las personas y el medio ambiente que hayan sido tratados por la jurisdicción penal, y aún menos que hayan terminado condenas (de hecho, ninguno o solo uno, si consideramos ese del que dado conocimiento). En muchas de las sentencias analizadas el amianto no desarrolla, en realidad, un papel esencial en la decisión del juzgador sino, a lo sumo, contribuye por así decirlo, a dibujar un contexto difuso de peligrosidad o de que no se estaban haciendo las cosas bien. Esta ausencia de recurso a lo penal diferencia España de lo que ha ocurrido en otros Ordenamientos, particularmente en Italia, como tendremos ocasión de oír en el presente Congreso. Por otra parte, algunas de las cuestiones teóricas que se plantean en la responsabilidad civil por daño por amianto, sea en controversia de competencia de la jurisdicción civil o de la jurisdicción laboral, son equivalentes, o podríamos analizar si son equivalentes, a las que uno esperaría hipotéticamente encontrar si es que en España también se hubiese desarrollado una línea jurisprudencial en la jurisdicción penal. Otras cuestiones, sin embargo, difieren, pero es interesante, en cualquier caso, hacer este análisis comparado. Por ejemplo, en cuanto a la causalidad también se hace uso en el derecho de daños de la terminología de la causalidad general y la causalidad individual, y no se aprecian problemas en la jurisprudencia en cuanto a la primera de ellas. Esto sucede, en particular, en cuanto al mesotelioma y la asbestosis, porque en la práctica totalidad de los casos estas enfermedades están asociados a la exposición al amianto. Pero ¿esta práctica totalidad sería suficiente para establecer también la causalidad general en Derecho penal? ¿Esa duda que quedaría sería una duda razonable o sería una duda no razonable? A los jueces penales españoles les ha parecido siempre que esa duda era una de las que se declina en el famoso principio de *in dubio pro reo*. No podemos estar seguros, de todas maneras, de qué habría sucedido.

Paso a la última de las conclusiones para no alargarme demasiado. Quisiera llamar la atención sobre la no utilización de una herramienta de la que dispone el Ordenamiento jurídico-penal, como es la responsabilización de las personas jurídicas en estos casos. Creo que los límites a la responsabilidad de cada una de las personas físicas que a lo largo del tiempo, en distintos grados y con distintos ámbitos competenciales, ocupan la posición gestores del riesgo, debido a la imposibilidad o a la gran dificultad, en muchos casos, de poder imputar objetiva y subjetivamente el resultado a la conducta de cada una de esas personas físicas de manera individual, tal y como exige justamente el Derecho penal, no serían óbice ninguno, desde un punto de vista hipotético, para que se considerase a la empresa, en sí misma, responsable penalmente. Incluso con algunos requisitos en caso de sucesión de empresas, aunque luego el Tribunal Supremo tiene una opinión distinta a lo que dice la Ley. No obstante, para que esto fuese posible sería necesaria una reforma legal que introdujese los delitos contra la seguridad e higiene en el trabajo, el homicidio y las lesiones (al menos, las producidas por la violación de dichas normas de higiene en el trabajo, como sucede en Italia) en el catálogo de conductas susceptibles de generar responsabilidad penal para las empresas.

Muchas gracias por la atención.

«LA CREACIÓN DEL FONDO DE COMPENSACIÓN PARA LAS VÍCTIMAS DEL AMIANTO EN ESPAÑA COMO MECANISMO EFICAZ PARA SU REPARACIÓN INTEGRAL»

Manuel José García Rodríguez
Universidad Pablo de Olavide

La promulgación en nuestro país de la Ley 21/2022, de 19 de octubre, por la que se crea el fondo de compensación para las víctimas del amianto, supone un hito decisivo para el reconocimiento de sus derechos a la reparación integral de los daños y perjuicios padecidos sobre la salud, como consecuencia de su exposición al amianto en el ámbito laboral, doméstico o ambiental en España, así como para sus causahabientes en caso de fallecimiento. Y, pese a que el desarrollo reglamentario de la Ley aún no se ha llevado a cabo, rebasándose con creces el plazo máximo de tres meses en que debía efectuarse, nosotros partiremos del proyecto de Real Decreto publicado en junio de 2023 por el Ministerio de Inclusión, Seguridad Social y Migraciones. Para tratar de determinar a partir de ambas regulaciones, en qué medida este nuevo fondo puede constituir un instrumento eficaz para conseguir la realización efectiva de la compensación propuesta. A partir de la evidencia científica que acredita la existencia de una relación directa entre la exposición al amianto y el desarrollo de determinadas enfermedades con diversos efectos para la salud[1], tal como ha puesto de manifiesto la reciente Directiva (UE) 2023/2668 del Parlamento Europeo y del Consejo, de 22 de noviembre de 2023, por la que se modifica la Directiva 2009/148/CE sobre protección de los trabajadores contra los riesgos relacionados con la exposición al amianto durante su trabajo[2]. Al declarar que, según las últimas estadísticas europeas sobre enfermedades profesionales, esa exposición es con diferencia la principal causa de cáncer profesional, con hasta un 78 % de casos reconocidos en los Estados miembros asociados a ella. Pues, «cuando se inhalan, las fibras de amianto suspendidas en el aire pueden provocar enfermedades graves, como mesotelioma y cáncer de pulmón, y los primeros signos de enfermedad pueden tardar una media de treinta años en manifestarse desde el momento de la exposición, dando lugar, en última instancia, a muertes relacionadas con el trabajo».

Dado que el gran problema del amianto radica en las graves enfermedades derivadas de las antiguas exposiciones, que como señala el propio preámbulo de la Ley 21/2022, afloran y seguirán aflorando aún con mayor intensidad en los próximos años[3] por su largo periodo de latencia[4]. Razón por la cual, en esta ponencia se valorará la oportunidad de crear este fondo de compensación para las víctimas, ante la gran cantidad de litigios que éstas se verán obligadas a promover para reclamar la reparación de los daños causados en su salud. Lo cual debe valorarse positivamente, pues a diferencia de los accidentes de trabajo, en las enfermedades profesionales los daños no son instantáneos, sino que aparecen muchos años después. Y concretamente en el caso del amianto, décadas más tarde, cuando las empresas responsables han podido desaparecer, dado que podemos estar

1 MINISTERIO DE SANIDAD, SERVICIOS SOCIALES E IGUALDAD, *Protocolos de vigilancia sanitaria específica Amianto* (3.ª ed.), 2013, p. 23 y ss., en: https://www.sanidad.gob.es/ciudadanos/saludAmbLaboral/docs/ProtoVigiAmianto1.pdf [Consulta: 07-05-24].

2 DO L de 30.11. 2023, pp. 1-13.

3 Según la Sociedad Española de Neumología y Cirugía Torácica (SEPAR), 20/07/20, «en España podría haber un total de 130.000 muertes a causa de la exposición al amianto para el año 2050, un 40 % por llegar», en: https://www.separ.es/node/1912 [Consulta: 07-05-24].

4 AZAGRA MALO, A., «Compensación de las víctimas del amianto en España», *Gerencia de Riesgos y Seguros*, N.° 102, 2008, p. 58.

hablando de exposiciones que se produjeron de veinte a cincuenta años antes. Situación a la que también debe añadirse el problema de que esos trabajadores han podido prestar servicios en diferentes empresas a lo largo de su vida laboral. Lo que, sin duda alguna, puede dificultar la identificación de la exposición concreta que generó la enfermedad y su responsabilidad en el pago de las indemnizaciones que correspondan a las personas afectadas o a sus familiares.

De manera que, ante estas circunstancias, la creación del nuevo fondo español para la compensación a las víctimas del amianto, puede ser una solución acertada para conseguir que estos trabajadores/as y sus familias que tengan vedada la vía judicial, por no tener empresa a la que reclamar su indemnización, puedan ver compensados los daños padecidos. Y si a ello se suma, que los procesos judiciales para reclamar esos daños suelen conllevar un coste económico muy elevado —honorarios de letrado, procurador y pruebas periciales, entre otros[5]—, cuyo desembolso no está disponible para todos estos trabajadores y sus familias, la gratuidad del procedimiento que ahora se habilita para reclamar la oportuna indemnización a cargo del nuevo fondo, también puede representar una vía más sencilla, ágil y rápida. Ante la ineficiencia del derecho de daños basado en la litigación, y en la prueba de los presupuestos de la responsabilidad civil extracontractual para compensar este tipo de daños[6].

Para cumplir con su finalidad, el fondo se integra por un conjunto de recursos económicos que se determinan en el propio texto de la Ley 21/2022 que lo regula (art. 4), cuya gestión se atribuye al Instituto Nacional de la Seguridad Social (INSS): a) Consignaciones o transferencias que se determinen cada año en la correspondiente Ley de Presupuestos Generales del Estado; b) Cantidades que se obtengan por subrogación de las personas afectadas por el amianto, o sus causahabientes, en vía judicial; y c) Aportaciones provenientes de las sanciones impuestas por la autoridad laboral correspondiente, a propuesta de la Inspección de Trabajo y

5 MORILLO GONZÁLEZ, F., «Algunos problemas en relación con la responsabilidad civil por daños personales producidos por la exposición a las fibras de amianto», *Cuadernos de Derecho Privado*, 1, 2021, p. 128.

6 Azagra Malo, A., «Los fondos de compensación del amianto en Francia y en Bélgica», *InDret Revista para el Análisis del Derecho*, N.° 3, 2007, p. 4.

Seguridad Social, por incumplimiento de las obligaciones en materia de seguridad y salud laborales relacionadas con el amianto, o cualquiera otros que se prevean en las leyes.

Sin embargo, no debe descartarse la posibilidad de completar esos recursos a través de otras vías, como las cotizaciones de los empresarios, tanto públicos como privados, por los trabajadores y trabajadoras por cuenta ajena, u otras procedentes de las mutuas de accidentes de trabajo y enfermedades profesionales[7]. Lo que está en línea con la regulación ya existente de este tipo de fondos en otros países, como en la vecina Francia o en Bélgica. Así, mientras el fondo francés se financia mediante contribuciones del Estado y la Seguridad Social y, en menor medida, por las donaciones y legados de particulares y por las acciones de subrogación contra los responsables de los daños que indemniza, el belga no solo lo hace a través de partidas presupuestarias estatales y con ocasionales donaciones y legados, sino también mediante las cotizaciones de los empleadores de las industrias del amianto. Lo que es considerado un acierto, ya que, de este modo, además de cargar parte del daño a quien lo causa, se consigue reducir el lastre que debe soportar el erario público[8].

Y en cuanto a su naturaleza, nos encontramos ante un fondo carente de personalidad jurídica[9], de los regulados en el art. 137 de la Ley 40/2015, de 1 de octubre, de Régimen Jurídico del Sector Público[10], encontrándose sujeto en cuanto a su régimen presupuestario, de contabilidad y control económico-financiero a las disposiciones previstas en la Ley 47/2003, de 26 de noviembre, General Presupuestaria, al

7 Aragón Bombín, R., *Guía para la Protección de las víctimas del Amianto, Secretaría de Salud Laboral y Medio Ambiente UGT-CEC*, 2019, p. 172, en: https://www.ugt.es/sites/default/files/guiaamianto_web.pdf [Consulta: 19-04-2024].

8 Azagra Malo, A., «Los fondos de compensación del amianto en Francia y en Bélgica», *op. cit.*, p. 10.

9 Guillén Subirán, C., «La creación de un fondo de compensación para las víctimas del amianto en España, tras veinte años desde la prohibición de su uso», *Gestión Práctica de Riesgos Laborales*, N.° 209, Diciembre de 2022, p. 2.

10 Cabero Morán, E., «La evitación de la exposición al amianto en el ámbito laboral y los nuevos derechos a la reparación integra de los daños», *Trabajo y Derecho*, N.° 97, Enero de 2023, p. 11.

formar parte según establece su art. 2.2. f) del sector público estatal[11]. Destacándose que la Ley 21/2022, para garantizar el cumplimiento de sus fines, crea una Comisión de Seguimiento adscrita al INSS, como órgano de consulta y asesoramiento, cuya composición valoramos positivamente que esté conformada por representantes de todos sectores interesados, Administración del Estado, organizaciones empresariales y sindicales más representativas, entidades y expertos de reconocido prestigio de la comunidad científica conocedores de las consecuencias y patologías derivadas del amianto, y de la Federación de Asociaciones de Víctimas del Amianto.

En cuanto a los beneficiarios, comprobamos que el propio texto legal delimita el conjunto de personas que pueden acceder a las compensaciones económicas del fondo (art. 6), señalando a las siguientes: a) personas que hayan obtenido el reconocimiento de una enfermedad profesional ocasionada por el amianto; b) personas con una enfermedad que no pueda ser reconocida como profesional, pero de la cual se haya determinado o pueda determinarse que su causa principal o coadyuvante ha sido su exposición al amianto, dado que el porcentaje de casos de afectados sin exposición laboral al mismo es también importante[12]; y c) causahabientes de los anteriores beneficiarios, en caso de fallecimiento, según se determine reglamentariamente.

Con relación al segundo grupo de la ley, el Proyecto de Reglamento se refiere a las personas que como consecuencia de su exposición al amianto de carácter laboral, ambiental o doméstico, padezcan mesotelioma o asbestosis «con repercusión funcional moderada o severa» según lo previsto en su anexo I. Reconociéndose de este modo a los denominados pasivos ambientales y domésticos[13], como viene haciendo el

---

11 *Benito Osma, F.*, «Gestión de riesgos y seguros. Reseña de actualidad», *La Ley Mercantil*, N.° 97, Diciembre de 2022, p. 2.

12 OSALAN, Instituto Vasco de Seguridad y Salud Laborales, *Los fondos de compensación para personas afectadas por el amianto*, 2012, p. 13, en: https://www.osalan.euskadi.eus/contenidos/informacion/a_informacionestudios/es_informe/adjuntos/fondo_compensacion_amianto_2012.pdf [Consulta: 07-05-24].

13 Vela Torres, P. J., «Responsable extracontractual. Indemnización de daños por amianto a los familiares de trabajadores de Uralita y a quienes residían en las proximidades de la fábrica», *Diario La Ley*, N.° 9880, Junio de 2021, p. 4.

Tribunal Supremo en su jurisprudencia sobre responsabilidad extracontractual, de la que es una buena muestra las SSTS 141/2021, de 15 de marzo, o 453/2021, de 28 de junio. Si bien, lleva razón FEDAVICA, CCOO y UGT en sus alegaciones formuladas al proyecto de Reglamento, al resaltar que el Real Decreto 1299/2006, 10 de noviembre, por el que se aprueba el cuadro de enfermedades profesionales en el sistema de la Seguridad Social y se establecen criterios para su notificación y registro, no distingue entre diferentes grados de asbestosis para reconocer la contingencia profesional, e incluye entre las enfermedades profesionales a las «afecciones fibrosantes de la pleura y pericardio que cursan con restricción respiratoria o cardíaca provocadas por amianto»[14]. Por lo que, de acuerdo a estas consideraciones, sería conveniente modificar la actual redacción de este apartado del art. 3 del Proyecto de Reglamento de la Ley 21/2022 para incluir estas patologías en los mismos términos previstos en el RD 1299/2006, sin restricción alguna.

Asimismo, por estar vinculada a la compensación reconocida a las personas beneficiarias, queremos hacer una breve referencia a la posible subrogación del Instituto Nacional de la Seguridad Social en todas las acciones y derechos que correspondan a las mismas, prevista en el art. 8.3 de la Ley 21/2022. Y para la que el Proyecto de su Reglamento establece un plazo de prescripción de cinco años a contar desde la resolución que reconozca esa compensación (art. 5). Que, a nuestro juicio, debe ser valorada positivamente, al representar una de las fuentes para la financiación del fondo de compensación español, que puede complementar al resto de sus recursos económicos. Siguiendo el modelo de otros fondos de compensación europeos, como el francés o el belga, que también se encargan de regularla en sus respectivos ordenamientos[15].

Acerca del procedimiento a seguir para hacer efectiva las compensaciones económicas a cargo del Fondo, la Ley

14 FEDAVICA, CCOO y UGT, *Alegaciones al Proyecto de Real Decreto por el que se regula el fondo de compensación para las víctimas del amianto en desarrollo de la Ley 21/2022, de 19 de octubre*, 2023, p. 2, en: https://www.ugt.es/sites/default/files/ALEGACIONES%20FONDO%20AMIANTO.pdf [Consulta: 07-05-2024].

15 Azagra Malo, A., «Los fondos de compensación del amianto en Francia y en Bélgica», *op. cit.*, p. 13.

21/2022, atribuye al Instituto Nacional de la Seguridad Social (art. 7) el diseño, implantación y seguimiento de los diferentes trámites que lo integran. Y determina que éste, se habrá de iniciar a solicitud de la persona perjudicada o de sus causahabientes, en caso de fallecimiento de aquella, aportando la documentación acreditativa e informes que se establezca reglamentariamente, para probar los daños y perjuicios a la salud resultantes de la exposición al amianto (art. 8). A cuyos efectos, debemos tener presentes las previsiones que sobre este particular se contienen en el Proyecto de Reglamento de la Ley 21/2022 (art. 7 a 13), que obliga a la persona interesada a presentar dos solicitudes, una primera para conseguir la certificación de patologías derivadas de la exposición al amianto, y otra segunda, para la compensación propiamente dicha.

De modo que, una vez recabada la certificación de patologías, la persona interesada deberá dirigirse a la Dirección General del INSS, cumplimentando el formulario de solicitud electrónico que a tal efecto se establezca en la sede electrónica de la Secretaría de Estado de la Seguridad Social y Pensiones. Se advierte, con razón, que esta previsión incluida en el Proyecto de Reglamento de la Ley 21/2022, contraviene el art. 14 de la Ley 39/2015, mediante el cual se establece que las personas físicas no tienen obligación de comunicarse, ni relacionarse con las Administraciones Públicas a través de medios electrónicos[16]. Motivo por el cual, se considera que debiera abrirse el abanico de posibles alternativas ofrecidas a los beneficiarios.

A continuación, la Dirección General del INSS procederá a aplicar el baremo indemnizatorio aprobado en el referido Proyecto de Reglamento para fijar la compensación a la persona interesada. Para acto seguido, dictar resolución reconociendo, en su caso, esa compensación que le será notificada a través de medios electrónicos en el plazo máximo de seis meses desde la fecha de entrada de la solicitud en el registro de dicha Dirección General. Para finalmente abonarla una sola vez y en pago único, mediante la oportuna transferencia bancaria en la cuenta de titularidad de la persona beneficiaria, de acuerdo con los plazos y procedimientos establecidos

16 FEDAVICA, CCOO y UGT, *Alegaciones al Proyecto de Real Decreto por el que se regula el fondo de compensación para las víctimas del amianto...*, *cit.*, p. 5.

en el art. 24.3 del Reglamento General de la gestión financiera de la Seguridad Social, aprobado por el RD 696/2018, de 29 de junio.

Debiéndose manifestar que las cuantías recogidas en el baremo indemnizatorio del Anexo I del actual Proyecto del Reglamento de la Ley 21/2022, nos parecen claramente insuficientes. Pues distan mucho de las indemnizaciones fijadas judicialmente, y como también se ha señalado en las alegaciones presentadas al citado Proyecto de Reglamento por FEDAVICA, CCOO y UGT, están muy alejadas de las previstas para otros colectivos de víctimas en los que concurren especiales circunstancias de vulnerabilidad, como las contempladas en la Ley 29/2011, de 22 de septiembre, de reconocimiento y protección integral a las víctimas del terrorismo[17], con las reconocidas a los afectados por el Virus de Inmunodeficiencia Humana (VIH) en el Real Decreto-ley 9/1993, de 28 de mayo, o las recientemente fijadas por el Real Decreto 574/2023, de 4 de julio, para regular el procedimiento de concesión de ayudas a las personas afectadas por la talidomida en España durante el periodo 1950-1985. Sin olvidar tampoco, que estas indemnizaciones del fondo de compensación para las víctimas del amianto tendrán que cotizar en el impuesto de la renta de las personas físicas, a pesar de que desde las diferentes asociaciones representativas de este colectivo y las organizaciones sindicales se insistió en la necesidad de que fuera reconocida la exención del IRPF[18].

Tras haber analizado el articulado de la Ley 21/2022, de 19 de octubre, mediante la cual se crea el fondo de compensación para las víctimas del amianto en España, poniéndolo en relación con las disposiciones del Proyecto de Reglamento que pretende desarrollarla, aún pendiente de aprobación por el Gobierno, consideramos que este nuevo fondo, que sigue el modelo de otros instaurados en el espacio europeo, puede constituir un instrumento eficaz para ellas a la hora de conseguir la reparación íntegra por los daños y perjuicios padecidos sobre su salud, tanto en el ámbito laboral, doméstico o

17 FEDAVICA, CCOO y UGT, *Alegaciones al Proyecto de Real Decreto por el que se regula el fondo de compensación para las víctimas del amianto..., cit.*, p. 7.

18 GUILLÉN SUBIRÁN, C., «La creación de un fondo de compensación para las víctimas del amianto en España...», *op. cit.*, p. 2.

ambiental en nuestro país, así como para sus causahabientes, en el caso de fallecimiento de las primeras.

Si bien, como hemos expuesto, existen algunos extremos de su regulación legal y del proyectado desarrollo reglamentario, que a nuestro juicio y en línea con las demandas formuladas por la Federación Española de Asociaciones de Víctimas del Amianto y las principales organizaciones sindicales de nuestro país, merecerían ser modificados con el fin de que éste pueda cumplir eficazmente con su finalidad. Entre los cuales, por su importancia, nosotros hemos destacado el relativo a la duplicidad de solicitudes exigida a los interesados para poner en marcha el procedimiento, y el que atañe al importe de las cuantías recogidas en el actual baremo indemnizatorio del Proyecto de Reglamento de la Ley 21/2022, que nos parecen muy insuficientes.

CONFERENCIA INVITADA

"CRIMINAL PROSECUTIONS FOR DEATHS FROM ASBESTOS IN ITALY: AN INTRODUCTION"

Barry Castleman
Environmental consultant

Thank you very much, Victor.

As a public health worker, I have also been involved in civil litigation in the United States, where companies were sued for failure to warn about the dangers of asbestos in their products, which subsequently caused grievous illness and death in product users. And so, I've spent also about the last 45 years going through corporate documents, and the corporate documents have been extraordinarily revealing about the mentality of the business world in dealing with public health issues like asbestos. But now, let me just again talking about what's going on in Italy.

Italy is exceptional in actually prosecuting businessmen, putting businessmen in jail, for failing to prevent occupational cancer among their workers and environmental cancers among the neighbours of their asbestos factories, and also other types of industries that are mentioned at the end.

So, in Italy it goes back to 1898 that the workers compensation law providing for compensation for injury and death on the job, also had requirements for heads of the enterprises to take preventive measures, and there were criminal and civil penalties for failure to do so. So, going back to the 1898 workers compensation law in Italy, they had this concept of criminal liability for failing to prevent preventable occupational injuries and diseases.

There was this case that was brought in Italy in the 1970's of the workers dying with bladder cancer. The workers were using these aromatic substances known as naphthalene and benzene, and these chemicals were recognized over 100 years ago by the ILO, the International Labor Organization, to be cancer causing substances, which had as their target organ the bladder. In Italy workers at this plant, the IPCA plant, became suspicious because they were noticing many of the workers had developed bladder cancer. They went to the union and this led to an investigation by the town officials, and the labor magistrate found 26 cases of bladder cancer in the workers and referred the case for criminal prosecution.

The dye plant owners, the managers and the long-time company doctor were charged. The employer's insurance has been required in Italy since 1935 for bladder cancer caused by manganese, so this was a long-standing legal requirement that employers carry insurance for injuries of this kind; and the workers urine had been subject to testing and analysis since 1961, but the workers were never told why.

There were over 100 workers who died from bladder cancer. The owners, and the plant managers were sentenced up to 6 years in jail; so, this is an extraordinary example of the state holding the owners and managers and even the company doctors responsible for not preventing preventable and long recognized risk of occupational cancer.

In Northern Italy, Hoffmann la Roche, the big Swiss company had set up a plant to make something called tetrachlorobenzene, which was used to make various types of soaps and disinfectants. The process was a very dangerous process, and this is why Hoffmann-La Roche set the plant up in Northern Italy rather than Switzorland. All of tho products were made for export to Switzerland and the United States, so this is a case where the hazardous process was exported by the Swiss multinational corporation to Northern Italy.

The plant operated for only 7 years after opening in 1969. It was well known that the process was dangerous because, if overheated, it would cause an explosive release of dioxin chemicals, which caused birth defects at extremely low levels of exposure. One Saturday the process ran out of control in 1976 and dioxins were blown all over the town of Seveso, and then, of course, there were pregnant women who were exposed to this air pollution and they did not want to have children with cleft palates and other kinds of grievous birth defects, and it was illegal to have an abortion in Italy at that time unless it was to save the life of the mother. This contributed to changes in the Italian abortion law and the EU law also on major industrial accident risks, which the people in Seveso were disappointed with; it was called the Seveso directive, published in 1982. Only the Italian managers were prosecuted, the Hoffmann-La Roche people and Switzerland managers were never prosecuted, and they paid a few million euros to compensate victims.

In Italy there was a fairly large asbestos enterprise called Eternit, it was a Swiss owned enterprise, and it was largely owned by the family of Stephan Schmidheiny. At the age of 29, in 1976, was made the Chief Executive Officer of this company which had asbestos manufacturing plants all over Europe, South America, Lebanon, India... They had plants all over the place, and they also owned asbestos mines; in Italy they owned an asbestos mine and several plants. One of the plants was a giant plant in the town of Casale Monferrato. In the town of Casale, only about 40,000 people live there, and every family has been affected; every family or friends of people living in Casale have been affected by this terrible asbestos catastrophe. So, the Italian prosecutors, after prosecuting the Italian managers of the Enterprise, went after the chief executive officer, the Swiss multi billionaire Stephan Schmidheiny. Schmidheiny, in the meanwhile, in the 1980s sold off most of his asbestos to cement plants, or closed them as demands on asbestos were spreading across Europe, and he was reinvesting the money in other things, I'll talk about that later but he was reinventing himself as a green businessman of all things, giving money to a conservation groups in Brazil and so on.

They had this trial in Italy and Schmidheiny was represented by very good lawyers, the best lawyers money can buy, and it was held in an auditorium, and the people could come in and observe what was going on. The Eternit trial began in 2009, the multibillionaire was charged with creating an environmental disaster, and there were an estimated 3,000 deaths from asbestos related cancer in the factory and in the neighbours who lived in the community who had only environmental exposure. Eternit documents were discovered that actually went back to 1931 talking about asbestosis, and then more documents in the 1950s. There were also the Italian prosecutors noticed that large payments had been made to a public relations firm called Belotti, which had offices in Milan. The prosecutors showed up one day at the Belotti offices with the police and seized the files for Eternit from Belotti. These documents revealed that Stephen Schmidheiny, upon taking control of that in 1976, had immediately organized training sessions for his managers in Germany in June of 1976 and then later in Switzerland, in October 1976. In these sessions, he trained the managers to threaten the unions and lie to the public about the hazards of asbestos, and some of these managers were probably hearing some of this for the first time, people who had worked for decades in these factories and had probably some breathing problems of their own because asbestos doesn't just cause cancer it can also cause a lung disease called asbestosis, which can be totally disabling or fatal.

Schmidheiny occasionally showed up at the Italian plant; being a young man, he was introduced as a Swiss technical specialist, not as the chief executive officer, to the Italian workers. There were letters exchanged between the Italian chief manager of the Enterprise and Schmidheiny, which went through Post Office boxes. The secretary of the Italian manager testified that she had never seen these letters, so these were letters that were meant to bypass everyone, except the top executives who were exchanging them. There were no dust counts done in the Casale plant, which is an indication that there was nothing done to protect the workers from the dust. If you actually install the proper industrial hygiene dust control system, you would think there would be some air sampling done before and after the system was put into operation to see how well it was working. No dust counts were ever found and there were no real records of the use of industrial ventilation at the plants. This plant also produced broken sheets and pipes, and the ordinary course of making asbestos cement pipes is that, if there's breakage, the broken sheets and pipes cannot be recycled. So, they had a huge operation outside the plant, crushing asbestos cement sheets and pipes, and then distributing the crushed asbestos to be used for surfacing roads. and driveways, and farm roads throughout the area. And so, the asbestos contamination was distributed to the environment in a massive and totally irretrievable way, and this is why most of the deaths from mesothelioma, the cancer that is seen as a signal tumor from asbestos, are on people who lived in the community but never worked in the factory.

There are 40 to 50 mesotheliomas a year in the town of Casale Monferrato, about once a week people are diagnosed with this cancer, which is always fatal, usually kills you in about a year from the time of diagnosis. It's a terrible disease, it's very painful. In one of the documents that was found in the Belotti files, the public relations people were bragging about the fact that they had confined all of the legal responsibility for what happened with it's contamination in Italy to level one Italian management, or level two Swiss Eternit Group, which is the Enterprise which by 1992 was just an empty shell. What they had done was selling off whatever they could and close the rest so that the Swiss Eternit group was nothing really, it was just an empty shell.

And level three there was Anova, which is where all the money went from selling asbestos mines and asbestos factories that they could sell, and this is a separate corporation that Schmidheiny had set up in Switzerland. And STS is level 4: Stephan Schmidheiny. And the memo goes on to explain that level three and four are not even to be mentioned in Italy, that the public relations people were only trying to focus all the media coverage and legal responsibility on the Italian managers and on the Swiss Eternit Group, the empty shell, the old company that had owned all the asbestos mines and factories.

So, this is a clear demonstration in a very clear way of just what the plan was, and it had worked very well. Through 1992 most of the people in Casale didn't know who Stephen Schmidheiny was. When the appeal court heard the case, they were so shocked by some of these documents that one of the judges compared Schmidheiny to Hitler, saying that this was like the final solution being planned in January 1942, when the industrial plan was developed to set up the crematoriums and the concentration camps on a vast industrial scale, so that they could kill people on the largest possible scale. So, this parallel was made by the judges and was picked up by the newspapers while the case was going.

The original trial found that Schmidheiny was guilty; he was sentenced to 16 years in jail. This is just all the people calling for justice for Eternit, in the town of Casale Monferrato. You can imagine: a town of 40,000 with one death per week for mesothelioma. Everybody knows somebody who's died from this. So Schmidheiny was sentenced to 16 years in jail, and the court judged that he had to pay about 100 million Euros in damages to individuals and families of individuals who had died from mesothelioma, the judgment was upheld by the court of appeal, where they commented on the comparison with the final solution and so that was they raise the sentence from 16 to 18 years in jail, adding some additional cases from Naples that hadn't been included in the original trial. Then, the Court of Cassation, in 2014, dismiss the case on the legal technicality of statute of limitations, saying that it's too bad that he did all these things but the law says that, as the court just determined, that the statute of limitations for creating an environmental disaster ends 10 years after the exposure, and the exposure was counted by the courts to end 10 years after the closure of the plant; even though all the contamination that they had put into Casale and all of the exposure of the workers were still in the bodies of the workers and ticking like a time bomb, and continuing death and disease month after month, year after year, after that 10 year period ended.

The prosecutor anticipated that there might be some funny business on the final appeal and so 6 months before that was decided, murder charges were prosecuted in turn, and Schmidheiny was charged with murder in the case of about 250 people in Turin in 2014. The Court of Cassation, and some other court that got involved eventually, it was determined that there would be four trials, one in each of the four regions of Italy where the deaths had occurred, and so the first of these trials went forward in Turin, in the case there was one death that went to verdict. Schmidheiny was sentenced to four years in jail, which was subsequently reduced to, I think, a year and a half in jail by the appeals court.

The Naples case needs their separate homicide trials. The case in Naples went to verdict in 2022 and again, for only one death that went to verdict. There were originally eight individuals in that group, and at the end only one death he was convicted of. There were other problems with statutes of limitations, even on manslaughter, there's no statute of limitation on murder, but the way murder is defined in Italian law made it impossible to sustain a verdict for murder. So, the charges may have been for murder, but the convictions were for manslaughter, and so the clock kept kicking, and there were cases that were thrown out on the basis of that. In the Novara trial for 392 deaths, Schmidheiny was sentenced to 12 years in jail, which went to trial last June 2023, so all of these are on appeal now. But Schmidheiny has been convicted by three courts, three trial courts for manslaughter based on the evidence that I described and other evidence.

I just want to talk briefly about criminal prosecution in Italy for other cases. There was a case involving the German company ThyssenKrupp, workers had been killed, burned to death, and the cause of this was because the company wasn't properly maintaining the plant, the plant was set to close in another year, most of the fire extinguishers didn't work when they reach for them to try and put out the fire when it began, and in the final appeal, the Italian managers were convicted in jail for years, the German managers were also sentenced one to 6 years and 8 months. The two German managers fled to Germany, initially the German government refused to turn them over to Italy and refused to prosecute them but ultimately the German law did imprison them German style.

But the way the Germans did it was these managers only had to show up in the evening and sleep in jail and then they could go back to work the next day, so it wasn't really jail the way you think of being in jail.

For a conclusion about all of this I mentioned I've been reading corporate documents for over 40 years, intern corporate documents about occupational cancer in the United States, and they show a very consistent picture that occupational health and safety decisions made by corporations were business decisions to the people who made them. That these decisions were matters of life and death to the workers or to the communities who live near the factories but to the people making the decisions of how much money to spend on things like dust controls, or how much financial risk to take by telling the workers how deadly this stuff was and how it could cause death and disease, these were business decisions and they were made by businessmen.

The corporate documents from numerous companies have dozens and dozens, hundreds of companies I think I must have seen, they all show the same picture. And so, I've concluded in the end that there's a five-part formula for the prevention of occupational and environmental disease.

Information, and that's the foundation of everything, information at the level of warning the workers, information at the level of doing the medical and scientific studies to identify the risks associated with the materials the workers are working with.

Regulations, number two, the industry has to meet at least some minimum standards that the government imposes to regulation, so that the companies don't have an advantage over each other by avoiding the costs of protecting their workers or protecting the communities from deadly pollution.

The third is compensation for the harm caused. Despite whatever information and regulation there is in place, people get injured from occupational or environmental disease. They deserve to be compensated by the industrial enterprises that cause those occupational environmental illnesses.

The fourth is humiliation. The corporations generally find people who are willing to say just about anything and to defend them, but it is an interesting thing to see in a jury trial as we have in the United States when an expert witness trying to tell a bunch of lies to a jury is practically laughed off by the time the cross-examination is concluded, showing what a liar he was.

And the last is incarceration, the idea that people will be held personally responsible for making business decisions that make workers die or suffer serious injury.

I think that all of these things, you don't have to choose, you need them all, in order to try to best prevent occupational and environmental disease.

So well, I'd be happy to discuss this with you further, this is basically what I wanted to talk about.

MESA III

LA EXPERIENCIA ITALIANA

INTRODUZIONE

Donato Castronuovo

Buenos días y bienvenidos a la tercera mesa de las jornadas de estudio sobre el «desastre lento». Voy a intentar hablar en español o cosa similar. Una vez más quiero dar las gracias a la profesora García Álvarez, y también al profesor Macías Caro, por su coordinación académica del congreso. Pero no quiero olvidarme de dar las gracias a Carmen Fernández y a Marta Rodríguez que nos han ayudado en la organización. Muchas gracias.

En esta tercera mesa de acuerdo con el método comparativo que anima estas jornadas de estudio os presentamos la experiencia italiana, gracias a las ponencias de nuestro amigo y colega Carlo Ruga Riva que hablará del desastre medioambiental a partir del caso Eternit; Luca Masera, con la exposición de las personas al amianto y sobre todo el problema de la causalidad; y Federica Carriero sobre el problema de la imprudencia y la culpa. Otra intervención italiana no tendrá lugar en la quinta mesa, la de la profesora Buoso, porque no puede conectarse.

Como ya se desprendía ayer de varias ponencias y en particular de la ponencia del señor Castleman, la experiencia italiana es en realidad la excepción italiana ya que, como confirman las investigaciones comparativas más recientes, la experiencia italiana se caracteriza fuertemente por la intención de ofrecer protección especialmente y casi exclusivamente, a través de la vía de la jurisdicción penal. En otras palabras, a pesar de que el fenómeno de la contaminación por amianto es más o menos el mismo en todos los países occidentales, sólo en Italia se opta por la vía de la protección mediante el recurso al derecho penal; un instrumento de tutela, el penal, que sin embargo se ha revelado a menudo disfuncional respecto a la finalidad de hacer justicia, no consiguiéndola, o a veces consiguiendo el objetivo, pero solo al precio de distorsiones evidentes de las categorías de imputación penales. Es decir, la reconstrucción del hecho objetivo típico, la identificación de los responsables, causalidad y culpabilidad, y, por lo tanto, a expensas de los principios constitucionales que rigen y limitan la responsabilidad penal al principio de legalidad y taxatividad, principio de personalidad y culpabilidad.

Sin duda, el amianto pone a dura prueba cualquier sistema de protección, sobre todo si es penal, por diversas razones de espacio, de tiempo, de personas... Razones que pueden resumirse en una crisis de complejidad, de incontenibilidad del Derecho y del Derecho penal frente a la sociedad del riesgo. Primera razón, el espacio. El amplio uso que se ha hecho del cemento amianto, del fibrocemento, y, por tanto, la producción masiva de artefactos de asbesto en Italia; prohibido solo desde el año 92; un material y una sustancia que se encuentran prácticamente en todas partes y de forma omnipresente, como nos recordó muy claramente YVONNE WATERMAN en la conferencia inaugural de ayer. Segunda razón: el tiempo, el enorme lapso de tiempo transcurrido entre la exposición al factor patógeno, las peligrosas fibras de amianto, y la aparición de enfermedades en la persona es calculable en varias décadas. Tercera razón: las personas. La victimización masiva, el enorme número de personas expuestas entre trabajadores y ciudadanos que viven en los alrededores de las fábricas o que, en cualquier caso, entran en contacto con las fibras. Piénsese en las mujeres que entraron en contacto masivo con el agente patógeno sólo por lavar los monos, los trajes de los maridos obreros que estaban expuestos directamente al amianto. Piénsese también en las numerosas ocasiones relacionadas con la renovación de edificios viejos.

Por lo tanto, desgraciadamente la del amianto es una tragodia, pero es una tragedia en la que las tres unidades aristotélicas de tiempo, lugar y acción con quedan completamente subvertidas, porque en su lugar nos encontramos con un tiempo ilimitado, un lugar sin fronteras y una multiplicidad inconmensurable de acciones y personas.

Esquematizando una historia judicial que empieza en los años 90 en Italia hemos tenido al menos dos fases, una primera fase en la que se utilizó el derecho penal de resultado lesivo, con los delitos de homicidio y lesiones culposos, y una segunda fase en la que, como alternativa a los delitos de resultado lesivo se utilizaron de los delitos de peligro contra la seguridad colectiva.

De los muchos casos judiciales dramáticos relacionados con el amianto, el caso Eternit es sin duda el más conocido, también en el extranjero. La notoriedad del caso se explica en gran medida por la magnitud de sus catastróficas consecuencias para la salud y el medio ambiente, pero también por su innovador paradigma de Derecho penal. Todos conocemos ya el gran éxito industrial y el triunfo comercial que han caracterizado la producción de materiales de cemento amianto durante al menos ochenta años el Eternit en Italia. El nombre comercial de los productos de cemento, lo que en España sería la Uralita, la Eternit, en cierto modo sigue formando parte de nuestro paisaje urbano industrial e incluso rural. Una presencia que es incluso omnipresente en las zonas de dentro y alrededor de las plantas de fabricación debido a la dispersión continua y masiva de fibras de amianto, así como, al menos en Casale de Monferrato, uno de los principales teatros de la tragedia del caso de Eternit debido a la costumbre de vender a los habitantes el llamado Polverino, el polvo residual del proceso industrial que luego se utilizaba para varios usos domésticos e incluso públicos.

Por tanto, dentro y fuera de los centros de producción de la llamada mala polvere, el mal polvo estaba por todas partes multiplicando con el tiempo inexorablemente el largo y triste catálogo de víctimas. Carlo Ruga Riva hablará del caso de Eternit antes de trazar sus reflexiones sobre aquel modelo de protección basado de forma innovadora ya no en los delitos de homicidio y lesiones, sino en los delitos de peligro común contra la seguridad colectiva; el desastre laboral y el desastre genérico en forma de desastre medioambiental y sanitario, ese innovador paradigma ha hecho posteriormente proselitismo y ha sido imitado en otros procesos penales relativos a la exposición industrial a sustancias tóxicas con proyección ofensiva dentro y fuera del lugar de trabajo.

A ese paradigma alternativo innovador de protección penal respecto del paradigma más tradicional para el orden penal italiano, basado en el homicidio y las lesiones culposas se había llegado una vez constatadas las enormes dificultades que entrañaba la utilización de los delitos de resultado de lesión en estos casos en la práctica judicial. La gestión de los criterios de imputación objetiva y subjetiva resulta en los casos de homicidio con nexo, con aspecto distinto respecto al del más riguroso cumplimiento de los estándares garantistas resumidos en el principio constitucional de la personalidad de la responsabilidad penal. En primer lugar, es el dogma de la *conditio sine qua non* el que muestra signos conspicuos de deformación praxiológica en los casos de exposición a sustancia tóxicas. Las dificultades del juicio de causalidad y de la relativa carga de prueba dependen de razones fácticas relativas a las modalidades y tiempos de exposición de las presuntas víctimas, pero también de razones cognitivas en función de posibles controversias científicas sobre los mecanismos de etiopatogenia.

En el caso del amianto basta pensar en las diferentes reconstrucciones patogénicas ofrecidas por las teorías de la correlación de dosis y respectivamente de la independencia de dosis, relacionada con la aparición de neoplasia. Reflejo jurisprudencial de esta complejidad puede verse en la tendencia a agotar el nexo condicional en un nexo de riesgo, reduciendo la averiguación de la causalidad del resultado a la mera constatación del aumento o no del riesgo en sí, y, en última instancia, estructurando la constatación causal según modelos reconstructivos de carácter epidemiológico mediante la valoración del aumento del riesgo de morbilidad o mortalidad como momento de la causalidad general, y mediante la devaluación correlativa de la verificación de la causalidad individual del caso concreto.

Las formidables y centrales cuestiones relativas a la causalidad en casos de amianto serán objeto de la ponencia de Luca Masera, pero la crisis del Derecho penal de resultado no depende únicamente de los problemas, a veces irreductibles, relativos a la comprobación del nexo causal en presencia de hechos delictivos vinculados a la exposición a factores de riesgo para la salud. Otras dificultades engrosan en torno a otros elementos esenciales de la estructura del delito, en particular los sujetos activos y la culpabilidad; en el caso del amianto la determinación de la responsabilidad penal suele referirse a actividades ilícitas que tienen lugar en un contexto organizado. De ahí la inevitable confrontación con determinados problemas propios del derecho penal de la empresa, capaces de representar un nervio en carne viva en el complicado intento de asegurar una protección eficaz de los bienes implicados y por tanto una respuesta punitiva eficiente, pero sin desbordar, por supuesto, los límites de las garantías trazados por los principios constitucionales.

En el caso del amianto la dificultad de reconstruir el hecho típico conforme al principio personalista se ve incrementada por un lado por los larguísimos tiempos de latencia de las enfermedades y, por tanto, por el desfase temporal entre la exposición y los hechos perjudiciales y, por otro lado, por la frecuente concurrencia de una pluralidad sincrónica y diacrónica de garantes dentro de una textura organizada. Por último, tampoco escapa a estas dinámicas de deformación praxiológica de la imputación penal el criterio de imputación subjetiva por imprudencia. FEDERICA CARRIERO nos dará cuenta de ello con referencia al homicidio imprudente, o incluso la imputación dolosa en referencia a los delitos de desastre laboral o medioambiental imputados de forma dolosa en los casos de homicidio.

La imprudencia en función de la considerable distancia entre la conducta y el hecho de la muerte o lesión tiende varias veces a ser distorsionada en valoraciones basadas en la visión retrospectiva, es decir, en datos cognitivos adquiridos solo ex post, y no según una correcta perspectiva de juicio ex ante. En ciertos casos judiciales, esta tendencia a formular juicios de imputación subjetiva enriquecidos por el patrimonio cognitivo madurado solo en momentos posteriores a la conducta se radicaliza aún más, se alude a aquellos modelos de decisión judicial que se inclinan por reconstruir las exigencias de reconocibilidad del riesgo y previsibilidad del hecho en situaciones de incertidumbre científica en el momento de la conducta, según una lógica próxima al principio de precaución.

Además, incluso la evitabilidad del resultado, especialmente en relación con la conducta consistente en la utilización de amianto antes de principios de los años noventa, resulta difícil de gestionar en los tribunales ante la identificación de las normas cautelares supuestamente violadas. A parte de un deber radical de abstención que no existía antes del noventa y dos, las normas infringidas según la inculpación son las que exigían desde los años cincuenta la reducción de todo tipo de dispersión de polvo en lugar de trabajo; normas de contenido muy general que son ciertamente infradimensionadas en comparación con la capacidad ofensiva y lesiva de la sustancia en cuestión. Es decir, en el caso del amianto, la mera reducción de la dispersión del polvo no es suficiente.

Todo ello contribuye al proceso de deformación de la categoría de la imprudencia relativa a los criterios de imputación objetiva y subjetiva del hecho dañoso contra la vida y la seguridad individual y, en particular, la dificilísima gestión de la dogmática causal en este proceso penal, han empujado por tanto a la jurisprudencia a buscar paradigmas alternativos e incluso experimentales.

En esta búsqueda destacan los desarrollos creativos practicados por la jurisprudencia italiana inaugurados precisamente en el asunto Eternit. El modelo del delito de resultado de lesión a un bien individual es sustituido por el modelo del delito de peligro común contra la seguridad colectiva. Este cambio de paradigma represivo ha producido un renacimiento de las figuras incriminatorias basadas en el desastre o, en todo caso, en el peligro común, especialmente en la forma dolosa, y en su caso, agravado por la realización efectiva del riesgo con proyección ofensiva dentro y fuera de la planta industrial o del lugar de trabajo. Una aplicación analógica de estos casos concebidos para una dinámica causal violenta e inmediata de fenómenos lesivos con causalidad serial y diluida en un período de tiempo muy largo, con la sospecha por tanto de una distorsión de la tipicidad y por lo mismo de una violación del principio de legalidad, la configurabilidad de esta hipótesis de delito con víctimas generalizada e indeterminadas en lugar de individuales tendría la ventaja de basarse en una causalidad de más fácil constatación al basarse exclusivamente en el conocimiento epidemiológico del aumento de casos de morbilidad o mortalidad de la población afectada por la exposición.

Pero de todo esto hablarán los siguientes ponentes. El orden de las ponencias, empezando por el profesor Masera, a quien cedo inmediatamente la palabra. El profesor Masera es profesor ordinario de la Universidad de Brescia y nos hablará de la cuestión de la causalidad precisamente el desastre medioambiental de amianto.

«L'ESPOSIZIONE ALL'AMIANTO E I REATI CONTRO LA VITA E L'INTEGRITÀ FISICA: PROFILI RIGUARDANTI LA CAUSALITÀ»

Luca Masera

Università degli Studi di Brescia

Prima di tutto voglio ringraziare gli organizzatori per questa bella occasione di confronto: le relazioni di ieri sono state per me davvero molto stimolanti e voglio altresì ringraziare di cuore i colleghi per la splendida ospitalità di questi giorni.

Nel mio intervento mi occuperò del problema dell'accertamento del *nesso causale* nell'ambito dei *reati di evento* (in modo particolare dei reati di omicidio e lesioni personali), quindi non mi occuperò del tema della configurabilità del reato di disastro, che sarà invece oggetto della relazione dell'amico Carlo Ruga Riva.

Strutturerò il mio intervento in due parti. La prima parte sarà relativa a una breve ricostruzione della *giurisprudenza*, dalle primissime decisioni dei primi anni 90 fino alla sentenza che rappresenta ancora oggi il punto di riferimento in materia di causalità e amianto, la sentenza *Cozzini* della Corte di Cassazione del 2010; nella seconda parte del mio intervento mi concentrerò sulle *questioni* ancora oggi *controverse*, e proporrò alcune *riflessioni critiche* di natura più generale, con particolare attenzione ai *profili epistemologici* del problema, che credo siano centrali per comprendere a fondo le difficoltà che ha incontrato la giurisprudenza italiana in questi anni.

1) L'evoluzione della giurisprudenza

Le prime decisioni in materia di morti da amianto sono degli anni Novanta del secolo scorso, e inizialmente la giurisprudenza ha un atteggiamento molto punitivo: la prima reazione dei giudici italiani è di stare dalla parte delle vittime, anche a costo di stravolgere il concetto di causalità. La nozione di causa *come condicio sine qua non* viene infatti sostituita dal concetto di *aumento del rischio*, con un'operazione che è molto diversa da quella tipica delle teorie di imputazione oggettiva di matrice tedesca, in cui il canone dell'aumento del rischio viene applicato *dopo* avere verificato il rapporto condizionalistico tra la condotta e l'evento: in questo orientamento, l'aumento del rischio va a sostituire la *condicio sine qua non*, con la conseguenza che le sentenze degli anni 90 consideravano sufficiente per poter accertare la causalità, e dunque per poter condannare per omicidio (colposo), la dimostrazione che l'esposizione all'amianto avesse aumentato il rischio per il singolo lavoratore esposto di contrarre la patologia da cui era poi risultato affetto.

Vediamo ora rapidamente gli snodi logici essenziali di questo indirizzo giurisprudenziale. Il primo passaggio importante è quello della qualificazione del *nesso causale* come *omissivo*, dal momento che il nesso di causalità sarebbe da instaurare non tanto tra la sostanza (l'amianto) e la patologia, ma tra la patologia e l'omissione da parte del datore di lavoro delle cautele necessarie per ridurre l'esposizione ad amianto. Il secondo passaggio logico consiste nell'affermare che la causalità omissiva è intrinsecamente, ontologicamente più ipotetica della causalità commissiva, e dunque non è possibile richiedere in questo contesto lo stesso grado di certezza richiesto per la prova del nesso di causalità commissivo: in ambito omissivo è sufficiente provare che la condotta omessa abbia aumentato il rischio di verificazione dell'evento.

Si tratta di una soluzione che non è poi così lontana da quella che è la soluzione adottata nell'ordinamento tedesco, in cui si riconosce espressamente una diversità ontologica tra causalità commissiva e omissiva. Questa impostazione viene tuttavia sottoposta a critiche molto forti da parte della dottrina italiana più autorevole (penso ad esempio agli scritti di Paliero del 1999 e di Donini del 2000, oltre che di Stella del 2001), secondo cui questo orientamento implica una distorsione del concetto di causalità, andando a sostituire surrettiziamente il criterio *prognostico* dell'aumento del rischio al criterio *ex post* della causalità in senso condizionalistico. Tale esito viene ritenuto in contrasto con due principi fondamentali del diritto e del processo penale: il principio di legalità, perché in questo modo si trasforma l'omicidio da reato d'evento in reato di pericolo, con cui si punisce taluno non perché abbia cagionato la morte di una persona, ma perché ha aumentato il rischio che una persona morisse; ed il principio di *in dubio pro reo*, perché nel dubbio se quella malattia e quella morte siano davvero da addebitare alla sostanza, invece di assolvere il responsabile dell'esposizione, il giudice emette una sentenza di condanna, in violazione del principio dell'oltre ogni ragionevole dubbio.

A queste critiche fa seguito un radicale cambiamento di orientamento della Corte di Cassazione, che in alcune sentenze dei primi anni 2000 arriva a richiedere, perché si possa ritenere validamente accertato il nesso causale, che il giudice abbia a disposizione una legge scientifica che correla la sostanza e la malattia con un coefficiente statistico prossimo al 100 %. Posto che in materia di danni legati all'amianto non esistono leggi scientifiche di tale forza statistica (nel senso che, per fortuna, non vi sono malattie che al 100 % si sviluppano in caso di esposizione ad amianto), tale orientamento conduceva alla pratica impossibilità di ritenere accertato il nesso causale in caso di malattie asbesto-correlate. Si tratta, tuttavia, di una teoria sostenuta da poche decisioni, e che risulta a ben vedere logicamente insostenibile. Faccio un esempio che può sembrare paradossale, ma che è la conseguenza logica di questa teoria: se Tizio spinge Caio dalla finestra al terzo piano e Caio muore, il giudice seguendo questo orientamento dovrebbe concludere che non c'è il nesso di causalità, perché non vi è una legge scientifica che consenta di affermare che la caduta dal terzo piano provoca la morte del soggetto nel 100 % o 99 % dei casi, posto che non sono così eccezionali casi di soggetti caduti dal terzo piano che sono rimasti in vita: identificare il concetto di causalità con il concetto di prevedibilità al 100 % dell'evento conduce ad aporie logiche, che portano ad un rapido abbandono di tale orientamento.

Il punto di svolta nel dibattito in tema di causalità è la sentenza *Franzese* delle Sezioni unite della Cassazione del 2002, che non ha ad oggetto un caso di responsabilità in materia di esposizione ad amianto, bensì un caso di responsabilità medica, ma afferma principi che vengono poi ripresi da tutta la giurisprudenza successiva, e quindi anche dalla giurisprudenza in materia d'amianto. Vale la pena dedicare un po' di attenzione a questa sentenza perché è vero che risale ormai a più di vent'anni fa, ma ancora oggi in Italia costituisce il punto di riferimento in materia di causalità, tutte le sentenze che si occupano di causalità ancora oggi partono dai principi della sentenza *Franzese*. Il modello di accertamento causale proposto in tale decisione ha una *struttura bifasica* (questa non è la terminologia che utilizza direttamente la Cassazione del 2002, ma è la terminologia con cui la dottrina ha interpretato la sentenza ed è poi la terminologia che la stessa giurisprudenza successiva ha preso ad usare): il primo passaggio è l›accertamento della *causalità generale*, cioè dell'idoneità lesiva della sostanza, della sua capacità di indurre la malattia da cui è risultata affetta la persona offesa; il secondo passaggio, decisivo, è l'accertamento della *causalità individuale*, cioè la verifica che la relazione causale ipotizzata dalla legge scientifica generale abbia trovato concreto riscontro nel caso specifico oggetto del giudizio. L'elemento poi che permette di passare dalla causalità generale alla causalità individuale non è il coefficiente statistico della legge di copertura (le Sezioni unite criticano apertamente l'orientamento del 100 %, ed affermano che anche una legge scientifica dal basso coefficiente statistico può fondare una sentenza di condanna), ma la verifica che nel caso concreto non ci siano altre *spiegazioni alternative* dell'evento. Il momento centrale da un punto di vista epistemologico è dunque la *fase abduttiva*, il giudice può accertare la causalità individuale anche qualora la legge di copertura abbia un basso coefficiente statistico (in altri termini, quando l'evento sia una conseguenza rara della condotta), se riesce ad eliminare possibili e ragionevoli spiegazioni alternative dell'evento. Ovviamente si potrebbe parlare a lungo di questa sentenza, sulla quale sono state scritte centinaia di pagine in Italia: ma vediamo qual è l'applicazione di questi principi al tema che ci interessa.

In relazione al problema della correlazione tra amianto e patologie tumorali, il punto di riferimento è la sentenza *Cozzini* della Corte di cassazione del 2010, relativa ad un caso di *mesotelioma pleurico* insorto tra lavoratori esposti ad amianto per ragioni professionali. Facendo applicazione del modello bifasico delineato da *Franzese,* la Cassazione ritiene possa ritenersi pacificamente provato che il mesotelioma pleurico sia una patologia riconducibile all'esposizione ad amianto, posto che si tratta di una *patologia firmata*, cioè una patologia che insorge in modo statisticamente significativo solo tra gli esposti alla sostanza. La questione dell'accertamento causale risulta, tuttavia, problematica, perché nel caso sottoposto alla Cassazione (come in quasi tutti i casi di esposizione ad amianto) si tratta di lavoratori che sono stati esposti a lungo (almeno per 10-20 anni) alla sostanza e in questi anni si sono succeduti diversi datori di lavoro: si è verificata una successione nelle posizioni di garanzia e, secondo il principio della personalità della responsabilità penale, ogni datore di lavoro è responsabile soltanto per la frazione temporale dell'esposizione a lui addebitabile. Il problema, quindi, non è se il mesotelioma è causato dall'amianto, ma se è possibile accertare scientificamente se ogni singola frazione dell'esposizione si può considerare causale rispetto all'insorgere della malattia: problema scientifico che già è stato discusso nelle relazioni che mi hanno preceduto e su cui quindi non mi soffermerò.

Nel dirimere la questione, la sentenza *Cozzini* affronta anzitutto il tema della relazione del giudice con la *conoscenza scientifica*: come deve orientarsi il giudice quando nel processo vengono proposte tesi scientifiche opposte dai consulenti tecnici delle parti? come fa a il giudice decidere? La sentenza del 2010 fa al riguardo delle affermazioni molto interessanti, che riprendono le conclusioni cui era giunta la Corte suprema americana nel *leading case* in materia, la sentenza *Daubert* del 1994, dove viene coniata l'espressione del *giudice* come *custode del metodo scientifico*, un giudice cioè che ovviamente non è in grado di risolvere la controversa scientifica, ma deve svolgere la funzione di custode della correttezza del dibattito scientifico all'interno del processo: tema di grande complessità, che qui non è possibile approfondire.

La sentenza *Cozzini* ritiene, alla luce di un'analisi del dibattito scientifico pertinente, che possa ritenersi affidabile la legge scientifica del mesotelioma come patologia *dose dipendente,* e quindi la tesi per cui ogni aumento dell'esposizione contribuisce ad accorciare il periodo di latenza, conducendo ad un'anticipazione dell'evento lesivo. Questa, però, secondo lo schema bifasico di *Franzese,* è la causalità generale: rimane il problema di accertare la causalità individuale, cioè di provare che proprio quel *singolo* lavoratore si sarebbe ammalato più tardi se fosse stato esposto per un periodo minore alla sostanza. Ma è possibile provare sul caso singolo l'effetto del prolungamento dell'esposizione? O è una *pro-*

batio diabolica, che conduce in sostanza sempre ad esiti di proscioglimento (come avvenuto nel caso *Cozzini*)?

2) I problemi aperti ed il ruolo della conoscenza epidemiologica nell'accertamento causale

Rispetto a tale domanda, la giurisprudenza italiana successiva a *Cozzini* mostra una radicale diversità di posizioni. Una parte consistente della giurisprudenza, anche di cassazione, ritiene che sia impossibile provare rispetto al singolo individuo il nesso di causalità, perché non sono disponibili sufficienti conoscenze scientifiche sul decorso della patologia per individuare il momento in cui è insorta e quindi per capire qual è il singolo datore di lavoro responsabile. Ci sono tuttavia altre sentenze che sostengono esattamente il contrario, cioè che la prova che il mesotelioma è una patologia dose dipendente consente di ritenere accertato il nesso di causalità anche sul singolo caso, perché la natura di dose dipendenza vuol dire che ciascuno di coloro che sono stati esposti ha visto ridotto il tempo di latenza della patologia in ragione della specifica frazione temporale addebitabile all'imputato.

Non è una situazione confortante, perché continuiamo ad assistere a decisioni opposte rispetto a casi pressoché identici: se la questione viene decisa da una sezione della Cassazione l'esito è la condanna, se viene decisa da un'altra sezione della Cassazione l'esito è l'assoluzione. Solitamente, in caso di contrasti giurisprudenziali, la soluzione è chiedere alle Sezioni unite della Cassazione di prendere una posizione, ma la Cassazione ha già risposto che in questo caso la remissione alle Sezioni unite non è possibile, perché non si tratta di una questione di diritto, ma di una *questione di fatto*, che deve essere decisa in sede di merito, e non di legittimità.

Venendo ora a qualche considerazione critica , il problema maggiore che deve affrontare la giurisprudenza in materia di amianto deriva a mio avviso dal fatto che il giudice si trova a confrontarsi con una disciplina scientifica «giovane», l'*epidemiologia*: una scienza che, come noto, viene fatta risalire alla metà del secolo scorso, con gli studi di Doll e Peto sugli effetti sulla popolazione del fumo di sigarette. L'epidemiologia è così difficile da maneggiare per il giurista penale, perché introduce una categoria epistemologica nuova, quella del *danno alla popolazione*. Il penalista è abituato a pensare al concetto di danno, declinandolo rispetto al *singolo* individuo che lo ha subito: l'omicidio o le lesioni tradizionalmente presuppongono che venga individuato il singolo soggetto che è morto o che ha subito una lesione, mentre l'epidemiologia non è in grado, per la sua stessa struttura epistemologica, di provare nessi di causalità individuale, posto che si occupa dei danni a collettività di individui. Quando pensa a danni alla popolazione, il penalista è abituato a ragionare in termini di *pericolo* per la salute o l'incolumità pubblica, ma l'epidemiologia non prova soltanto l'esistenza di pericoli o di rischi per la popolazione, ma può provare la causazione di veri e propri *danni* alla popolazione. Il concetto di danno alla popolazione non corrisponde quindi esattamente né ai reati di danno come l'omicidio, che secondo l'impostazione tradizionale richiedono l'individuazione della singola persona offesa, né ai reati di pericolo contro l'incolumità pubblica, perché non esprime solo un pericolo, ma un danno. Proverò ad essere più chiaro perché si tratta di un punto centrale. Quando l'epidemiologia afferma che il fumo di sigarette provoca un aumento dei tumori al polmone nella popolazione dei fumatori, non esprime solo la prova di un rischio per la salute pubblica, ma consente di affermare che migliaia di persone sono morte per il fumo di sigarette, anche se non è in grado di stabilire se il singolo soggetto fumatore è morto proprio per il fumo di sigarette, posto che ci sono molti soggetti non fumatori che muoiono di tumore al polmone.

Questa particolare capacità euristica del metodo epidemiologico si è tradotta in un problema giuridico tutt'altro che semplice: se si raggiunge la prova scientifica (certa oltre ogni ragionevole dubbio) che una determinata sostanza ha provocato un certo numero di vittime, questo è sufficiente per accertare il nesso di causalità per il reato di omicidio, o è necessario provare la derivazione causale della singola morte? Facendo un esempio, si accerta con sicurezza, sulla base di una affidabile legge epidemiologica, che dei 50 operai di una certa fabbrica morti per tumore al polmone, 30 sono addebitabili all'azione di una sostanza cui sono stati esposti, in violazione delle norme sulla sicurezza sul lavoro: su questa base probatoria, può il giudice condannare per omicidio (colposo), o la prova di un danno alla popolazione dei lavoratori basta solo per l'accertamento di reati contro l'incolumità pubblica, ma non di reati contro la vita, come l'omicidio?

In un libro del 2007 ho sostenuto la tesi che è sufficiente l'evidenza epidemiologica di un danno alla popolazione per accertare il nesso di causalità nell'ambito dei reati di omicidio, facendo riferimento all'istituto di origine tedesca dell'*accertamento alternativo* (*Wahlfeststellung*), che si applica proprio nei casi in cui si raggiunge la prova certa che c'è stata la commissione di un reato (in questo caso l'omicidio, visto che si accerta che la condotta ha provocato la morte di un certo numero di persone), ma non è possibile ricostruire in modo certo alcuni elementi del fatto (nel nostro caso, l'identità delle singole vittime addebitabili alla condotta), senza che questa incertezza comprometta la certezza della colpevolezza dell'imputato. Il tempo a disposizione non mi permette ora di sviluppare in modo più disteso questa tesi: se qualche studioso di lingua spagnola fosse interessato, nel 2017 ho pubblicato un lavoro su questi temi sulla rivista cilena *Politica criminal*. Il tentativo che ho fatto nel lavoro del 2007 e in diversi contributi successivi è di mostrare che in realtà l'idea per cui, per condannare per omicidio, sarebbe necessario individuare univocamente l'identità della persona di cui si è cagionata la morte, rappresenta solo un postulato, non imposto da alcun principio penalistico di garanzia. Sostituire la *condicio sine qua non* con l'aumento del rischio, come faceva la giurisprudenza degli anni Novanta, può in effetti condurre ad uno stravolgimento della nozione di causalità; ma nella prospettiva qui proposta, rimaniamo in una prospettiva *ex post*, perché l'evidenza epidemiologica prova la causazione di un danno, e non solo di un pericolo, per la popolazione, e non vi è quindi alcuna violazione dei principi di legalità e di *in dubio pro reo*.

Come è facile immaginare, è una tesi che ha suscitato moltissime critiche, ed anche a questo tavolo ci sono amici e colleghi che non la condividono; ma ci sono anche autori che invece l'hanno sostenuta, come Francesco Viganò, uno dei più autorevoli penalisti italiani, o Stefano Zirulia, giovane studioso che ha scritto una monografia in cui, senza percorrere la strada dell'accertamento alternativo, argomenta perché l'evidenza epidemiologica sia sufficiente per l'accertamento causale nei reati di omicidio.

Aderire a tale tesi può poi risultare rilevante in contesti anche molto diversi dall'esposizione ad amianto. Pensiamo a quello che è accaduto qualche anno fa in Grecia, in seguito alle politiche di austerità imposte dall'Unione europea e dalle istituzioni finanziarie internazionali dopo la crisi del debito pubblico. Diversi studi epidemiologici, pubblicati sulle maggiori riviste scientifiche internazionali, hanno accertato che la riduzione dei fondi alla sanità pubblica, imposta nell'ambito di tali politiche, ha comportato un aumento netto e significativo della mortalità infantile, o in altri termini ha cagionato la morte di migliaia di bambini. Sembra impossibile immaginare che ci possa essere responsabilità per omicidio, perché non si riesce ad individuare il singolo bambino che è morto in ragione del taglio della sanità, anche se si ha la certezza scientifica che migliaia di bambini non sarebbero morti se i fondi non fossero stati tagliati, ed essi fossero stati adeguatamente curati. La tesi che ho sostenuto vuole provare a mettere in discussione l'effettiva fondatezza del tradizionale modo di concepire le relazioni causali in ambito penale, che impedisce in casi come quello della Grecia financo di «vedere» i danni in termini di vite umane cagionati da ben precise scelte politiche ed economiche.

Avviandomi a concludere, l'attuale situazione della giurisprudenza penale italiana in materia di amianto non va esente da critiche, perché a nostro avviso non è stata compresa sino in fondo la novità epistemologica del metodo epidemiologico: o, nelle sentenze di assoluzione, si considera il dato epidemiologico insufficiente perché è necessaria la prova della causalità individuale, come fa la sentenza *Cozzini*; oppure, nelle sentenze di condanna, si prova a forzare il concetto di causalità individuale, ricorrendo in modo surrettizio alla teoria dell'aumento del rischio; o ancora, come vedremo nelle relazioni successive, si utilizza l'epidemiologia per provare la commissione di reati di pericolo contro la salute pubblica. Ma così come non è corretto utilizzare l'epidemiologia per provare il nesso causale singolare, così non è corretto affermare che l'evidenza epidemiologica possa provare solo un pericolo, e non un danno, per la vita e la salute. L'uso dell'epidemiologia pone, insomma, al penalista problemi complessi, perché propone una nuova categoria epistemologica, il *danno alla popolazione*, che rappresenta un inedito *tertium genus* tra le categorie classiche del danno individuale alla vita, e del pericolo per la salute pubblica: trovare una soluzione coerente con le capacità euristiche del metodo epidemiologico, e rispettosa dei principi di garanzia della materia penale, è obiettivo che non ci pare possa ancora considerarsi raggiunto dalla giurisprudenza italiana in tema di amianto.

Grazie per l'attenzione.

«L'ESPOSIZIONE ALL'AMIANTO DELLE PERSONE: PROFILI RIGUARDANTI LA CAUSALITÀ»

Federica Carriero
Sapienza Università di Roma

1. Quadro normativo di riferimento

Vorrei innanzitutto fare un ringraziamento a Victor e a tutti coloro che hanno contribuito alla realizzazione di questo magnifico evento.

La maggior parte delle condotte che vengono in rilievo nei processi di amianto sono collocabili in un arco temporale compreso tra la fine degli anni '50 e la fine degli anni '80 del secolo scorso. Ai tempi non esistevano, però, norme specificamente dedicate al rischio di amianto, fatto salvo quanto previsto nell'ambito dei d.p.r. nn. 547/1955 e 303/1956, recanti rispettivamente «Norme per la prevenzione degli infortuni sul lavoro» e «Norme generali per l'igiene del lavoro». Rilevano, in particolare, gli artt. 4 e 21 del d.p.r. n. 303/1956[1]

1 Art. 4. (Obblighi dei datori di lavoro, dei dirigenti e dei preposti) «I datori di lavoro, i dirigenti e i preposti che esercitano, dirigono o sovraintendono alle attività indicate all'art. 1, devono, nell'ambito delle rispettive attribuzioni e competenze: a) attuare le misure di igiene previste nel presente decreto; b) rendere edotti i lavoratori dei rischi specifici cui sono esposti e portare a loro conoscenza i modi di prevenire i danni derivanti dai rischi predetti; c) fornire ai lavoratori i necessari mezzi di protezione; d) disporre ed esigere che i singoli lavoratori osservino le norme di igiene ed usino i mezzi di protezione

e gli artt. 377 e 387 del d.p.r. n. 547/1955[2], che obbligavano i garanti della salute sul lavoro ad adottare, tra l'altro, misure idonee a ridurre la diffusione delle polveri nell'ambiente di lavoro e la loro inalazione da parte dei lavoratori (ZIRULIA, 93 s.). Si trattava di norme generiche che, per quanto concerne il «problema amianto», erano essenzialmente volte a prevenire il *rischio di asbestosi*, e non già anche quello di patologie

---

messi a loro disposizione». **Art. 21. (Difesa contro le polveri)** Nei lavori che danno luogo, normalmente alla formazione di polveri di qualunque specie, il datore di lavoro è tenuto ad adottare i provvedimenti atti ad impedirne o a ridurne, per quanto è possibile, lo sviluppo e la diffusione nell'ambiente di lavoro. Le misure da adottare a tal fine devono tenere conto della natura delle polveri e della loro concentrazione nella atmosfera. Ove non sia possibile sostituire il materiale di lavoro polveroso, si devono adottare procedimenti lavorativi in apparecchi chiusi ovvero muniti di sistemi di aspirazione e di raccolta, delle polveri, atti ad impedirne la dispersione. L'aspirazione deve essere effettuata, per quanto è possibile, immediatamente vicino al luogo di produzione delle polveri. Quando non siano attuabili le misure tecniche di prevenzione indicate nel comma precedente, e la natura del materiale polveroso lo consenta, si deve provvedere all'inumidimento del materiale stesso. Qualunque sia il sistema adottato per la raccolta a la eliminazione delle polveri, il datore di lavoro è tenuto ad impedire che esse possano rientrare nell'ambiente di lavoro. Nei lavori all'aperto e nei lavori di breve durata e quando la natura e la concentrazione delle polveri non esigano l'attuazione dei provvedimenti tecnici indicati ai commi precedenti, e non possano essere causa di danno o di incomodo al vicinato, l'ispettorato del lavoro può esonerare il datore di lavoro dagli obblighi previsti dai commi precedenti, prescrivendo, in sostituzione, ove sia necessario, mezzi personali di protezione. I mezzi personali possono altresì essere prescritti dall'Ispettorato del lavoro, ad integrazione dei provvedimenti previsti al comma terzo e quarto del presente articolo, in quelle operazioni in cui, per particolari difficoltà d'ordine tecnico, i predetti provvedimenti non sono atti a garantire efficacemente la protezione dei lavoratori contro le polveri.

2 **Art. 377**. «Il datore di lavoro, fermo restando quanto specificatamente previsto in altri articoli del presente decreto, deve mettere a disposizione dei lavoratori mezzi personali di protezione appropriati ai rischi inerenti alle lavorazioni ed operazioni effettuate, qualora manchino o siano insufficienti i mezzi tecnici di protezione. I detti mezzi personali di protezione devono possedere i necessari requisiti di resistenza e di idoneità nonché essere mantenuti ma buono stato di conservazione». **Art. 387**. «I lavoratori esposti a specifici rischi di inalazioni pericolose di gas, polveri o fumi nocivi devono avere a disposizione maschere respiratorie o altri dispositivi idonei, da conservarsi in luogo adatto facilmente accessibile e noto al personale».

tumorali, quali ad esempio *cancri ai polmoni* e *mesoteliomi pleurici*.

Sebbene, infatti, la consapevolezza della pericolosità dell'amianto sia piuttosto risalente —potendo, in effetti, farsi risalire agli anni '30 del secolo scorso (BARTOLI, § 5)— il consenso scientifico sulla necessità di *eliminare radicalmente* tale sostanza costituisce il risultato di un costante progresso della ricerca scientifica che è, poi, culminato negli anni '90 nell'adozione di un testo che ne ha previsto la (quasi) totale messa al bando. Si è in questo modo passati da un sistema improntato alla *gestione di un rischio lecito* ad uno volto alla *totale eliminazione del rischio* [PERINI, *passim*; PIERGALLINI, *passim*].

Per un lasso di tempo considerevole (che si è protratto almeno fino alla fine degli anni '80 e inizi anni '90) il nostro Paese si è infatti preoccupato di *contenere*, e non già di *azzerare* del tutto il *rischio* di diffusione delle polveri: l'obiettivo finale era pertanto quello di identificare dei *limiti di tolleranza di esposizione* capaci di individuare un *rischio consentito* di utilizzo della «sostanza maledetta» [DI AMATO, 1].

Si trattava di una strategia condivisa dagli organi sia pubblici che privati, essenzialmente volta a salvaguardare l'impiego dell'amianto dato il suo successo in ambito industriale, essendo questo un materiale a basso costo, resistente al fuoco, all'attrito, all'abrasione, agli agenti chimici, con alto potere coibente e fonoassorbente [NANO, 1602 ss.]. Non era però, una scelta arbitraria, essendo di fatto corroborata dalle opinioni di scienziati ed esperti sia italiani che stranieri.

Possiamo, ad esempio, ricordare come nel 1968 sia intervenuto il professore Vigliani, in un convegno dedicato proprio al tema dell'amianto tenutosi a Torino, sostenendo che «gli esposti professionalmente all'amianto vanno incontro a queste possibilità: asbestosi, cancro polmonare, mesotelioma della pleura». Avendo, poi, riguardo a quest'ultima patologia (che è quella che più ci interessa sotto il profilo della colpa) rilevava come «dai molti studi e ricerche pubblicate risultasse che in realtà si trovavano dei mesoteliomi pleurici con accresciuta frequenza non solo tra gli asbestosici, ma anche in persone esposte per poco tempo a polvere di amianto, oppure che hanno avuto una esposizione estremamente esigua» [VIGLIANI, 163 ss.; CENTONZE, 1030].

Nella medesima direzione, nel 1985 Girolamo Chiappino rimarcava come in nessun Paese avesse avuto credito l'ipotesi di bandire l'asbesto dagli impieghi industriali e che «l'azzeramento del rischio da fibre minerali è utopia, mentre la possibilità di ridurre le esposizioni fino ai limiti di buona sicurezza può esistere, per gli amianti, come esiste per decine di altri agenti chimici e fisici. [...]. Si deve oggi ritenere che l'uomo possa "convivere" con le fibre minerali purché, nello sfruttare gli indubbi vantaggi, eserciti quei controlli ed utilizzi quelle cautele che le conoscenze attuali consigliano: si tratta, cioè, di applicare anche in questo campo il comportamento che è correttamente attuato per il controllo di numerosi altri agenti quali le radiazioni, il benzene, il cloruro di vinile, il berillio, gli esplosivi ed altri. [..]. Il contenimento delle dispersioni ed il controllo sistematico delle concentrazioni può comportare una riduzione del rischio da asbesti, per la popolazione fino ad un livello che è stato definito "trascurabile"» [CHIAPPINO, 105 s.; CENTONZE, 1030].

Tale situazione, come si diceva, si è protratta fino a più o meno la metà degli anni '80, quando il legislatore è intervenuto avviando il progressivo abbandono dell'asbesto dapprima con una *circolare del Ministero della Sanità del 10 luglio 1986, n. 45* (Piano di interventi e misure tecniche per la individuazione ed eliminazione del rischio connesso all'impiego di materiali contenenti amianto in edifici scolastici e ospedalieri pubblici e privati); e poi, successivamente, con la *l. del 27 marzo 1992 n. 257* recante norme relative alla cessazione dell'impiego dell'amianto.

Eppure, a ben vedere, persino la l. n. 257 del 1992 —precipuamente dedicata alla «Cessazione dell'impiego dell'amianto»— costituisce la concretizzazione di una *regolazione normativa del rischio consentito* nell'esposizione a tale materiale. Se da un lato, infatti, l'art. 1 vieta «l'estrazione, l'importazione, l'esportazione, la commercializzazione e la produzione di amianto, di prodotti di amianto o di prodotti contenenti amianto», è la medesima disposizione a riconoscere *expressis verbis* una deroga a tali divieti per una «quantità massima di 800 chilogrammi e non oltre il 31 ottobre 2000, per amianto sotto forma di treccia o di materiale per guarnizioni non sostituibile con prodotti equivalenti disponibili». Abbiamo, poi, l'art 3 dedicato ai «valori limite» alla «concentrazione di fibre di amianto respirabili nei luoghi di lavoro che rinvia per la determinazione degli stessi all'art. 31 del d.lg. 15 agosto 1991, n. 277; l'art. 9 si occupa, infine, del «[c] ontrollo sulle dispersioni causate dai processi di lavorazione e sulle operazioni di smaltimento e bonifica» richiedendo una relazione annuale alle «imprese che utilizzano amianto, direttamente o indirettamente, nei processi produttivi, o che svolgono attività di smaltimento o di bonifica dell'amianto» [Centonze, 1041].

Questo, quindi, il quadro storico-normativo di riferimento. Proviamo, a questo punto, a delineare quelli che si ritengono essere i principali problemi sollevati in punto di colpa.

2. La colpa

(a) Responsabilità per «tipo» e «modo» di produzione

Al fine di comprendere quelle che sono le principali questioni che si possono sollevare rispetto all'accertamento della colpa, è utile partire dall'analisi di qualche caso concreto [per ambedue le ricostruzioni, v. Blaiotta, 266 ss.].

(i) Partiamo da un caso degli anni '90 (per l'esattezza, del 1995), in cui il giudice di prime cure ha ritenuto colpevole un datore di lavoro di omicidio colposo per la morte di un lavoratore, addetto all'applicazione a spruzzo di un prodotto contenente amianto, colpito da *mesotelioma* moltissimi anni dopo l'esposizione a polveri di amianto[3].

Il lavoratore aveva lavorato senza che fosse stata adottata alcuna misura tecnica, organizzativa o procedurale per eliminare o almeno ridurre lo sviluppo e la diffusione della polvere. All'epoca dei fatti, mentre erano da molto tempo note le potenzialità lesive dell'amianto in relazione all'asbestosi, non erano conosciuti gli effetti cancerogenetici. Il giudice ritenne comunque configurabili profili di colpa sia *generica* che *specifica*. La pronunzia è poi stata censurata dalla Corte d'Appello, essendosi ritenuto che fossero stati adottati caschi ventilanti, ritenuti gli unici strumenti utili in quelle con-

3 Pret. Torino, 9 febbraio 1995, Barbotto Beraud, in *Riv. it. dir. proc. pen.*, 1997, 1447, con nota di Piergallini, *Attività produttive*, cit.

dizioni di lavorazione. La suprema Corte, infine, ha riformato la pronunzia d'appello, confermando la sentenza del giudice di primo grado.

(ii) In un'altra sentenza, afferente alla morte di lavoratori che avevano manipolato amianto in un'officina per la riparazione e demolizione di carrozze ferroviarie, la Corte ha affermato che la prevedibilità dell'evento non riguardasse soltanto le specifiche conseguenze dannose che possono discendere da una certa condotta, ma si riferisse a *tutte le conseguenze lesive* che derivano da un certo tipo di comportamento. La *mancata eliminazione*, o *riduzione significativa*, della fonte di assunzione del pericolo comportava pertanto il rischio, del tutto prevedibile, dell'insorgere di una malattia gravemente lesiva della salute dei lavoratori addetti; non rilevava, viceversa, il fatto che fossero state successivamente conosciute altre conseguenze di particolare lesività derivanti dalla medesima esposizione. D'altronde —si sostiene nella sentenza— le misure di prevenzione da adottare per evitare l'insorgenza della malattia conosciuta (asbestosi) erano le stesse di quelle richieste per eliminare o ridurre gli altri rischi, anche non conosciuti; con la conseguenza, sotto il profilo obiettivo, che la mancata adozione di quelle misure ha cagionato l'evento, e sotto il profilo subiettivo che l'evento era prevedibile perché erano conosciute conseguenze potenzialmente letali della mancata adozione di quelle misure[4].

Ciò posto, un primo aspetto che emerge dalle sentenze poc'anzi riportate è che nella maggior parte (anche se non in tutti) i processi di amianto si contestano morti avvenute a causa di mesoteliomi pleurici. Sotto tale profilo, non intendiamo soffermarci sulla differenza che sussiste tra la natura *dose-dipendente/dose-indipendente*, che pure però pare rilevare sotto il profilo della colpa.

La qual cosa si comprende soprattutto se si considera che sussiste, ancora oggi, un dibattito a livello scientifico che si traduce in un vero e proprio *stallo epistemico* da cui sembra difficile uscire in ambito giuridico, e che ci fa dire che pro-

4 Cass., Sez. IV, 11 luglio 2002, n. 988, Macola, in *CED Cass.* n. 227000. L'indirizzo giurisprudenziale è stato ribadito in altre pronunzie: Cass., Sez. IV, 16 ottobre 2012, n. 49215, Gastaldi; Cass. 12 giugno 2014, n. 39516, Lania; Cass., Sez. IV, 30 marzo 2000, Camposano, in *CED Cass.* n. 21942 e in *Foro it.*, 2001, II, c. 278; Cass., Sez. IV, 11 maggio 1998, Calamandrei, *ivi*, 1999, II, c. 236.

babilmente il giudice più che *consumatore di leggi scientifiche* sia, ad oggi, un creatore di *massime giurisprudenziali* in grado di soppiantare il dato scientifico [CARRIERO, Cap. IV].

Ciò che intendiamo, al contrario, sottolineare è la differente eziologia sottesa alla contrazione rispettivamente dell'asbestosi e del mesotelioma: a differenza della prima (che è provocata da tutte le fibre inalate, medie, fini e ultrafini), il mesotelioma è causato da fibre ultra-fini che passano dal polmone alla pleura peritale. Ne deriva che se le misure applicabili fino agli anni '90 per eliminare o ridurre i rischi da polveri erano efficaci per prevenire, tra i danni da amianto, quelli per asbestosi, lo stesso non può sostenersi avendo riguardo al mesotelioma. Le fibre ultrasottili non erano, infatti, né visibili né eliminabili con le misure preventive allora disponibili: sia le maschere antipolvere individuali, che i filtri per gli impianti di aspirazione fissi e mobili erano, dunque, completamente inefficaci perché sicuramente permeabili alle fibre di diametro sub-micronico [BARTOLI, 7].

L'insieme di queste considerazioni ci orienta nel senso di affermare che la giurisprudenza ha probabilmente confuso la *responsabilità per il modo di produzione* (cioè le modalità attraverso cui si lavorava l'amianto) con quella per il *tipo di produzione* (cioè l'utilizzo dell'amianto *tout court*) [BRICOLA, 1234], cancellando *ex post* quella che —sino al divieto del 1992— era un'*area di rischio consentito* [ZIRULIA, 99; CENTONZE, 1027 ss.].

Tale logica produce una serie di scompensi sotto diversi profili.

Innanzitutto, sul piano della prevedibilità dell'evento, per cui occorre: a) non solo chiedersi quale sia l'evento oggetto di prevenzione da parte del soggetto agente, tra quello astratto (per cui sarebbe sufficiente richiamare u*n evento del tipo di quello che si è venuto a manifestare*, a prescindere dalla eziologia e dalla concreta lesività) e quello concreto; b) ma anche individuare il grado di soggettivizzazione del referente cui parametrare tale prevedibilità. Da quest'ultimo punto di vista, sembra infatti che agli imprenditori si sia «contestato di non aver precorso i tempi, supplendo all'inerzia delle autorità statali e anticipando il divieto di utilizzo dell'amianto attraverso il suo totale abbandono» [ZIRULIA, 99]. Contestazioni di questo tipo necessitano, nondimeno, di chiarimenti sul piano degli *obblighi di approfondimento* e di *aggiornamento* posti eventualmente in capo ai soggetti garanti nelle situazioni di incertezza scientifica [Ruga Riva, 1762].

In secondo luogo, sul piano della evitabilità, per il quale occorre valutare l'effettiva tenuta della condotta alternativa lecita, anche se si è visto come non fosse chiaro il rimprovero mosso nei riguardi dei garanti della salute.

Ciò posto, proviamo a valutare tutti questi punti, procedendo per gradi.

(b) La descrizione dell'evento prevedibile

Emerge, in primo luogo, la centralità del tema della *descrizione dell'evento prevedibile* [in generale: Forti, *passim*; Fornari, *passim*]. In particolare, occorre chiedersi se ai fini di una corretta imputazione di un accadimento nei riguardi di un soggetto (che soprattutto rispetti il *principio della responsabilità per fatto proprio e colpevole*, ex art. 27 coo. 1 e 3 c.p.) sia sufficiente richiamare un *generico evento di danno*, costituito da una qualsiasi patologia; oppure, se sia, al contrario, necessario individuare l'oggetto delle affermazioni predittive di rischio in un evento che *quantomeno contenga* quello specificamente realizzatosi [Castronuovo, *Il principio*, 168].

Il tema non è nuovo, avendo conosciuto importanti studi condotti sia in Italia che all'estero, che ci portano a chiedere quale sia l'evento che rileva sotto il profilo giuridico-penalistico: quello astratto (*abstrahierende Erfolgsbetrachtung*), oppure quello concreto (*konkretisierende Erfolgsbetrachtung*)?

In relazione, poi, a quest'ultimo orientamento —che è quello ad oggi maggioritario, in tema di causalità, soprattutto nella versione che ci deriva da Stella e da Engisch— occorre inoltre specificare se la «concretezza» dell'evento debba essere valutata alla luce di aspetti meramente *fenomenologici* (mero evento *hic et nunc*), oppure anche *normativi* [Stella, *passim*; Engisch, 41].

Se si avalla la prospettiva dell'evento concreto, è necessario che quello che si è venuto a manifestare possieda un'intensità lesiva quantomeno analoga a quella dell'evento pensato dal legislatore prima della cristallizzazione della regola cautelare (es. tumore ad esito mortale) [Castronuovo, *Il principio*, 168].

Sennonché, si è visto, come la giurisprudenza sembri essere compatta e univoca nel ritenere che «l'agente è rimproverabile se agisce —in contrasto con regole cautelari— sapendo (o dovendo sapere) che la sua condotta può avere conseguenze dannose, anche se questi esiti della condotta non sono determinabili preventivamente, purché si tratti di conseguenze del tipo di quelle prese in considerazione nel momento in cui la regola cautelare è stata redatta anche se non ancora interamente descritte e conosciute»[5]. E poiché, «tali conseguenze dannose consistevano nei danni alla salute, anche letali, derivanti dall'esposizione alle polveri nocive, non esistono motivi ragionevoli idonei ad escludere da tale categoria anche le patologie di carattere tumorale» [Zirulia, 94].

Non sembrerebbe essere, tuttavia, dello stesso avviso la dottrina. Alcuni hanno, ad esempio, sostenuto che «la descrizione di un generico evento di danno costituito da una qualsiasi patologia dilata e svuota il fondamentale giudizio di prevedibilità; e rende di conseguenza pure vacuo l'apprezzamento sull'evitabilità *ex ante* dell'evento per effetto delle condotte appropriate. Si finisce in questo modo col ritenere «prevedibili anche patologie per le quali non era scientificamente nota la derivazione dall'esposizione lavorativa [...] così estendendo l'imputazione colposa in modo smisurato» [Blaiotta, 271].

In effetti, un evento di massima genericità, come un indistinto danno alla persona, non consente di articolare in modo penetrante i giudizi di *prevedibilità* ed *evitabilità*, per la semplice ragione che non è chiaro a cosa tali giudizi debbano concretamente riferirsi [Blaiotta, 273; Forti, *passim*; Fornari, *passim*].

Avallare questa prospettiva significa, d'altronde, legare la prevedibilità dell'evento a considerazioni orientate dal *senno di poi*, e quindi al patrimonio cognitivo acquisito soltanto in epoca successiva a quella in cui si realizzavano le condotte [Castronuovo, *Fenomenologie*, 221]. Il punto di vista *ex ante* (che è quello dei destinatari dei precetti, della colpa, della prevedibilità e/o rappresentabilità delle conseguenze di determinate condotte) viene, così, inevitabilmente inquinato da considerazioni attinenti al piano *ex post* (che appartiene invece alla causalità), andando di fatto a fondersi con quest'ultimo.

---

5 Cass. pen., IV Sez. n. 4675 del 17.05.2006 Ud. —dep. 06/02/2007— Rv. 235661 (P.G. in proc. Bartalini e altri.)

Ne deriva la possibilità di attribuire valore anche a comportamenti che, nonostante non potessero (quantomeno non sempre) ai tempi essere effettivamente calibrati nell'ottica di prevenire eventi del tipo di quelli che si sono materialmente realizzati, si ritengono comunque in grado di integrare gli estremi dei fatti tipici contestati.

Purtuttavia, affinché un evento (di danno o di pericolo) assuma rilevanza in relazione ad una determinata condotta è necessario che questo rappresenti e concretizzi il rischio che si è attivato *ex ante* mediante lo specifico disvalore dell'azione compiuta; se ciò non avviene, può sorgere una questione di *(nesso di) disvalore*, e quindi anche di *(nesso di) di rischio* [DONINI, *Disvalore*, §§ 1 ss.].

Non basta, in effetti, una semplice noncuranza, o una mera rappresentazione (o eventualmente anche volizione) di un evento, se poi quello verificatosi *hic et nunc*: i) non appartiene alla classe di eventi che dovevano essere prevenuti/evitati da parte di una determinata categoria di soggetti, secondo un criterio che tenga conto della specifica "competenza dei rischi"; ii) non concretizza il rischio e il disvalore d'azione attivato *ex ante*.

Pur potendo, pertanto, il datore di lavoro essere formalmente in colpa sul piano del disvalore di azione, il «fatto colposo» non si esaurisce in una «pretesa inosservanza» di una regola di condotta (che, al contrario, rappresenta un mero indice del disvalore complessivo del fatto), dovendosi necessariamente concretizzare/identificare nell'offesa prodotta.

(c) Mesoteliomi ed evitabilità dell'evento

Nei processi ancora in corso, a fronte di una malattia professionale come il mesotelioma pleurico, si pone altresì il problema di stabilire con ragionevole certezza cosa sarebbe successo là dove si fossero adempiuti gli obblighi ai tempi imposti, che si è visto che si sostanziavano nella riduzione della diffusione delle polveri nell'ambiente di lavoro [DONINI, *Imputazione*, 118]. Dubbi, questi, che si alimentano se si considera —come si è già detto— che il mesotelioma è causato da *fibre ultrafini*, non visibili né eliminabili con le misure preventive allora disponibili.

L'unica misura che avrebbe, senza ogni ombra di dubbio, scongiurato eventi del tipo di quelli che si sono verificati consisteva, infatti, nella totale messa al bando della «sostanza maledetta». Altro è, in questo senso, chiedersi se l'adozione di una misura di questo tipo fosse, ai tempi, concretamente esigibile nei riguardi dei garanti della sicurezza, anche ed eventualmente a titolo di *colpa generica.* Sistematico, sul punto, è il richiamo al principio racchiuso nell'art. 2087 c.c. che impone l'adozione di misure secondo il *principio della massima sicurezza tecnologicamente fattibile ed attuabile* [ZIRULIA, 95]. Ma si tratta di un argomento su cui torneremo.

(d) Principio di precauzione

I problemi di cui *supra* si sollevano soprattutto per via della natura delle *regole cautelari* che stiamo analizzando: si trattava di norme cautelari che, pur essendo *modali* erano talmente *generiche* e *aperte*, da poter essere in grado di reggere qualsivoglia tipo di addebito colposo, limitandosi appunto a prescrivere la riduzione della dispersione di (qualsiasi tipo di) polveri sul luogo di lavoro. La natura e l'entità di siffatte cautele era naturalmente pensata in funzione delle caratteristiche delle sostanze che entravano nelle lavorazioni, che potevano essere inerti o altamente tossiche. Non solo. In tali situazioni è subentrato spesso anche il paradigma della *colpa generica*.

In relazione ad ambedue i profili, proprio l'assenza o l'incompletezza delle informazioni scientifiche avrebbe dovuto condurre —ad avviso della giurisprudenza— i garanti della sicurezza ad adottare l'approccio dell'incertezza proprio del *principio di precauzione* [BLAIOTTA, 273].

Trattasi, come è noto, di un «principio di legittimazione di interventi di autorità pubbliche» [PULITANÒ, 652], essendo essenzialmente volto a gestire *rischi non solo ontologicamente, ma anche nomologicamente ignoti* [*ex multis*: CASTRONUOVO, *Il principio*, *passim*; RUGA RIVA, 1761].

In dottrina, generalmente si ritiene che se tale principio possa essere posto alla base di *norme cautelari scritte e rigide* (es. disciplina in tema di limiti soglia), talune difficoltà possono sorgere, al contrario, in relazione a profili di *colpa generica*, fatti salvi i casi in cui vengano prese le opportune cautele ed accorgimenti [CASTRONUOVO, *Il principio*, 167 ss.; RUGA RIVA, 1761 ss.; DONINI, *Imputazione*, 75, nt. 16]. Cautele che non sono state evidentemente prese rispetto ai casi di cui si discute, in relazione ai quali, al netto delle regole cautelari che sono state già esaminate, si è frequentemente ravvisata la presenza di "residui" di colpa generica [Bartoli, § 8].

In questo senso, è utile soffermarsi su altre sentenze da cui emerge in maniera esplicita il richiamo a tale principio [tali sentenze sono state riprese da: Castronuovo, *Il principio*, 134].

(i) Nel caso del mesotelioma nei *cantieri navali Breda-Fincantieri di Porto Marghera*, gli imputati erano stati condannati dal Tribunale di Venezia (con sentenza poi confermata dalla Corte d'appello lagunare e dalla S.C.[6]), per aver colposamente cagionato la morte di undici operai esposti alle polveri di amianto, e in tre casi, anche delle loro mogli, le quali erano venute a contatto con le polveri tossiche lavando gli indumenti da lavoro dei coniugi [Castronuovo, *Il principio*, 134 ss.].

I giudici della quarta Sezione hanno, in primo luogo, ritenuto che: «[l]'esercizio di attività pericolosa avrebbe imposto all'imprenditore l'approntamento di ogni possibile cautela, dalla più semplice ed intuitiva (proteggere le vie respiratorie con maschere altamente filtranti; imporre accurati lavaggi alla cessazione dell'orario di lavoro con cambio degli indumenti da lavoro da sottoporsi, anch'essi, a lavaggio; riduzione al minimo delle polveri; loro appesantimento mediante acqua; loro aspirazione, ecc.), alle più complesse e sofisticate seconda quel che la scienza e la tecnica consigliavano. Non solo nulla di tutto questo venne fatto, ma, al contrario, emerge dall'istruttoria una grossolana indifferenza di fronte all'inalazione del le polveri tossiche» (§ 8.1).

Dopodiché, viene evocato il principio di precauzione avendo riguardo alle correlazioni patologiche non tumorali. Si è così sostenuto che: «anche a voler considerare che fosse nota solo la generica tossicità delle polveri d'amianto, causa di asbestosi, avrebbe risposto al principio di precauzione trattare con ogni cautela le polveri che si sapevano assai sottili (e, quindi, di agevole infiltrazione e fissazione polmonare) di sostanza comunque tossica» (§ 8.1). Non solo. Si è specificato, altresì, che la nozione di prevedibilità è parametrata sulla figura dell'agente modello, «ossia il modello dell'uomo che svolge paradigmaticamente una determinata attività, che importa l'assunzione di certe responsabilità, nella comunità, la quale esige che l'operato si ispiri a quel modello e faccia tutto ciò

6 Cass. pen., IV Sez. n. 33311 del 24.5.2012.

che da questo ci si aspetta. Un tale modello impone, nel caso estremo in cui il garante si renda conto di non essere in grado d'incidere sul rischio, l'abbandono della funzione, previa adeguata segnalazione al datore di lavoro» (§ 8.1).

In definitiva, si è ritenuto che non potesse assumersi che le conseguenze nefaste sulla salute derivanti dal contatto con le polveri d'amianto non fossero prevedibili.

(ii) Un altro caso particolarmente interessante è quello nei *cantieri navali Fincantieri di Riva Trigoso*[7], riguardante il delitto di omicidio colposo per la morte di un lavoratore rimasto esposto alle polveri di amianto presenti nell'ambiente di lavoro e ammalatosi di mesotelioma pleurico [CASTRONUOVO, *Il principio*, 134 ss.].

Anche qui, si è sostenuto che «ai fini della imputazione soggettiva dell'evento al soggetto agente, ai sensi dell'art. 43 c.p., la prevedibilità dell'evento dannoso, ossia la rappresentazione in capo all'agente della potenzialità dannosa del proprio agire può riconnettersi, invece, anche alla probabilità o anche solo alla possibilità (purché fondata su elementi concreti e non solo congetturali) che queste conseguenze dannose si producano, non potendosi limitare tale rappresentazione alle sole situazioni in cui sussista in tal senso una certezza scientifica. Tale conclusione è fondata sul condivisibile rilievo che le regole che disciplinano l'elemento soggettivo hanno funzione precauzionale e la precauzione richiede che si adottino certe cautele per evitare il verificarsi di eventi dannosi on che se scientificamente non certi ed anche se non preventivamente e specificamente individuati. I giudici di legittimità [...] affermano che il principio della concretizzazione del rischio va inteso con criteri di ragionevolezza interpretando la regola cautelare non in senso formale e statico ma secondo la sua *ratio* e secondo criteri che tengano conto dell'evoluzione delle conoscenze e della possibilità di ricondurre comunque l'evento alle conseguenze della violazione della regola di condotta [...] Sotto tale profilo, la S.C. distingue proprio in funzione della *ratio*, le regole cautelari per «aperte», nelle quali la regola è dettata sul presupposto che esistano o possano esistere conseguenze dannose non ancora conosciute, ed altre c.d. «rigide», che prendono in considerazione solo uno specifico e determinato evento».

---

7 Cass. pen. IV, Sez. n. 5117 del 22.11.2007.

(e) Agente-modello e obblighi di approfondimento scientifico

Nelle sentenze poc'anzi citate, ad un certo punto, si legge che la *nozione di prevedibilità* deve essere parametrata sulla *figura dell'agente modello*, «ossia il modello dell'uomo che svolge paradigmaticamente una determinata attività, che importa l'assunzione di certe responsabilità, nella comunità, la quale esige che l'operato si ispiri a quel modello e faccia tutto ciò che da questo ci si aspetta. Un tale modello impone, nel caso estremo in cui il garante si renda conto di non essere in grado d'incidere sul rischio, l'abbandono della funzione».

Un principio di questo tipo trova, come si diceva, terreno fertile soprattutto nei casi in cui si abbia a che fare con norme cautelari a carattere *aperto*, oppure nelle ipotesi in cui si contestino «residui» di *colpa generica*. Sotto tale profilo, al netto delle critiche che si possono svolgere rispetto alla contestazione in combinato dei profili di colpa generica o specifica, occorre evidenziare un altro dato. Soprattutto nelle ipotesi in cui si presentano *fattori di rischio a spettro inizialmente incerto*, si dovrebbe rendere, di volta in volta, necessario valutare l'effettivo patrimonio conoscitivo posseduto (o che avrebbe dovuto possedere l'/) dall'agente concreto al momento della condotta [con parole simili, v. Castronuovo, *Il principio*, 167], al fine di verificare se questo abbia o meno rispettato il *carattere dinamico del dovere di diligenza*, con riferimento al progresso delle conoscenze scientifiche [Marinucci, 29].

D'altronde, in dottrina frequentemente si sostiene che regole cautelari presentano il medesimo statuto delle leggi scientifiche, essendo queste valide in funzione della loro efficacia preventiva, e non già in virtù del loro recepimento in una fonte normativa formale [Castronuovo, *La colpa*, 279 ss., 284 ss.; Cornacchia, 501 ss.]. Non devono, pertanto, necessariamente avere natura giuridica, in quanto si fondano su un paradigma etiologico e nomologico. Ciò, di fatto, comporta la necessità di intendere e definire in dovere di diligenza in un'ottica appunto (non statica, bensì) dinamica, in funzione dei tempi che corrono, e anche talvolta a prescindere dalla *concreta cristallizzazione* di regole di condotta in apposite normative.

«*Dati fattuali* "anomali" (tipo, numero di malattie o di decessi significativamente superiori a quelli attesi; comparsa di malattie o di accadimenti ambientali mai osservati prima, specie dopo innovazioni nei sistemi di produzione o nel tipo di prodotto o sostanza, ecc.) possono [ad esempio] far sorgere in capo ai garanti, oltre che a taluni obblighi operativi, anche specifici obblighi di *conoscenza scientifica*», che cambiano a seconda del caso concreto, potendo variamente consistere in obblighi *di approfondimento scientifico* e/o in obblighi di *aggiornamento scientifico* [così, RUGA RIVA, 1762; v., inoltre PIERGALLINI, *passim*, sui c.d. «obblighi di ritiro»; BLAIOTTA, 272].

Siamo, d'altronde, al fuori dalle ipotesi di «fattori non conoscibili da nessuno *ex ante*», cioè quelli che pur essendo esistenti al tempo dell'azione non potranno evidentemente essere imputati ad alcun tipo di garante, non essendo possibile costruire su di essi né una colpa, né un dolo «sensati» *ex ante*. Nelle situazioni qui ipotizzate esistevano, infatti, pur sempre regole cautelari a tutela dell'integrità fisica (contro l'asbestosi), dalla cui violazione risulta, poi, anni più tardi, che sono derivate malattie non preventivabili al tempo della costruzione (e della violazione) della cautela, perché accertabili solo sulla base di leggi scientifiche scoperte in seguito (mesotelioma pleurico) [DONINI, *Imputazione*, 75].

Proprio in virtù della natura delle situazioni di cui si discute, si rende pertanto necessario valutare la presenza: (i) di eventuali *nozioni aggiuntive* o *superiori* del garante rispetto a quelle possedute dalla comunità scientifica, che siano tali da giustificare il superamento della figura dell'agente modello; (ii) delle *nozioni ragionevolmente raggiungibili*, soprattutto nei casi in cui ci si muova all'interno di organizzazioni complesse, altamente specializzate, dotate di dimensioni, capacità e risorse economiche tali da pretendere un innalzamento delle pretese cognitive e operative [CASTRONUOVO, *Il principio*, 167].

L'identificazione —secondo un metro di identificazione sociale— di cautele *ad personam* dell'*homo eiusdem* esigibili, ma *generalizzabili* a una categoria di agenti, costituisce una fondamentale garanzia per l'esercizio del diritto di difesa, che porta l'accusa ad indicare positivamente e concretamente che cosa *quel determinato soggetto* avrebbe dovuto o potuto fare in alternativa [DONINI, *L'elemento soggettivo*, § 5.6].

Ciò che, invece, la prassi insegna è che nella maggior parte delle volte si assiste ad una autentica «spersonalizzazione» dell'agente modello: le capacità predittive ed impeditive di cui è accreditato quello concreto diventano così pressoché illimitate in funzione della estensione «a tappeto» degli obblighi di sicurezza dei garanti apicali. Ciò determina un'eccessiva normativizzazione nella ricostruzione della colpa che produce esiti di iper-oggettivazione che dissolvono qualunque tentativo di individualizzazione del giudizio [Con parole simili, CASTRONUOVO, *Fenomenologie*, 222]. Si approda, così, ad una forma di *culpa in re ipsa* che è tutto, però, «fuorché quell'elemento soggettivo [...] che aveva in mente l'art. 43 c.p., ma soprattutto quella componente di colpevolezza esigibile da una figura umanizzata e differenziata di *homo eiusdem condicionis et professionis*» [DONINI, *Nesso di rischio*, § 9].

«L'ESPOSIZIONE ALL'AMIANTO DELL'AMBIENTE»

Carlo Ruga Riva
Università degli Studi di Milano-Bicocca

Ringrazio gli organizzatori per questo invito, che è stato molto gradito. Cercherò di parlare piano e mostrare più immagini rispetto alle parole che dirò. Questo per contenere anche i danni. Io parlerò del caso Eternit. Purtroppo, ieri non sono stato presente. Credo che sia già stato evocato, quindi cercherò di fare una specie di sintetico riassunto di quello che è accaduto. È stato un caso molto sentito nelle comunità locali, cioè nelle città e nelle fabbriche dove letteralmente veniva prodotto, ma poi ha avuto un'eco molto vasta sull'intera opinione pubblica perché parliamo di migliaia di morti in diversi stabilimenti e quindi volevo farvi un po' la storia di questa fabbrica e trarne qualche riflessione più ampia sulla figura, come vedremo controversa, del disastro innominato e nella sua accezione di disastro ambientale.

Come si diceva ad opera di altri, l'amianto ha avuto una storia industriale e una diffusione ubiquitaria nell'edilizia, nell'industria navale, nell'industria automobilistica e quindi era presente un po' ovunque in Italia. Viene vietato solamente con legge del 1992. I processi per morti d'amianto che si fanno e si sono fatti in Italia riguardano quasi sempre esposizioni che si sono verificate prevalentemente negli anni 70 e 80. Non ovviamente dal 92 in poi, ma già prima le grandi industrie chimiche e siderurgiche in Italia avevano chiuso oppure erano state molto ridimensionati; quindi, parliamo di esposizione negli anni 70 e 80, con tempi di latenza, come sappiamo, che possono arrivare anche a 40 o 50 anni.

E, in particolare, la società Eternit aveva in Italia quattro stabilimenti. Due in Piemonte, Casale Monferrato, che era più grande, un altro paesino che si chiama Cavagnolo, e altri due: uno in centro Italia e uno vicino a Napoli. Erano quattro gli stabilimenti, ma è stato fatto poi un processo unico, come vedremo, per disastro ambientale o innominato e poi adesso da ultimo sono stati fatti o sono pendenti processi per morti o ammalati di amianto rispetto a questi quattro stabilimenti in quattro diverse corti d'Assise italiane. È un capo di imputazione che ha caratteristiche molto particolare. L'anno di inizio di questo contestato disastro viene stabilito nel 1966, un arco temporale di circa 50 anni all'interno del quale curiosamente si sono verificate poche successioni nelle posizioni di garanzia, nel senso che la fabbrica o, meglio, la società che gestiva le fabbriche, è sempre o per lungo tempo stata o nelle mani di questi due soggetti, svizzero e belga, i due principali imputati.

È un processo penale, un maxiprocesso ambientale, con tutti i problemi processuali che derivano dalla grandezza della magnitudine di questa contestazione. Pensate che nel processo Eternit ci sono circa 6.000 parti civili tra parenti delle vittime, enti locali, comuni, province, associazioni sindacali, associazioni ambientaliste, insomma, una difficile gestione. Questo processo è un processo che ha dato come frutto una sentenza di primo grado di 700 pagine, una sentenza di secondo grado anche lì di 700 pagine, quindi potete immaginare i problemi di accertamento non tanto rispetto agli imputati, che erano solo due, ma rispetto alla esposizione a pericolo di così tante parti offese, parti civili, e quindi io qua ho messo due slides: una montagna iconica e un topolino, perché alla fine questo grande sforzo dello Stato, della magistratura, ha partorito un topolino nel senso, non vorrei svelarvi il finale, non è un finale ovviamente, come dire, a lieto fine, perché la vicenda è tragica: migliaia di morti. La cassazione ha detto che il reato era prescritto già prima della pronuncia della sentenza di primo grado; quindi, il processo non avrebbe dovuto neanche iniziare dal punto di vista del giudice di cassazione.

È stata una costruzione giuridica innovativa nel senso che, a partire dagli anni 90, sono stati fatti tanti processi per morti di amianto o per ammalati di asbestosi e altre patologie, però, quasi mai rispetto industria che producevano amianto, ma rispetto a particolari industrie chimiche e siderurgiche

che usavano l'amianto come prodotto di solito per coibentare tubazioni o per raffreddare determinati processi produttivi. Questo è un processo, però, che la procura di Torino ha voluto, non so se per dare un segnale o per intima convinzione, utilizzare la figura che si prestava a questa contestazione di disastro, che era, ed è, perché tuttora è presente nel nostro codice penale, una figura un po' paradossale... «innominata», senza nome, ed è paradossale rispetto al principio di tipicità che dovrebbe guidare il diritto penale.

«Chiunque con atti diretti a causare un crollo o un altro disastro», recita l'art. 434 c.p. Quindi in realtà la norma, il tipo penale è costruito su due parole, «altro disastro»; disastro si può più o meno capire. Poi vedremo la definizione giurisprudenziale che ha specificato questa nozione legislativa piuttosto vaga; «altro» si intende diverso, ma simile agli altri disastri tipicizzati che sono classicamente l'incendio: la frana, la valanga, l'inondazione, il naufragio ecc. Quindi, la fattispecie del 1930 —perché come voi sapete noi abbiamo ancora il codice fascista, ovvero il codice del periodo bellico— riflette una fase di sviluppo industriale e di evoluzione scientifica e tecnologica che lasciava presagire nuovi pericoli, non ancora ben delineati, per un numero indeterminato di persone; una norma programmaticamente aperta per il futuro, che servirà ad abbracciare futuri eventi, diciamo così, disastrosi per l'incolumità pubblica.

Quindi, l'articolo 434 in questa parte nasce appunto come capace di abbracciare tutta una serie di eventi che ancora non si immaginavano nella loro concretezza, ma nella loro, diciamo, tipologia astratta; tra questi eventi pericolosi per la pubblica incolumità la giurisprudenza, a partire dagli anni 80 e 90, include anche il cosiddetto disastro ambientale, cioè, le contaminazioni massicce dell'ambiente, delle matrici ambientali del suolo, dell'aria, dell'acqua, capaci poi di avere una proiezione offensiva verso la salute delle persone e, quindi, la Procura della Repubblica di Torino pesca dal cilindro dell'articolo 434 questo coniglio, diciamo così, e contesta due reati. Io parlerò del disastro ambientale ma, in realtà, l'imputazione prevede anche un'altra contestazione che, non so come si farà a tradurre, di omissione dolosa di cautele contro gli infortuni sul lavoro, detto più semplicemente, un reato dell'articolo 437 del codice penale, che punisce il datore di lavoro o l'imprenditore che non fornisce ai lavoratori strumenti di protezione o non crea un'organizzazione di lavoro capace di evitare malattie o infortuni.

Nel caso Eternit si contestava, lo vedete in questa slide, di non avere per esempio messo a disposizione sistemi di aspirazione delle polveri, di non avere arieggiato in modo adeguato i locali, di non aver previsto la pulizia dei vestiti (come sapete gli operai portavano a casa vestiti contaminati con l'asbesto, da qui diciamo anche casi di malattie asbesto correlate a danno di famigliari, tipicamente la moglie che lavava i vestiti del marito), quindi tutto questo viene contestato sia diciamo così come disastro interno ai luoghi di lavoro, dentro il recinto della fabbrica sia come disastro ambientale, cioè come contaminazione dell'ambiente esterno alla fabbrica, in parole povere della città o dell'aria diciamo contigua agli stabilimenti industriali; sono entrambi reati contestati in forma dolosa perché dalle carte raccolte, secondo la Procura vi era la prova della piena consapevolezza in capo ai due gestori della pericolosità dell'amianto, e anzi di campagne di finanziamenti volte a diciamo far passare nell'opinione pubblica un messaggio di scarsa pericolosità dell'amianto, oppure di possibilità di contenerne gli aspetti dannosi.

Dal punto di vista giuridico una questione interessante che ha posto questo caso è se valutare le morti e le malattie asbesto correlate come prova del pericolo contro l'incolumità pubblica; diceva prima l'amico Masera che in realtà l'eccesso di morti, considerato tale sulla base di studi epidemiologici seri, è un danno, non è un pericolo, quindi lì si contavano migliaia di morti il cui elenco viene allegato in queste sentenze e ancor prima nel capo di imputazione, e quindi era da valutare come dovessero considerarsi questi morti sia dal punto di vista delle eventuale elemento costitutivo del reato oppure della prova di un diverso elemento costitutivo che non era la morte ma era il pericolo per l'incolumità pubblica, cioè per l'integrità fisica di un numero vasto e indeterminato di persone.

Poi il tema collegato era da quando iniziassero a decorrere i termini di prescrizione del reato; questo perché fabbrica Eternit, parliamo di quella più grande di Casale Monferrato, chiuse negli anni Ottanta perché c'è il fallimento nel 1986 a seguito di varie voci sulla pericolosità dell'amianto. Entra in crisi la fabbrica, nell'86 fallisce e gran parte dei morti «arrivano» nel 2000-2020, a causa dei lunghi tempi di latenza. Quindi il reato quando si è consumato? Quando si è chiusa la fabbrica? Quando si è arrivati al picco dell'eccesso epidemiologico di morti, cioè quando i morti attesi continuano a essere superiori a quelli diciamo che ci si aspetterebbe? Questo elemento è stato diversamente valutato nei vari gradi di giudizio, però da subito la difficoltà è stata ad inquadrare i morti rispetto a un reato che non era di evento, come viceversa l'omicidio; non si puniva la causazione della morte dell'operaio o dell'ammalarsi del cittadino che viveva vicino alla fabbrica, appunto, con il disastro innominato, un pericolo per l'incolumità pubblica.

In primo grado è arrivata una condanna per sedici anni di reclusione per disastro doloroso e si è considerato però che il reato fosse prescritto rispetto ai due stabilimenti industriali di cemento amianto rispetto ai quali erano state effettuate bonifiche (nelle fabbriche di Napoli Bagnoli e di Rubiera), e quindi i giudici hanno detto il pericolo là non c'è più o comunque è stato contenuto, non c'è più un pericolo persistente e permanente di esposizione dei soggetti non soltanto perché la fabbrica è chiusa e gli operai non ci sono più, ma anche perché i cittadini non sono più a rischio, perché diciamo la bonifica ha permesso di confinare l'inquinamento; mentre è condannato a 16 anni di reclusione degli altri due stabilimenti perché perché non eran intervenute opere di bonifica e quindi, dicevano i giudici di primo grado, l'ambiente era ancora inquinato alla data del processo

In particolare, a Casale Monferrato le fibre di amianto si sono disperse per tutta la città attraverso il meccanismo di cessione gratuita o quasi di un residuo di produzione dell'amianto che era rappresentato dal cosiddetto polverino, che viene utilizzato per lastricare strade; ancora, le tegole non perfette venivano date agli operai che poi le utilizzavano su piccole strutture in campagna; tutto ciò ha comportato una contaminazione di tutto l'ambiente di vita intorno alla fabbrica.

Dopodiché, come spesso accade in questi processi molto discussi,c'è stato una riforma della sentenza; si è confermata la sentenza di condanna e anzi si è aumentata la pena da 16 a 18 anni di reclusione, per disastro doloso, ma è cambiata l'impostazione: si è parlato di un unico grande disastro che comprendeva sia l'area interna alla fabbrica,sia l'area esterna, quindi sia la fabbrica che la città; soprattutto i giudici di appello hanno dato una diversa interpretazione della consumazione del reato, dicendo che quello che conta non è la data di cessazione della produzione dell'amianto, quindi il reato non si sarebbe consumato fino al 1986 nel caso di Casale Monferrato; in realtà come elemento costitutivo del reato non ci sarebbe soltanto la diffusione nell'ambiente delle fibre di asbesto, ma uno degli elementi costitutivi, anzi il più importante, sarebbe il cosiddetto fenomeno epidemico, cioè l'epidemia di morti (l'eccesso di morti) per mesotelioma per asbestosi ed altro, che lungi dall'essere finito deve ancora vedere il suo picco più alto, perché qua siamo nel 2010 circa, ma le previsioni del numero maggiore di morti sono mi pare per il 2020.

Quindi la Corte d'Appello ha detto non soltanto che il reato non si è prescritto, ma addirittura che non si è ancora del tutto consumato nella sua pienezza, e questo accadrà quando comincerà a diminuire il numero di morti entro limiti diciamo diversi dall'eccesso calcolato dall'epidemiologia; quindi la Corte di Appello ha dato un'interpretazione molto come dire dilatata nel concetto di consumazione, arrivando ad inserire il cosiddetto fenomeno epidemico dentro i requisiti di fattispecie del disastro nominato, e dando vita così come ha sintetizzato la dottrina al concetto di disastro sanitario.

C'è una situazione di grave pericolo tuttora in essere per un numero indeterminato, in questo caso molto ampio di persone; dice espressamente la Corte d'Appello che soltanto nel momento in cui l'eccesso numerico dei casi di soggetti deceduti ammalati rispetto agli attesi diminuirà, allora verrà meno la consumazione del reato e quindi da lì cominceranno a decorrere i termini di prescrizione. Dal punto di vista civilistico la Corte d'Appello fa una interessante osservazione perché dice che il danno risarcibile non è soltanto quello legato alla perdita della vita, al prezzo del dolore subito dai familiari dei morti, ma che tutti i soggetti esposti, quindi anche quelli che non si sono ammalati, hanno diritto al risarcimento, perché la loro qualità di vita è diminuita, perché sanno di essere dentro il target di una classe di persone a rischio; tu operaio sei stato esposto, sei stato molto più fortunato dei tuoi compagni di lavoro ma sai che avendo vissuto quella situazione di vita potresti subire l'insorgenza della malattia; quindi il risarcimento è stato previsto anche per i soggetti che non hanno contratto alcuna malattia.

Si giunge in Cassazione con grandi aspettative delle parti civili e delle parti sociali, perché appunto si vedeva la fine vicina di questa questione molto controversa, ma la Corte di Cassazione, su richiesta conforme del Procuratore generale, ha annullato la sentenza di condanna, ritenendo che in realtà la consumazione del reato si sia esaurita negli anni 80, e che quindi è spirato il termine di prescrizione previsto dalla legge italiana per questo tipo di reato; ha quindi assolto tutti i due gli imputati, ma quel che è peggio, ovviamente per le parti civili, è stata la revoca delle disposizioni di condanna al risarcimento del danno; al di là poi degli aspetti monetari, che non sono quelli probabilmente principali, «brucia» l'idea che questo processo non si sarebbe dovuto nemmeno iniziare perché termini di prescrizione sarebbero già esauriti al momento della sentenza di primo grado. Si è trattato di una vicenda molto complicata e di difficile gestione processuale, che però, come anticipavo all'inizio, non ha prodotto i risultati sperati dalle parti civili che erano quelli appunto di una condanna e di un risarcimento congruo.

Come ha reagito la Procura di Torino e in generale la magistratura? Ha cercato di rispondere a questa debacle processuale modificando l'approcci, tornando se vogliamo a quel filone che avevamo visto all'inizio, e cioè ha instaurato diversi nuovi procedimenti penali, questa volta non per omicidio colposo o per lesioni colpose, ma per omicidio e lesioni dolose di centinaia di persone (operai e cittadini nel caso di Casale Monferrato), o di numeri minori per varie ragioni negli altri processi.

Non si tratta più di un processo unico per un reato di pericolo, ma di tanti processi quanti erano gli stabilimenti e quanti sono i soggetti morti che sul piano causale si ritengono correlabili a certi datori di lavoro.

Gli ultimi procedimenti sono stati giudicati da Corti di Assise, essendo un'imputazione per omicidio doloso, ovvero una Corte composta da cinque giudici popolari da due giudici togati; le Corti di Assise di Novara, di Napoli e di Torino hanno ad oggi condannato in primo grado, però riqualificando il fatto da omicidio doloroso a omicidio colposo. Io non ho letto queste sentenze perché sono ancora sentenze di merito, non mi risulta ancora pubblicate, però capite bene che nel caso di condanna per omicidio doloroso avrebbero dovuto dare l'ergastolo o poco meno e quindi forse è stata anche una scelta legata a una sorta di equità e proporzionalità.

Però insomma la storia della risposta giudiziaria penale al problema dell'amianto, come si vede, non è ancora finita, e quindi si è passati dalle contestazioni per omicidio colposo degli anni 90 poi finite spesso con annullamenti da parte della Cassazione al tentativo diciamo pionieristico del disastro innominato o sanitario o ambientale e infine si ritorna si è ritornati all'omicidio però nella versione dell'omicidio doloso; come vedete tra impostazioni diverse che tradiscono diverse opzioni. Prima di concludere volevo fare un breve riferimento al reato di disastro ambientale, che è stato introdotto in Italia nel 2015, nell'ambito di un pacchetto più vasto di nuovi delitti ambientali, il quale prevede anche una figura che un po' a cavallo tra il disastro ambientale e il disastro sanitario; si tratta dell'articolo 452 quater n.3 c.p., secondo cui costituisce disastro ambientale l'offesa alla pubblica incolumità in ragione della rilevanza del fatto; pertanto si intende un fatto di contaminazione dell'ambiente anche attraverso sostanze chimiche o patogene, per l'estensione della compromissione o dei suoi effetti lesivi ovvero per il numero delle persone offese esposte a pericolo.

Si tratta di un reato «ibrido», che ha tra le sue proiezioni di tutela sia l'ambiente sia soprattutto direi l'offesa alla pubblica incolumità.

Dalle tante pagine che ho letto, perché queste sentenze come vi dicevo sono di 700 pagine l'una, una cosa mi è saltata all'occhio; soprattutto la Cassazione riprende la giurisprudenza in materia di disastro ambientale e parla della necessità di verificare la cosiddetta immutato loci, cioè una modifica dei luoghi dovuti a una contaminazione ambientale; in questo caso, con l'esposizione alle fibre di asbesto, non c'è nessun dato probatorio, non è stata fatta nessuna consulenza che abbia studiato gli effetti dell'amianto per esempio sulla fauna, sugli animali, sull'acqua o sul suolo. Non so se ne avete parlato ieri, però in questo processo i giudici non si sono posti minimamente il problema del grado di tossicità o di pericolosità dell'amianto per la flora o per la fauna o per il suolo o per le altre matrici ambientali. Perché?

Una ultima cosa che forse c'entra poco con l'amianto, ma lo dico per un futuro convegno, e cioè il tema complesso della sindacabilità penale di scelte politiche. Si è fatto l'esempio della Grecia, e cioè di drastici tagli alla sanità pubblica su richiesta del Fondo Monetario Internazionale e dell'Unione Europe, tagli che hanno causato in ipotesi molti morti.

Si tratta di scelte politiche che prevedono bilanciamenti di interessi molto delicati; questo è evidente così come evidente è prevedibilità degli eventi, probabilmente. Ma questo basta a condannare o c'è un problema di scelte politiche che devono essere e devono rimanere tali? e la sanzione può o dovrebbe essere che perdi le elezioni la volta dopo?

Traslando questo discorso al caso del disastro ambientale, può menzionarsi il caso Ilva (enorme stabilimento siderurgico a Taranto, il più grande d'Europa). Abbiamo avuto un grande processo penale, ancora pendente, nel quale si contesta ai gestori della fabbrica di avere causato danni ambientali e morti attraverso emissioni di diossina, pur conformi ai valori di legge all'epoca vigente. Anche lin quel caso si può riflettere sul concetto di rischio consentito, e più in generale ci si può interrogare su scelte politico amministrative rivelatesi poi inadeguate.

Il vero tema, secondo me, non è tanto la causalità, e neppure l'elemento soggettivo, quanto invece un tema vertiginoso: quanto possiamo tollerare socialmente, quanto possiamo sindacare giuridicamente determinati assetti produttivi, determinate scelte politiche che naturalmente hanno ricadute pesanti sull'uomo, sulla salute, sull'ambiente eccetera?

Adesso vi faccio un ultimo esempio: sto seguendo come avvocato un processo penale per l'incendio di un palazzo a Milano, edificio che era rivestito di materiale spagnolo prodotto dalla ditta Alucoil, che, credo, è la stessa ditta che ha rivestito il palazzo di Valencia che sia incendiato di recente con morti. Ecco questo prodotto (pannelli di alluminio che contengono all'interno polietilene) all'epoca della posa era assolutamente commerciabile, e di fatto utilizzato per rivestire palazzi anche di lusso; quindi, non era un prodotto usato per risparmiare. Tuttavia, negli ultimi anni sono bruciati palazzi rivestiti con questo materiale, in Spagna, in Italia, negli Emirati Arabi e altrove.

Questo è un problema che sarà sempre più sentito nel futuro e ci saranno tanti processi per incendio; sul piano causale non ci sono dubbi Il problema è anche quello appunto di intervenire ex post rispetto a ad assetti produttivi e legislativi che consideravano lecito quel prodotto, che a distanza di anni si rivela pericoloso Quindi, e concludo, ho toccato temi diversi tra loro, collegabili però idealmente da un filo rosso, e cioè dal rapporto tra scelte politiche amministrative, da un lato, e sindacato penale dall'altro.

È vero, da un lato, che il diritto penale si deve occupare di cose serie, e dunque di vicende che causano decine di morti. Al tempo stesso però l'interferenza con scelte politiche e amministrative è assai delicata, ed è perlomeno problematico che il diritto penale, ex post, intervenga sulla libertà di persone che, ex ante, potevano talvolta fare affidamento su di un quadro normativo e di conoscenze diverso da quello esistente al momento del giudizio.

Grazie.

MESA IV

LA PERSPECTIVA DE LAS VÍCTIMAS

«LA EXPERIENCIA DE LAS ASOCIACIONES Y COLECTIVOS DE VÍCTIMAS DEL AMIANTO: HISTORIA, LOGROS Y REIVINDICACIONES ACTUALES»

Juan Carlos Paúl Hernández

Presidente de la Federación de Asociaciones y Colectivos de Víctimas del Amianto (FEDAVIDA)

Quiero agradecer a los alumnos que están aquí a estas horas su presencia, sé que es duro he preparado un kahoot para después para que estéis un poquito atentos porque, además, parece ser que me lo ha pedido la organización para luego valorar vuestro interés y vuestra atención, así que yo no digo nada.

Como ha dicho Manuel, soy presidente de la Asociación de Víctimas del Amianto inicialmente y, posteriormente, desde ese inicio de trabajo en la Asociación de Madrid, y también por una cuestión casual de centralidad, empecé a dinamizar la creación de asociaciones en todo el territorio nacional. Bien es verdad que la Asociación de Víctimas de Madrid no es la primera, precisamente la primera Asociación de Víctimas de amianto se crea aquí, en Dos Hermanas, muy relacionada con la fábrica de Uralita en Bellavista, y que son ellos los que me piden asistir a un encuentro informativo que organicé en Getafe. Y de ellos parte la iniciativa de que nos creemos también en Getafe como asociación, y nos cedieron su nombre, o sea que el nombre de Avida Asociación de Víctimas del amianto es una creación de aquí, de Andalucía, concretamente de Sevilla; y con esas siglas al final en todo el año, en todo el territorio nacional, hemos ido creando asociaciones: Agavida, Asociación Gallega de Victimas do Amianto en Galicia, Alviamie, que significa lo mismo en euskera, etcétera, etcétera.

Yo lo que vengo a contaros es un poquito la perspectiva de la víctima y también entraré, que ayer salió el debate, en por qué nos consideramos víctimas, no personas enfermas, personas que somos víctimas.

Vale, duelo eterno. ¿Qué ocurre con las personas que están afectadas con amianto? Ayer se comentó, hoy lo recalco, que las enfermedades relacionadas con el amianto son todas incurables, no hay cura para ninguna enfermedad del amianto, y no hay cura precisamente por cómo se provocan. Se provocan por inhalación de microfibras, partículas muy pequeñas, casi siempre o la mayoría de las veces por vía respiratoria, que se van acumulando finalmente en los alvéolos pulmonares, en otros lugares también, se ha demostrado después, pero básicamente, fundamentalmente, en los alvéolos pulmonares. Esas fibras, como son tan pequeñas y tienen una dispersión tan grande, una vez dentro del pulmón no se pueden realizar operaciones de rescatar ese pulmón, es decir, de cortar una parte donde se me ha generado el tumor y ya está. No, porque están por todo el pulmón, y lo que vienen haciendo es que los pulmones, sabíais que es un músculo que se expande, esponjoso, vayan perdiendo esa capacidad; y algo que tiene que expandirse cuando se llena de aire y comprimirse para expulsarlo, cada vez es más rígido.

Entonces fijaros cómo es la agonía de esas personas que tienen este tipo de enfermedad pulmonar, se mueren ahogándose, se ahogan y los familiares que están al lado lo están viendo de hecho. Aprovechando que están los compañeros italianos, yo escuché a Romana, la presidenta de la Asociación de víctima de amianto de Casale, recién salida de la primera vista del juicio de Turín, que le preguntaban: «Bueno Romana, ¿qué esperas, qué deseas que le pase a Schmidheiny, al dueño de la fábrica de Eternit?», y lo único que deseaba es que Schmidheiny, el responsable de la muerte de cinco personas de su familia de las que solamente una había trabajado con el amianto, lo que deseaba es que sufriera o que tuviera que acompañar a un enfermo de mesotelioma en sus últimos meses de vida, para que supiera el daño y la agonía que ha provocado.

Esto tiene que ver también con por qué nos conformamos con compensaciones económicas y no queremos meter a alguien en la cárcel, luego cuál es el proceso de una persona de este tipo. Daros cuenta, como ya sabéis porque lo hemos dicho varias veces, que estas enfermedades aparecen entre los 25 y los 45 años después de haber estado expuestos. Imaginaros Sevilla, estamos aquí en la fábrica Uralita, una fábrica *superpotente*, una media de 400 trabajadores anuales, que —estamos hablando de los años sobre todo 80 o 70— recoge mucha inmigración, posiblemente aquí vendría gente de Huelva, pero también de Extremadura, gente que desarrolla su vida en esa fábrica, pero que luego, una vez que se jubila, que no está enferma, se vuelve a su pueblecito de Extremadura o se va a Córdoba y sigue con su vida y, después, un día no puede respirar. «Vamos a ver qué le pasa», se va al médico. Acaban en el neumólogo y le dice: «Pues usted tiene un mesotelioma». Se ha atinado que os diré ahora cuál es el problema de esto, no, bueno, «¿y eso qué es?» «Pues es una enfermedad que tiene que ver con el amianto». «¿Amianto?» «Sí, en la fábrica dónde usted trabajó, en Uralita, pues ahí». «Pero si ya ha pasado mucho tiempo, si me jubilé hace 15 años».

Entonces, esa es la primera dificultad, que es el diagnóstico, se ve además agravado porque posiblemente ese señor ha tenido suerte, pero habrá habido otros muchos que han ido a su pueblecito, y el médico de familia cuando ve que tiene esa enfermedad esa dificultad para respirar dice «¿usted fumó?» «Hombre sí, pero ya no fumo». «Ya está, ha sido el tabaco», y ese diagnóstico se queda sin hacer completo, que como veremos es uno de los problemas que tienen estas enfermedades, que existe un infrarregistro tremendo; no solamente en España, en España del 7 %, pero en toda Europa, porque muchas veces es difícil encontrar la relación entre la enfermedad desarrollada y el origen y perdemos la pista.

En Getafe, bueno igual, es un pueblo al sur de Madrid con un número muy importante de casos, y es verdad que los servicios de Neumología se especializan, identifican este tipo de enfermedad con donde ha trabajado, relación causa efecto rapidísimo. Entonces claro, el trabajador se ve una situación de desconcierto diciendo «¿cómo me pasa a mí, si a mí nunca me han dicho que trabajo con algo peligroso, qué está ocurriendo si me han tratado muy bien?» Volviendo al caso que tenemos cerquita: Uralita. Uralita era una fábrica en teoría ejemplar, luego hemos entendido por qué. ¿Por qué? Porque daba ayudas de libros para sus trabajadores, para los niños de los trabajadores, tenía un economato, que es algo como un supermercado moderno, en los que solamente iban sus trabajadores y que tenía precios especiales para hacer la compra. Tenían Reyes, en el caso de Getafe tenía la mejor piscina de verano que había en toda la zona sur de Madrid, tenía campos de fútbol y todo eso para sus trabajadores.

¿Qué se estaba pretendiendo en aquel momento, y empiezo también a dar indicios de la criminalidad? El empresario quería mantener contenta a su gente y crear un vínculo que le evitase luego posteriores demandas y denuncias. Ante esa dicotomía nos hemos encontrado: «Pero ¿cómo voy a denunciar a mi fábrica con lo bien que me ha tratado?» En España las características de nuestro mercado laboral es entrar en una empresa y pervivir ahí toda la vida, y al final la empresa es que es tuya, tú sientes que has sacado adelante a la empresa.

Entonces otra de las cosas que nos pasa cuando decimos podemos exigir tus derechos es eso: «Pero ¿yo cómo ir contra la fábrica?» o como me decía hace unas semanas Juan, un amigo personal mío que va a ser el primer caso que vamos a llevar contra lo que es ahora Airbus, decía «Pero bueno, ¿cómo vamos a denunciar el caso de mi padre si es que mi hijo acaba de entrar a trabajar en la fábrica? A ver si van a tomar algún tipo de represalia». Volvemos otra vez con la ecuación y la posición de represión y de adecuación hacia los trabajadores.

Lo siguiente, es decir: «¿Pero esto no tiene cura? ¿cómo que no tiene cura? Vamos a ver, vámonos al Hospital de Navarra, que son muy buenos en oncología, o vamos a ver en Estados Unidos». Y cuando intentas explicar no, no tiene cura, los tratamientos que estamos llevando en España son los mismos tratamientos que se dan en el resto de Europa y en el resto del mundo, no hay. Es verdad que últimamente hemos avanzado en la reducción del dolor, vale, no curamos, pero estamos haciendo que al menos la calidad de vida de los enfermos vaya siendo mejor. Pero, el final está allí, además, es un final indeterminado, sobre todo en el caso de los mesoteliomas, que hemos visto casos de tres meses o seis meses de vida a lo más extremos de cinco años desde que se hace el diagnóstico hasta que se produce el fallecimiento.

La negación, es lo que decía antes, es la culpa: «No mi empresa no, si me ha tratado muy bien, cómo va a ser de la empresa, porque no puede ser, tiene que ser otro sitio». Y luego ya empieza la rabia y el temor. La rabia porque finalmente te dices se han aprovechado de mí, se han enriquecido a mi costa, ya le demostramos que lo sabían, que incluso en el caso de Getafe se pasaban cada dos años un reconocimiento médico con una cartilla y, curiosamente, cuando había una anotación del neumólogo esa hoja desaparecía de la cartilla, y sería entonces de haberla arrancado. Ahí empieza la rabia. Y luego el temor, porque ya vas cogiendo información, tienes información, y dices bueno igual no tengo un mesotelioma, que es el cáncer que es 100 % provocado por el amianto, el 10 %, el 5 % que dicen que no está, no es que se haya encontrado otro origen distinto, sino que no se ha demostrado la exposición al amianto, por eso nunca se dice que sea el 100 %, se habla entre el 90 % o el 95 % de origen por la exposición al amianto.

Y es lo que comento, cualquier enfermedad relacionada con el amianto significa que has inspirado fibras de amianto, y de estas enfermedades que pueden ir de las que se llaman beneficiosas, que pueden ser unas placas plurales o puede ser una asbestosis, te puedes morir en el momento que tengas que morir, sin que sea por esto, pero ya tienes fibras de amianto.

Pero, claro, estas fibras de amianto en cualquier momento pueden provocar un mesotelioma, o un cáncer de pulmón. O sea, no es una progresión de enfermedades, son distintas enfermedades, pero todas te dicen que tienes amianto en tu cuerpo. Y puedes tener unas placas pleurales incluso sin restricción funcional y a los dos días tener un mesotelioma, y es cuando tus días están contados, en meses prácticamente.

Ese temor a estar enfermo es algo que marca siempre ya toda la vida del enfermo, más allá, marca la vida del enfermo y de su familia. ¿Por qué? Porque venimos de la época que venimos, de la situación de España después de la guerra, y era tradicional llevarse la ropa de trabajo a casa. Y os acordáis, vosotros los más mayores, vosotros los más pequeños igual lo habéis visto en algún sitio, tenéis una referencia de la madre sacudiendo la ropa antes de meterla a la lavadora. Claro, cuando esas fibras de amianto venían impregnadas en los monos, es más en contra la normativa venían con bolsillos, luego cargaban bien el amianto, y lo sacudían. Quien estaba expuesta era la esposa y los críos correteaban por allí.

Ya no es solamente tu temor «estoy enfermo, es más tengo una enfermedad que puede llegar a ser mortal», sino «qué pasa con mi mujer, qué pasa con mis hijos». Porque es una realidad que mujeres, incluso hijos de trabajadores han enfermado y han fallecido sin estar el trabajador enfermo. Evidentemente tenían fibras de amianto, pero por lo que sea, no se sabe por qué, no ha enfermado, en cambio la mujer ha fallecido o la hija ha fallecido. Voy metiendo coletillas: hace un año y medio o así llamamos a una familia, tenían el caso del padre, Fernando los había defendido, y los llamamos porque tenemos sentencia, una buena sentencia. Le llamamos para comunicarle a la mujer y tres hijos, dos hijos y una hija, la noticia «hemos ganado, bueno pues perfecto, se ha hecho justicia, al menos tu madre va a poder vivir un poquito mejor, al menos vosotros vais a poder...» Bueno, vale, es verdad que esa victoria no resarce la pena, no resarce el daño, pero bueno, compensa y sobre todo da a las empresas donde más les duele, que es en la economía.

Se van, y la hija se queda un poquito para atrás, la mujer de unos 44 años. «Bueno, ¿qué tal? ¿Todo bien?» «Sí, sí. De todas maneras» me dice «Juan Carlos, guárdame un hueco en la semana que viene, que voy a traer mis papeles». «¿Tus papeles?». «Sí, es que la semana pasada me diagnosticaron un mesotelioma». O sea, en el mismo día que le daban la noticia de haber ganado contra la empresa, la multinacional Uralita, una hija que jamás había estado expuesta al amianto en el ámbito laboral nos comunicaba que también tenía una enfermedad relacionada con el amianto. Falleció a los seis meses, la mujer de cuarenta y cinco años sin haber estado expuesta.

Por ahí el temor. Otro ejemplo que os pongo es Nicola Pondrano, uno de los activistas que han estado trabajando también con la sección de víctimas de Casale en Italia y el juicio de Turín. En el propio juicio decía el que su mayor temor del trabajo en la fábrica era que recordaba que cuando venía de trabajar, lo que más le gustaba a su hija era sentarse a las rodillas y quitarle las virutas blancas que traían el pelo. Esas virutas blancas son polvo de amianto, son fibras de amianto. Pues claro, Nicola decía: «bueno, es que, si yo estoy enfermo, estoy enfermo, pero que mi hija enferme por mi negligencia» —no lo sabían— «por haber traído esto», dice, «me consume». Esta es la tragedia de los enfermos del amianto y las personas expuestas al amianto, pues la enfermedad es compartida. No es que yo ya esté expuesto, es que esto lo he podido traer a mi casa.

Pasa lo mismo con los compañeros del metro. Julián Martín es el primer caso del Metro de Madrid que ganamos. A Julián lo conozco, vivía en mi pueblo, casualmente, su compañero Óscar. Y Oscar ha estado trabajando 25 años con Julián. Julián ha fallecido ya, y Óscar no tiene ningún síntoma. Pero él sabe que ha estado expuesto igual que Julián al amianto. Este hombre está en tratamiento psicológico porque no sabe cuándo, qué le pasará seguramente, con un poco de mala suerte, o por un cálculo de probabilidades, empezará a sentirse enfermo. No sabemos con qué intensidad, con cuál de las enfermedades, pero él sabe que el diablo lo tiene dentro, en cualquier momento se puede despertar y puede salir; y así toda la vida.

¿Qué tipos de afectados nos encontramos en estas circunstancias? Evidentemente los laborales, son personas que han estado expuestas en el ámbito laboral al amianto; los domésticos, que son aquellos que el trabajador ha llevado el amianto por desconocimiento a casa; y los ambientales. ¿Por qué los ambientales? Porque no se han hecho las cosas bien, también porque han sido más de dos millones de toneladas de amianto que se han importado en España, con más de 3000 productos que han contenido amianto. Productos que habéis tenido o que habéis visto, los más jóvenes yo creo que ya no, pero que hemos tenido todos en casa. O sea, desde los guantes para sacar la comida del horno, hasta los tapetes de las tablas de planchar, las pastillas de los frenos, además, antiguamente había la buena costumbre que cuando no te frenaban «es que se han ensuciado las pastillas porque son muy porosas», entonces lo llevas un taller y las lijas.

Durante un tiempo se habló de la enfermedad del policía. En blanco y negro, en algunas películas que habéis visto, sobre todo si están rodadas en Madrid, veréis a un guardia con un gorro redondito subido en un tapete en medio de lo que antes era Atocha, no lo que es ahora Atocha, dirigiendo el tráfico. Claro, había muchos frenazos: parabas, freno, desgaste de la pastilla, liberación de partículas de amianto. Y esos guardias enfermaban, no sabían por qué, pero enfermaban. Esos son, digamos, enfermos ambientales.

Pero igual que ha pasado en los estudios de Radiotelevisión Española. Todos los recubrimientos ignífugos y para aislar del ruido estaban hechos con placas de amianto, que bien, si no manipulas no son peligrosas, a no ser que vayas a cortarlas. Es que fijaros cómo ha sido la legislación en este país, y por eso tampoco nos acompleja pedir el fondo de indemnización al Estado, porque ha habido normativas, en Madrid, sobre todo, que han obligado la utilización del amianto para ciertos materiales. Los telones de los teatros tenían que llevar amianto, porque hacían de cortafuegos. Las sábanas en los hoteles durante un tiempo tenían que llevar amianto. En España, a partir de la séptima planta había que construir con amianto porque era ignífugo. ¿Qué ocurre? Que se cae el edificio Windsor y la dispersión que hay ahí de amianto es tremenda. Lo mismo que las Torres Gemelas, la dispersión de amianto, y eso llega, nos llega a todos.

Luego, que desarrollemos una enfermedad, no se sabe por qué unos sí y otros no. De hecho, la Organización Mundial de la Salud establece que la única exposición al amianto segura es la exposición cero. Y, ¿por qué dice cero? Porque no sabemos por qué a algunas personas les afecta, entonces, para no estar en riesgo, es exposición al amianto cero. ¿Cuánta gente tenemos en España? Esto son datos oficiales, antes hablaba del registro y luego os lo voy a decir, pero en la propia memoria del proyecto para la aprobación del Real Decreto que va a desarrollar la ley del fondo de amianto, es decir, documento oficial y reciente, habla que hay, contabilizados, 70.842 trabajadores expuestos al amianto según el registro RTEA, registro de trabajadores expuestos al amianto.

Os repito, 70.000 en este momento. El RTEA es un registro voluntario, es más, es un registro que, si te llaman para hacer un control médico de salud y no te presentan, te das de baja, por lo que estos 70.000 se quedan muy por debajo, y trabajadores, no estamos hablando personas, estamos hablando de trabajadores, personas que han tenido alguna relación, que han trabajado en presencia de amianto. En el registro aparece además que el 17 % de esos trabajadores, de esos 70.000 son andaluces, y, además, Andalucía es la comunidad que más trabajadores tiene inscritos en el RETEA. De esos 70.000, hay 20.000 que ya están enfermos, y, además, nos dicen que en el periodo 2007-2021 ha habido 119.000-120.000 personas que han fallecido por enfermedades relacionadas con el amianto. Y, aun así, y aparece así en un informe EUROGIP, está reconocido por la comunidad científica que hay un subregistro del 9 %, o sea solamente estamos contabilizando el 9 % de lo que se estima que es real.

Porque os digo, todos estos registros han sido voluntarios. En España existe el RERA, que es el registro de empresas relacionadas con el amianto, que es un registro voluntario. Hay muchas empresas, por ejemplo, la factoría de Repsol en Cartagena, no se quieren dar de alta en el RERA, porque va a facilitar que lleguen casos de denuncias por haber trabajado en presencia de amianto, y digamos que ya asumes que has trabajado con amianto. ¿Ahora por qué hay muchas empresas inscritas en el RERA? Porque es una condición indispensable para lo que hablábamos ayer de cumplir con el protocolo de trabajos a realizar en presencia de amianto, tienen que ser empresas que estén inscritas en el RERA. Digamos que ahora se ha convertido en una certificación y cualquier empresa constructora de servicios se da de alta, antes no era así.

¿Cuánto amianto se ha importado en España? Como decía antes, han sido más de 2.300 toneladas y más de tres mil productos. Su curva, si la comparamos con las de resto de Europa, la nuestra viene un poquito más hacia la derecha, viene más atrasada, viene más atrasada porque pasamos la guerra civil, supuso un retraso en las importaciones, del desarrollo del país, no se construye tanto, no hacía falta; cuando se empezó a construir de manera masiva empezamos a importar. Luego vamos a volver a ver este gráfico cuando estemos hablando de los responsables y de la criminalidad.

Este gráfico, fijaos en la forma que tiene, en las industrias sobre todo de fibrocemento. El fibrocemento es la mezcla entre amianto y cemento, las cascas uralitas, las jardineras que había en las casas, aquí en Andalucía, sobre todo en los pueblos, todavía se ven mucho unos depósitos grises encima de las casas: contienen amianto, las bajantes etcétera. Eso es fibrocemento. Hay una gran parte en los aislamientos, siempre en altos hornos, o todas las maquinarias eléctricas o mecánicas que generan mucho calor llevaban recubrimientos de amianto para que ese calor no saliera, lo que hablamos de los recambios y elementos de fricción, que son las pastillas de freno.

Incluso en el cartón, vosotros ahora estáis acostumbrados a ver los acetas, que es un color negro y gris que llevan dos anillas y clasificas. Esos acetas antes se hacían con fibrocemento, y si vais a los antiguos archivos vais a ver que esas carpetas empiezan a deshacerse, y se deshacen porque lo que compacta está llegando al final de su vida útil. ¿Qué ocurre con el amianto? Que no tiene final de vida útil, es imperecedero. ¿Cuándo se vuelve peligroso? Cuando esté en fibrocemento, el cemento llega al final de su vida útil, que es lo que compacta las fibras. Empieza a desaparecer el cemento y lo que hacen es que se liberan fibras. Con los acetas antiguos pasa lo mismo.

Ahora sí, fijaros en la primera gráfica, son las importaciones. La siguiente gráfica son las enfermedades y los fallecimientos por mesotelioma. Veis que hay una separación por el periodo de latencia, pero que la gráfica sigue apareciendo hasta el año 2040. Todos estos datos están hechos con trabajadores, sin tener en cuenta sobre todo los ambientales que vendrán. ¿Esto cómo se vendía? «Uralita, una ciudad sana». Esto son anuncios de prensa. «Cada vez fabricamos más partes de un edificio» Te ponen un desmontable de una casita como los que había antes para montarlos con sus cositas, y veis que están las jardineras, que están las bajantes, que están las chimeneas. «Alguno de estos puntos le cae a usted encima». Son la red de venta de Uralita en España; y este es el mapa de disposición del amianto en España. Sobre todo, en tres grandes sectores: el fibrocemento, que hemos hablado, el material ferroviario y el de la industria naval, que son realmente los tres sectores más importantes, donde se concentran el mayor número de afectados, y como veis Sevilla y Cádiz. Sevilla sobre todo por la parte de Uralita, Cádiz por la parte naval, por lo que es ahora Navantia. Pero está también Cartagena, Barcelona, Málaga, que tiene talleres de Renfe, Ferrol también está muy asociado con la industria naval. En Barcelona estaba la primera fábrica de fibrocemento creada en España.

Empezamos con la criminalidad, la conspiración del silencio. No os doy estos datos, la mayoría porque ya han salido antes, pero sí que es importante que en 1929 se crea el cártel del amianto, del amiantocemento se llamaba, el SAIC, que era un cártel europeo en el que estaban todos los importadores europeos de amianto, y España formaba parte de ese cártel. Incluso en el juicio de Turín, aparece una carta en francés que se manda desde España al SAIC, a este cártel, en el que entre ellos anualmente preguntaban: «oye, ¿cómo van los tuyos?, ¿cuántos tienes enfermos? ». Estábamos hablando del año 72-73. O sea, por entonces, en aquellos años ya la industria del fibrocemento sabía los enfermos e iban haciendo sus cálculos, estaban midiendo. «Oye que tenemos enfermos, a ver, calladitos, nosotros no contamos y establecemos estrategias, sacamos un científico que diga que esto no es así». O sea, eso estaba ahí.

De hecho, en España en el siglo XX, hay cinco familias europeas que controlan el amianto. Una de ellas es la familia March, la Banca March que habéis oído aquí en España, ahora saldrán un poquito más adelante, y había cuatro multinacionales a nivel mundial que lo controlaban la Cape plc en Inglaterra, Eternit de origen belga, JM en Estados Unidos, y otra inglesa, eran cuatro. Y esta es la presencia del grupo Eternit en amarillo en todo el mundo.

La familia March y Uralita, ¿qué ocurre con Roviralta? La familia March compró Uralita y a partir de entonces ha tenido una posición de privilegio en el Estado español, una familia que llegó a ser la séptima fortuna del mundo, y que, entre otras cosas, patrocinó el viaje en avión en el alzamiento nacional. O sea, su presencia y su influencia en los gobiernos, no solamente durante la dictadura, sino posterior, ha sido tremenda. De hecho, cuando a nivel europeo empiezan a salir las directivas, el representante español en esas reuniones de la Comisión Europea para ver qué pasa con el amianto era uno de los integrantes de la familia March. Imaginaos la posición que tenían.

De hecho, España hasta la última directiva, siempre había pedido que se aumentase el plazo para poder tomarlas en consideración. Realmente fue un gobierno de Aznar, después de la última directiva, la que dos años antes del plazo que había prohíbe el amianto. De una manera muy peculiar, dice, bueno vamos a prohibir el amianto porque sabemos que mata, pero oye, no construyas más, no fabriques más, pero lo que tienes te dejo que lo vendas. Y se ha estado vendiendo material con amianto hasta menos de 10 años, por que lo que estaba prohibido era fabricarlos.

Y ahora, quería hacer unas reflexiones sobre el fondo que salieron ayer. Bueno, inicialmente los colectivos del amianto nacimos para acompañar a las víctimas, hacer un acompañamiento que ni los médicos podían hacer, evidentemente la empresa no iba a hacerlo, pero que los sindicatos tampoco podían hacerlo. Los sindicatos, dentro de sus objetivos de trabajo son muy diversos y el amianto era uno más. ¿Por qué nos empezamos a constituir como asociaciones? Porque podíamos ser irreverentes, no teníamos por qué sentarnos en una mesa negociación colectiva con muchos temas y a ver a cuál le dábamos prioridad. Entonces nosotros creamos una alianza con los sindicatos en el que nosotros éramos los gamberros, los golfos, los que acudíamos a las manifestaciones, y ellos, porque entonces nosotros no podíamos, se sentaban en las mesas de negociación; pero ellos se sentaban en la mesa de negociación con nuestras reivindicaciones y con la presión que hacíamos en la calle. De hecho, algo que consiguió Fernando cuando en Madrid se dio la vuelta a toda la producción de las sentencias que había hasta el momento, es que cuando él iba a celebrar sus juicios había ruido ensordecedor en la calle y éramos nosotros haciendo jaleo.

Sobre el fondo, en ese camino que hemos hecho, hemos sido siempre sobre todo con los sindicatos UGT y Comisiones, no por ser excluyentes, sino porque legalmente son los que se sientan en ciertas mesas, nos hemos juntado con cualquier otro colectivo y partido político, el que ha sido haya sido necesario para sacar adelante nuestras reivindicaciones. Y llegamos al fondo, el fondo como ya se dijo ayer, lo dijiste tú mismo, nace de una iniciativa singular, que es que las Comunidades Autónomas pueden incluir una proposición de ley en el Parlamento, es una de las prerrogativas que tienen. En Euskadi se crea esa ley y se aprueba en Euskadi con unanimidad en el Parlamento Vasco. Esa ley ha tardado finalmente siete años en poder ser aprobada, porque hubo que retirarla dos veces, porque acababa la legislatura, y todo lo que no está aprobado tiene que empezar de nuevo todo su peregrinaje, había que presentarlo a la mesa, la mesa lo aprobaba, se llevaba a las comisiones pertinentes...

Y, ¿por qué —y salió ayer— hay algunas cosas que nos chirrían en el preámbulo? Porque, como venía de un consenso no quisimos tocar el espíritu inicial de la ley, es una barbaridad lo que pone, es más yo tengo una transparencia que critica una afirmación como esa de un diputado de Ciudadanos en la Asamblea de Madrid. Entonces lo único que hicimos, y lo hicimos conscientemente, fue actualizar el número de cifras, por respeto a lo que había salido del Parlamento vasco lo dejamos ahí. O sea, bien sabiendo que no era lo ideal, pero lo que nos interesaba venía después. Esa es la explicación de por qué aparece eso.

Las negociaciones fueron arduas, conseguimos que se aprobara por unanimidad en el Congreso de los Diputados y que se aprobara por unanimidad en el Senado. Fijaros los tiempos que tienen conseguir que una ley se haga con ese respaldo mayoritario, y eso fue porque nos sentamos con todos y cada uno, hay un grupo que no quiso sentarse, Vox, lo siento había que decirlo, porque se lo merecen, nos sentamos con todos los grupos incluso en momentos de crisis, aunque las iniciativas habían partido de partidos de izquierda, fue una diputada del PP quien se sienta encima de la mesa tres minutos antes del pleno y coge a todos los partidos y dice: «vamos a ver, señores, vamos a dejarnos de tonterías. Esto sale hoy sí o sí». Y salió, o sea que agradecidísimo con toda la clase política que ha participado.

Antes lo comentaba en la mesa, inicialmente estuvo la ministra Yolanda Díaz trabajando durante cuatro años con nosotros, era la portavoz de Podemos en la comisión de trabajo y, además, viene de Ferrol. Ferrol habéis visto que es unos puntos negros del amianto, entonces le tocaba muy de cerca.

Y ya sí que voy a acabar, uno de nuestros principales objetivos es que el fondo fuera universal. Hasta ahora quedaba mucha gente que no tiene ningún tipo de derecho. Los trabajadores sí, pueden encontrar compensación porque se reconoce una enfermedad profesional, porque tiene un recargo de prestaciones y porque pueden ir a litigar. Las personas que no han trabajado pero que han estado en contacto con trabajadores, tenemos la vía civil, porque la exposición es muy directa. Pero el resto de las personas, ambientales o trabajadores que no hemos sabido identificar donde han estado expuestos, o esas empresas en las que estaban expuestos ya no existen, se quedan sin ningún tipo de derecho. Entonces hemos conseguido que este fondo sea universal, por eso algo que chocaba también en los procedimientos, que ahí es verdad que están tocados, es que se ha intentado simplificar y ya no hay que aportar la prueba de carga, no hay que demostrar que se ha estado expuesto al amianto. Simplemente, si tienes una de las enfermedades que aparecen recogidas, tienes derecho a la indemnización, simplemente por tenerla.

Y parece muy simplificado, porque la idea es que sea un procedimiento electrónico no de presentación y tramitación electrónica, es un procedimiento electrónico porque el Ministerio lo que quiere es que, cuando ese expediente llegue a un funcionario, rellene los campos que estén hechos, botonazo y a tramitar la subvención, que es distinto la presentación y cómo nos relacionamos con la administración a cómo va a ser el expediente. No quieren acumular papeles, no quieren que venga el papelito del médico, que traigamos informes médicos, etcétera.

Es por eso por lo que aparece de esa manera. Y ya sí que me callo.

«LA PRIMERA DEMANDA COLECTIVA CONTRA URALITA»

Fernando Morillo González

Abogado de la Federación de Asociaciones y Colectivos de Víctimas del Amianto (FEDAVIDA)

Hola, buenas tardes a todos.

Lo primero es darle las gracias a la Universidad Pablo Olavide, y en particular a su Departamento de Derecho Penal, y al doctor Macías por haberme invitado a estar aquí en este congreso sobre el amianto.

Bueno, el tema que tenía previsto exponer era un tema muy técnico y problemático para todos los que en el ejercicio de la abogacía nos dedicamos a la defensa de las víctimas, pero, atendiendo básicamente al foro mayoritario que hay en esta sala de alumnos, me parece que voy a invertir o voy a cambiar mi ponencia, y voy a dedicarle una parte final a lo que era el tema que iba a tratar.

Pero, me parece que puede ser muy interesante para todos contaros el primer caso que yo llevé. Siendo letrado de la Asociación de Víctimas del Amianto he hecho más de cien juicios de amianto, pero siempre pues el primero tiene un sabor especial para mí. Creo que fue un juicio verdaderamente importante para la defensa de las víctimas, y pues, contaros un poco la historia e intrahistoria de este caso, de este juicio.

Bien todo empieza en el año 2007, cuando acude a mi despacho profesional Juan Carlos como acompañante de una serie de personas y nos piden que les hagamos un informe, que desde el punto de vista jurídico se llama dictamen, sobre las opciones que podrían tener de iniciar un procedimiento de reclamación de daños y perjuicios en favor de una serie de afectados por el amianto, en concreto trabajadores de la fábrica de Uralita de Getafe.

Cuando este caso me llega os confieso yo no sabía ni lo que era el amianto, no sabía nada. Cuando digo nada, es nada, desinformación total. ¿Qué hacemos? Estudiar, no queda otro remedio, nos ponemos a estudiar pues antecedentes, jurisprudencia, doctrina, y, al final, después de un estudio, concienzudo, la conclusión a la que llegamos es que se habían perdido la práctica totalidad de los casos que se habían presentado de manera individual. En concreto, todas las demandas que se habían presentado contra la factoría de Uralita de Getafe se habían perdido todas, no se había ganado ningún juicio, todos en la jurisdicción laboral.

En ese momento existía la opción de poder elegir en este tipo de procedimientos si litigar en la jurisdicción laboral o acudir a la jurisdicción civil. Lógicamente la respuesta era fácil, si en la jurisdicción laboral se habían perdido todos los procedimientos tratemos de llevarlo a la jurisdicción civil, a ver si en la jurisdicción civil tenemos alguna opción más de éxito. También teniendo en cuenta que la jurisprudencia de los tribunales civiles en estos casos era más más fácil, por decirlo alguna forma, por una aplicación que se llama la teoría del riesgo, que os voy a explicar, que se aplica la jurisdicción civil y que, en aquel momento, no se aplicaba en la jurisdicción social, por tanto, la primera decisión la teníamos clara: prepararíamos el juicio en la jurisdicción civil.

Segundo problema: todos los juicios habían sido individuales, una persona sola, un solo trabajador, contra una megaempresa que cotiza en bolsa con todos los recursos en abogados, peritos, técnicos... imaginaros, David contra Goliat, ejemplo clarísimo. Bueno, tenemos que hacer algo, tenemos que contrarrestar en alguna medida esta situación. ¿Y qué hacemos? Pues nos planteamos presentar una demanda colectiva, es decir tratar de agrupar en un solo procedimiento cuantos más casos mejor, todos los que se pudieran.

Tardamos dos años en preparar la demanda, estuvimos dos años recopilando información, seleccionando casos, mirando los que podían ser, los que no podían ser, estudiando. Tuvimos entrevistas con el Servicio de Neumología del Hospital Universitario de Getafe, hablamos con los médicos, hablamos con técnicos, hablamos con ingenieros químicos, es decir, teníamos que tener una demanda que no se pudiera perder, o sea, no podíamos arriesgarnos a volver a incurrir en los mismos errores.

Por tanto, preparamos este caso a conciencia. Todo este trabajo jurídico y médico lo unimos también a la presencia de las asociaciones al apoyo, en este caso de FEDAVIDA, y de la Federación de Asociaciones. Estoy completamente seguro de que la decisión del juez no hubiera sido la misma, o por lo menos no hubiera sido tan clara, si no hubiéramos tenido ese apoyo de las asociaciones, que se tradujo también en un apoyo en prensa. Empezamos a sacar comunicados de prensa, información para que la gente tuviera conciencia del problema del que el que está aquí sentado no sabía absolutamente nada. Por tanto, necesitábamos también ese apoyo de los medios de comunicación.

Con todo esto montamos una demanda, pues imaginaros, eran al final 52 casos agrupados. Cada caso era distinto, cada caso tenía una historia; era una historia de cincuenta y dos personas que habían sufrido daños, la gran mayoría fallecidos ya. Esto es un caso verdaderamente complicado de montar, pero bueno, creemos que logramos el objetivo.

La cuestión era si el juez sería capaz de leerse semejante mamotreto, de no solo la demanda, sino los más de 10.000 folios de documentación que la acompañaban, pero había que intentarlo. Bien, esta demanda recayó en el Juzgado de Primera Instancia de Madrid, el número 18, y bueno, como os podéis imaginar la defensa de la empresa Uralita no escatimó en medios, porque se estaban jugando su futuro. Ellos eran conscientes de que, si este caso colectivo lo perdían, detrás de él iban a venir cientos, y podría ser su propia supervivencia. Por tanto, invirtieron todo tipo de medios. Contrataron a Luis Diez Picazo, que es un glorioso catedrático de Derecho Civil, ya fallecido, que hacía diez años que no hacía un juicio, y le pagaron expresamente para que volviera a los tribunales e hiciera ese juicio. Él no ejercía ya, pero le pagaron, y bien me imagino, para que ejerciera la defensa. Llevaron al juicio pues, por supuesto, equipo médico, por supuesto, ingenieros industriales, por supuesto, directivos a declarar.

En fin, lógicamente, y por supuesto, pues todo tipo de trabajo por su parte también de defender que ellos habían actuado cumpliendo la normativa vigente en cada momento, protegiendo a los trabajadores, y que realmente era un daño imprevisible e inevitable. Esa fue básicamente la defensa, el juicio duró dos días, algo bastante inusual en la jurisdicción civil, se hizo en una sala más amplia, ellos estaban fuera haciendo mucho ruido. Salió en todos los medios de comunicación del momento y la verdad es que bueno, finalmente, pues el juicio pese a toda la defensa de Uralita pues logramos que se estimara en primera instancia la defensa nuestra.

Por supuesto, llevamos también a nuestro médico, llevamos también a los médicos del Hospital Universitario de Getafe y llevamos a trabajadores testigos de lo que había ocurrido. La demanda también tuvo una peculiaridad y es que, junto a los trabajadores, había dos esposas de trabajadores que estaban también diagnosticadas de mesotelioma. Hasta ese momento, no se había hecho jamás una reclamación de nadie expuesto al amianto que no hubiera sido un trabajador en este país. Es decir, es la primera vez que alguien decide pues meter dentro de esa demanda a dos señoras que estaban afectadas también, como nos ha contado Juan Carlos, por la manipulación de la ropa de trabajo de sus esposos cuando la llevaban a lavar a casa.

Bien, como decía, la empresa esgrimió todo tipo de argumentos, uno de ellos, el principal, es el argumento que le había dado sus frutos a lo largo de todos estos procedimientos previos individuales y es que la empresa podía acreditar que a partir de los años 81-82 había cumplido las medidas de seguridad específicas para la protección de los trabajadores que se recogían en la normativa. Este cumplimiento a nuestro modo de ver no era completo, ni muchísimo menos. Probamos que no era así, pero esto les había garantizado el éxito en el resto de los procedimientos. ¿Qué hicimos nosotros? Nosotros lo que optamos fue por defender que había una normativa previa del año 1940, una normativa genérica, un reglamento de seguridad e higiene en el trabajo, que también era de obligado cumplimiento para las empresas aunque no fueron reglamentos sobre la amianto y, en ese reglamento del año 1940 entre otras cosas decía que los trabajadores en ambientes pulvígenos tenían que llevar una mascarilla, que no se podía llevar a cabo el barrido de ambientes pulvígenos, que tenía que utilizar sistemas especiales... Cosas muy básicas pero cosas muy básicas que Uralita no podía demostrar que había cumplido. Y no sólo eso, sino que además aplicamos una doctrina a la que he aludido anteriormente, que es la doctrina que se conoce como doctrina del riesgo. Esta doctrina, en la jurisdicción civil, de forma muy simple, significa que cuando alguien causa un riesgo y ese riesgo le produce un beneficio, se invierte la carga de la prueba, es decir, que no es el trabajador el que tiene que probar que la empresa ha incumplido las medidas de seguridad, sino al revés, que es la empresa quien tiene que probar que ha desarrollado todas las medidas de seguridad vigentes en cada momento. Y no sólo eso, sino que esta doctrina dice que la empresa tiene que ir incluso más allá de esta normativa de protección y adoptar cualquier otra medida que, aunque no esté recogida en la normativa legal, sea necesaria para la protección de los trabajadores.

Esta doctrina es esencialmente civil y esa doctrina es la que nos hizo darle la vuelta a la tortilla y conseguir que esa demanda se estimara. Uralita argumentó de todo, por ejemplo, nos argumentó que era un daño imprevisible porque con los conocimientos científicos no se puede evaluar lo que ocurría. Ya os han dicho las enfermedades por amianto tienen un periodo de latencia que puede estar entre 20 y 40 años más o menos, y lo que decía uralita es que los conocimientos sobre el amianto existentes en los años 70-80 no eran los conocimientos sobre el amianto que existían en el año 2009, cuando se celebró el juicio, y que, por tanto, no se puede enjuiciar lo que ocurría en esos años con la información que tenemos a día de hoy.

Nosotros frente a ese dato de la imprevisibilidad del daño también hicimos los deberes y estudiamos y llegamos a la conclusión de que esto no era cierto, de que la peligrosidad del amianto se conoce desde el principio del siglo XX, desde el 1900 poco, incluso de 1800 hay algún estudio, y, sobre todo, que la relación de causa efecto entre la exposición al amianto y el cáncer de pulmón y el mesotelioma, que son las dos principales enfermedades que causan el fallecimiento de los trabajadores, se conocería al menos desde el año 1960. Se conocía por un estudio de un patólogo, el doctor Wagner, que hizo un estudio en las minas de Sudáfrica y que, en ese estudio, quedó constatado tanto que los trabajadores como sus familiares, como las personas que vivían en las inmediaciones de las fábricas generaban este tipo de tumores. Y este estudio se publicó en la revista *The Lancet*, que es una revista científica médica superprestigiosa, y además, en un congreso de Medicina Legal del Trabajo que hubo en Madrid en el año 1963, donde expuso sus conclusiones el doctor WAGNER.

Todo esto lo documentamos y lo sacamos en el juicio, por tanto, el primer argumento de fondo de fuerza de Uralita lo desmontamos. Luego también sostenían que el daño era inevitable, porque por muchas medidas de seguridad que hubiera podido adoptar la empresa, el daño se hubiera producido igualmente, porque, como ha dicho Juan Carlos, la Organización Mundial de la Salud dice que no hay exposición segura. Bien, esto puede ser cierto, pero no lo es menos, y este era nuestro argumento, que lógicamente, si a un trabajador se lo hubiera proporcionado, al menos, una mascarilla, y se le hubiera informado de la peligrosidad del material que estaba manejando, hubiera podido tener alguna opción más de impedir esa exposición, es decir, su exposición se hubiera minimizado. Por tanto, no estamos ni ante un fortuito, ni ante un caso de fuerza mayor.

Más argumentos, bueno, podría estar tres horas contando argumentos, pero, por ejemplo, otra de las cuestiones que nos alegaron, esta cuestión sí que era más complicada, nos argumentaron que la jurisdicción competente no podía ser la jurisdicción civil, que tenía que ser la jurisdicción laboral, y que, por tanto, este procedimiento se tenía que ventilar en la jurisdicción laboral. Esto significaba que tendríamos que peregrinar a la jurisdicción donde nos habían sacudido una y otra vez, por tanto, para nosotros esto era catastrófico.

Bien continúa el procedimiento, se celebra el juicio, y la juez del Juzgado de Primera Instancia número 18 de Madrid, de memoria no me acuerdo del número de la sentencia del 2009, estima la demanda. No la estima íntegramente, porque hay algún caso que nosotros a sabiendas de que era un caso dudoso lo incluimos en la demanda con un problema de prescripción el plazo para reclamar. En este tipo de demandas es un plazo de tan solo un año, nosotros defendíamos que las demandas que este tipo de patologías es un daño continuado y que mientras que la patología está evolucionando no comienza el plazo de prescripción. Vale, esto lo hicimos para tratar de incorporar a la demanda una serie de casos, este argumento no prosperó, y, por tanto, esto significó, que, si no recuerdo mal, fueron cuatro casos de los 52 que la juez consideró que tenía la acción prescrita.

Vale, esto fue duro para nosotros porque queríamos ganar todos los casos, pero realmente el éxito de la demanda fue muy importante. ¿Por qué? Porque se logró ganar por primera vez a Uralita, se logró con una demanda colectiva, una sentencia bien trabajada y una juez que a mi modo de ver fue bastante valiente.

Bien recurre Uralita, lógicamente, y nos vamos a la Audiencia Provincial de Madrid. La Audiencia Provincial de Madrid confirma íntegramente la sentencia del Juzgado de Primera Instancia número 18, pero, entre tanto, ocurre un dato sorprendente, ocurre algo que nos incidió de manera muy negativa: en el año 2008 el Tribunal Supremo pues decide cambiar la jurisprudencia, y decide que a partir del año 2008 todas las reclamaciones de trabajadores por enfermedades profesionales se deben tramitar en la jurisdicción social, no en la civil. Pero nuestro procedimiento ya estaba en curso, este fue el argumento de la Audiencia Provincial de Madrid, pese a que Uralita aporta la documentación relativa a esa jurisprudencia, aporta la Sentencia del Pleno del Tribunal Supremo. Pero la Audiencia Provincial dice que no se puede aplicar a este caso porque este caso ha nacido antes, la demanda se presenta en el año 2007 cuando estaba vigente otra jurisprudencia, y está jurisprudencia nueva no puede tener carácter retroactivo, no se puede aplicar a casos que han nacido y se han cursado conforme a una jurisprudencia anterior.

Bien nosotros, este argumento, pues creíamos en él y por tanto la Audiencia Provincial de Madrid desestima el recurso. Nos vamos al Tribunal Supremo, este caso tiene toda la trayectoria, llegamos al Tribunal Supremo y el Tribunal Supremo desgraciadamente para nosotros en sentencia de cinco de diciembre del 2015, esta no se me olvida, estima íntegramente el recurso de Uralita en cuanto a los trabajadores, y nos dice que aplica de manera retroactiva esta jurisprudencia y que tenemos que iniciar de nuevo los procedimientos en la jurisdicción social. Imaginaros el palo, imaginaros el hundimiento que tuvimos, fue terrible para nosotros, para las víctimas, pero no nos podíamos dejar caer, teníamos que tratar de seguir ahí, de seguir luchando y seguir luchando con argumentos jurídicos.

Bien, la sentencia del 2015 sí que tuvo una cosa al menos buena. Fue la primera sentencia que nos dijo que, a los trabajadores a la jurisdicción social, pero, había, acordaros, os he dicho dos esposas, desgraciadamente fallecidas, de trabajadores. Dos esposas con una exposición exclusivamente ambiental, estas señoras no tenían ninguna relación contractual ni laboral con Uralita, por tanto, la Sala de lo Civil del Tribunal Supremo a estas dos señoras no las podía mandar a la jurisdicción laboral, tenía que resolver el caso. Y en este caso, el Tribunal Supremo entra y confirma todos y cada uno de nuestros argumentos y nos da la razón, es decir, nos manda la jurisdicción laboral porque se considera incompetente, pero todos los argumentos de fondo los compra, le valen, y estima estos dos casos con dos sentencias firmes.

Por tanto, nos manda la jurisdicción laboral, pero, a la vez, la puerta que queríamos abrir se abre con estas dos señoras, a partir de ese momento, lógicamente a partir del 2008, una vez que ya sabíamos que era la jurisdicción laboral, presentamos una nueva demanda colectiva paralela a esta en la jurisdicción social con 60 casos.

Procedimiento que se gana en sentencia el 30 de junio de 2013, porque en ese momento ya la Jurisdicción Social abre la puerta por decirlo de alguna forma los casos, y entran en tropel. Esa demanda, con 60 casos insisto, se gana en el 2013.

¿Qué ocurrió?, os preguntaréis, ¿qué hicimos? Pues había dos opciones: una, recurso de amparo ante el Tribunal Constitucional por aplicación retroactiva de una ley que no se debió aplicar retroactivamente; dos, irnos a la jurisdicción laboral. Lo analizamos Juan Carlos y yo, y, al final, pese a que yo anuncié el recurso de amparo al Constitucional, no lo presenté. ¿Por qué? Porque al final lo que buscábamos era justicia, las víctimas estaban ya desesperadas y necesitábamos una reparación lo más rápida posible, y pensamos que si acudíamos a la jurisdicción social con todo el bombo que le habíamos dado a esto la Jurisdicción Social no nos iba a tratar mal, este procedimiento se iba a tramitar con relativa ligereza, rapidez, porque todo estaba ya aprobado. y concluimos que teníamos que ir a la jurisdicción social.

Como habíamos tenido problemas con la acumulación de procedimientos en la jurisdicción social, decidimos presentar cuatro demandas distintas, una por cada patología, agrupamos por patologías: aquí van los del mesotelioma, aquí van los del cáncer de pulmón, aquí van los de asbestosis, aquí otras patologías como placas pleurales y patologías benignas. Iniciamos cuatro procedimientos judiciales y, sorprendentemente, nos señalaron los juicios rapidísimo, en cuestión de meses, todos menos uno, que cayó en el juzgado de lo Social número 1. A nosotros nos importaban más los más importantes cuantitativamente. Nos señalaron y rápidamente se celebraron los juicios y se ganaron todos los juicios, lo que nos había negado a la jurisdicción civil lo conseguimos en la jurisdicción laboral finalmente, para que os hagáis una idea, la última de las sentencias que puso definitivamente fin a este procedimiento que se inició cuando llegó FEDAVIDA al despacho en el 2007 es de 23 de julio del 2021. Estuvimos, pues, 14 años de juicios pero, al final, se consiguió que estos estos casos insisto, menos los tres o cuatro que se cayeron por el camino por prescripción, logramos que se estimara, logramos abrir la puerta y a partir de ahí, a partir de este primer juicio primitivo —lógicamente cuando tenemos un juicio en el que hay afectados de cónyuges, familiares, o personas que han vivido en los inmediaciones de la fábrica nos vamos a la jurisdicción civil, y cuando son trabajadores nos vamos a la jurisdicción social— a partir de ahí pues, como os decía, yo he hecho más de cien juicios de amianto y bueno, pues algunos se pierden, pero estamos en torno a un 90 % de éxito en los procedimientos.

De hecho, el viernes, por ejemplo, estoy con juicio de amianto, un trabajador de Renfe, que es una de las empresas en las que últimamente tenemos nos salen más casos, trabajadores del sector ferroviario, pues tengo un juicio de un fallecido por mesotelioma.

Bien, pues nada. Creo que no me da tiempo a poner la otra parte. Muchas gracias, espero haberlos ilustrado de todas maneras.

MESA V

COMUNICACIONES

«LA ACCIÓN DEL TRIBUNAL CONSTITUCIONAL EN LA PROTECCIÓN DEL DERECHO FUNDAMENTAL A LA SALUD DE LOS TRABAJADORES POR RIESGOS DERIVADOS DEL EMPLEO DE AMIANTO: DE LA STC DE 13/1998, DE 22 DE ENERO A LA STC 21/2011, DE 14 DE MARZO»

Francisco Manuel Silva Ardanuy
Universidad de Sevilla

I.- Introducción

La jurisprudencia del Tribunal Constitucional en materia de atención a recursos interpuestos por afectados/as por patologías derivadas del uso o manipulación por razones profecionales o particulares de amianto no es muy numerosa y se centra más en los aspectos procedimentales, es decir, si son susceptibles de amparo las demandas planteadas, sin pronunciarse sobre el fondo: SSTC 215/2001, de 29 de octubre; 16/2004, de 23 de febrero; 196/2004, de 15 de noviembre y 21/2011, de 14 de marzo.

Hasta cinco sentencias (STC 2018/2006, de 3 de julio; 16/2008, de 31 de enero; 135/2008, de 27 de octubre;

192/2009, de 28 de septiembre y la ya citada 21/2011, de 14 de marzo) se refieren a la cuestión del recargo en las prestaciones, bien en caso de accidente de trabajo o de enfermedad profesional derivada del amianto, si bien el objeto de la controversia no versaba sobre la justificación o naturaleza del recargo sino en la institución responsable.

La STC 13/1998, de 22 de enero, relativa a la distribución de competencias en materia de medio ambiente, en la que entre otras cuestiones se refiere a cuestiones relacionadas con el amianto. Así entre las instalaciones que deben ser objeto de evaluación de impacto ambiental deben figurar las instalaciones productoras de amianto y productos derivados

La sentencia más importante que relaciona el tema del amianto con la legitimación procesal de los sindicatos es la STC 2015/ 2001, de 29 de octubre, en la que se reconoce la legitimación de los sindicatos para ser parte en los procesos que se susciten en relación con pretensiones individuales, siempre que afecten a cuestiones de interés general, se acredite implantación real en la empresa y haya sido parte en el procedimiento administrativo.

La presente comunicación explora la posición adoptada en el periodo 1998-2011 por parte del Tribunal Constitucional en la administración de justicia constitucional y la forma en que el Alto Tribunal salvaguarda los elementos contenidos en el art. 43.1 CE.

II.- De la intervención de los distintos órdenes jurisdiccionales ante las acciones individuales y colectivas de personas afectadas por la exposición al amianto

Los primeros estudios sistemáticos sobre trabajadores expuestos a los efectos del amianto se realizaron por el Doctor López-Areal en empresas de la provincia de Vizcaya dedicadas a la fabricación textil amianto. En 1971 se estimó que el número de trabajadores expuestos al amianto a finales de la década de los setenta se cifrase en 8.000 trabajadores afectados[1]. Dicha cifra ascendía en 1991 a 60.488 a partir

1 A partir de las estimaciones realizadas por A.C. Cárcoba el número

de los datos del Instituto Nacional de Seguridad e Higiene en el Trabajo (INSHT)[2]. Será a principios de la década de los noventa del pasado siglo cuando comience la aplicación del sistema internacional de información sobre cancerígenos en el lugar de trabajo (CAREX) que permitió cifrar el número de trabajadores expuestos al amianto a finales de la década de los noventa se situase en 56.600 afectados, siendo las manifestaciones más comunes enfermedades y patologías derivadas de la exposición al amianto son la asena, irritación de las vías aéreas, neumociosis, silicosis, asbestosis y aluminosis[3].

Mediante el denominado Programa Integral de Vigilancia de la Salud de los Trabajadores expuestos al Amianto (PIVISTEA) tenía registrado a finales de 2008 un total de 22.158 trabajadores a partir de los datos extraídos de un total de catorce Comunidades Autónomas y sobre un ecosistema de 306 empresas[4].

El análisis geográfico de la distribución de los casos reconocidos entre 1990 y 2010 muestra una clara asociación con la ubicación de las fábricas de amiantocemento en nuestro país, emplazadas en las provincias de Alicante, Barcelona, Cádiz, Guipúzcoa, Madrid, Sevilla, Valencia, Valladolid, Viz-

---

de trabajadores afectados por los efectos del amianto alcanzaría los 240.000 para un total de 2.300 empresas dedicadas a actividades de riesgo de amianto. CÁRCOBA, A. C., Ed. (2000) *El amianto en España. Ediciones GPS*. Madrid. Colección Estudios, págs. 76-83. LÓPEZ-ABENTE, G., et al (2007) *Atlas municipal de mortalidad por cáncer en España*, 1989-1998. Instituto de Salud Carlos III. Madrid.

2 ALLEMAN, J. E. y MOSSMAN B. T. (1997) "Reconsideración del amianto". *Investigación y Ciencia*. Septiembre 1997. Págs. 56-62. MÁÑEZ, J. A. y ROEL, J. M. (2006). *La interminable herencia del amianto. Revista* Por experiencia n.º 31 enero 2006. http://www.porexperiencia.com/ [Consultado en línea: 02/05/2024]. REGUEIRO, M. (2002). «Asbestos: Riesgos y mitos». En *Riesgos Naturales*. F. J. AYALA-CARCEDO y J. OLCINA CANTOS (coord.). Ed. Ariel Ciencia, págs. 99-103.

3 GÓMEZ, R. y GONZÁLEZ, P. (2006). *El amianto, un contaminante lento pero mortal*. Tribuna, abril 2006. NEMERY, B., DE RAEVE, H.,VERSHAKELEN, S., LEUVEN, K.V. (2000) «The Berlaymont building. Arethere measurable health effects associated with works in a building contained flocked asbestos? ». *Global Asbestos Congress*. Payt, Present an Future". Osasco. Brazil, págs.112-115.

4 Véase https://www.sanidad.gob.es/ciudadanos/saludAmbLaboral/docs/PIVISTEA2018.pdf [Consultado en línea: 02/05/2024].

caya y Toledo, y con la localización de los astilleros en la costa. En el mapa que representa el sector naval, los casos de asbestosis de Madrid y Zaragoza están vinculados a la fabricación de frenos y embragues, la fabricación de material ferroviario y la construcción aeronaútica y espacial, actividades incluidas en el mismo código CNAE que la construcción y reparación naval[5].

La experiencia adquirida tras un largo periodo de lucha y denuncia pública en el Estado español así como en otros Estados miembros de la Unión Europea, muestran que la acción ante los distintos Tribunales de justicia en sus distintos niveles y órdenes competenciales incluyendo la justicia constitucional y con independencia d si las acciones se realizan de forma individual o colectiva, no resultan en ocasiones la vía más eficaz para alcanzar un escenario que auné acciones compensatorias y reparadoras para las personas afectadas por la exposición al amianto y acciones preventivas más allá de lo establecido en el Real Decreto 396/2006, de 31 de marzo, por el que se establecen las disposiciones mínimas de seguridad y salud aplicables a los trabajos con riesgo de exposición al amianto[6], que neutralicen la proyección de los efectos del amianto por su perdurabilidad y friabilidad[7].

La solución individual, mediante demandas individuales sustanciadas en vía judicial presenta serias deficiencias y

---

5 ARTIEDA, L., BELOQUI, A, LEZAUN, M. (2005): *Cohorte poblacional de trabajadores expuestos a amianto*. Navarra 1999-2004. An Sist Sanit Navar.;28, págs. 335-344. GARCÍA GÓMEZ, M., CASTAÑEDA, R., GARCÍA LÓPEZ, V., MARTÍNEZ VIDAL, M., VILLANUEVA, V., ELVIRA ESPINOSA, M. *et al.* (2008): *Evaluación del programa integral de vigilancia de la salud de los trabajadores que han estado expuestos a amianto en España*, Gac Sanit. 2012.
TARRÉS, J., ABÓS-HERRÀNDIZ, R., ALBERTÍ, C., MARTÍNEZ ARTÉS, X., ROSELL MURPHY, M., GARCÍA-ALLAS, I. *et. al.* (2009): *Enfermedad por amianto en una población próxima a una fábrica de fibrocemento*. Arch Bronconeumol; 45(9), págs. 429-434.

6 BOE n.º86, de 11 de abril de 2006.

7 UZKUDUN, J. (2006). *Amianto: con la prohibición no basta. Revista Por Experiencia n.º 33 julio 2006*. http://www.porexperiencia.com/ [Consultado en línea: 03/05/2024]. VELASCO, P. (2022). «Sanidad vigila a 4.730 trabajadores con exposición al amianto: El Gobierno acaba de aprobar un fondo de compensación para las víctimas veinte años después de su prohibición». *Diario Palentino*. En www.diariopalentino.es [Consultado en línea: 03/05/2024].

limitaciones (alta litigiosidad, disparidad de trato, complejidad del proceso y exigencia de culpa). Los afectados por la exposición al amianto son un colectivo uniformemente afectado, donde el origen de su enfermedad radica en la exposición a las fibras de amianto[8].

Teniendo el daño por amiento naturaleza de daño masivo, cabría interpretar el necesario reconocimiento de reparación en los términos que establece el art. 1902 CC, si bien esta apelación del Código Civil hace alusión al ámbito de la responsabilidad extracontractual, es más claro lo establecido en el art. 4.2 apdo. d) del Real Decreto Legislativo 2/2015, de 23 de octubre, por el que se aprueba el texto refundido de la Ley del Estatuto de los Trabajadores[9], cuando afirma el derecho de los trabajadores a su integridad física y a una adecuada política de seguridad e higiene.

Tanto en un contexto de responsabilidad extracontractual como contractual han de tenerse en cuenta los aspectos subjetivos de ambas partes con intensa exigencia hacia la parte empleadora, donde opera el reconocimiento en el orden contencioso administrativo otorgado por la SSTC 76/1990, de 26 de abril, en la que se establece la potestad sancionadora de la Administración se rige, entre otros, por el principio de culpabilidad.

La reparación de los daños a personas por exposición al amianto se ha abordado mediante dos mecanismos básicos; por un lado, los mecanismos de indemnización colectiva y por otro la litigiosidad derivada de las reclamaciones colectivas. Atendiendo a lo manifestado en las distintas jurisdicciones:

a) Jurisdicción penal.

No se han sustanciado muchas demandas por daños para la vida y la salud de los trabajadores afectados por la exposición al amianto a pesar de la prevalencia del orden jurisdiccional penal. No hay pronunciamiento de la Sala Tercera del

---

8 GIL, R. (2018) *El amianto invisible: más de dos toneladas repartidas por toda España ponen en riesgo a los trabajadores*. En https://www.rtve.es/noticias/20180309/amianto-invisible-mas-dos-toneladasrepartidas toda-espana-ponen-riesgo-trabajadores/1689805.shtml. [Consultado en línea: 03/05/2024].

9 BOE n.° 255 de 24 de octubre de 2015. Véase lo establecido en el art. 14 de la Ley 31/1995, de 8 de noviembre, de Prevención de Riesgos Laborales (BOE n.° 269, de 10 de noviembre de 1995).

Tribunal Supremo, ni de los Tribunales Superiores de Justicia, debiendo apelar a la existen de tres sentencias y un Auto de Audiencias Provinciales.

- Sentencia de la Audiencia Provincial de Alicante de 28 de diciembre de 2006 (rec. 188/2006) que confirma la sentencia absolutoria del Juzgado de los Penal n.º 3 de Alicante por un delito contra los derechos de los trabajadores y homicidio por lesiones de imprudencia.
- Audiencia Provincial de Guipúzcoa, Sección 3.ª, Auto de 24 de mayo de 2004 (Jur 2004/294532) en el que se aprecian delitos contra la seguridad y salud por los trabajadores por la exposición de los trabajadores al amianto en las operaciones de demolición de una nave en la estaban instaladas placas de fibrocemento.
- Audiencia Provincial de Albacete, Sección 1.ª, Sentencia de 28 de diciembre de 2006 (Rec. 188/2006) por un delito contra los derechos de los trabajadores. · Sentencia de la Audiencia Provincial de Valencia de septiembre de 2009, dictada de conformidad por la que se reconoció por parte de la empresa Unión Naval de Valencia (Unión Naval de Levante) por la que se reconocía la responsabilidad del representante de la sociedad y tres jefes de prevención de riesgos laborales de la misma en la exposición de los trabajadores a los riesgos del amianto. Juzgado de lo Penal n.º 3 de Alicante, Sentencia de 4 de agosto de 2006 (Pro. 475/2005) Caso «Fibrocemento» donde se absuelve a los acusados porque al tomar medidas no se puede afirmar que sus conductas tengan encaje en los tipos penales.

Tiene relevancia, aunque no se sustanciaron en la vía penal la demanda planteada por cuarenta y siete vecinos de la localidad Cerdanoyla del Vallés y Ripollet (Barcelona) contra la empresa URALITA, como afectados por la actividad industrial de la planta de la empresa dedicada a la fabricación de fibrocemento. La condena inicial del Juzgado de Instrucción n.º 46 de Madrid que había fijado una cuantía de 3.918.954 euros fue revocada por la Audiencia Provincial de Madrid al estimar la prescripción de las acciones.

El 23 de enero de 2012 en el Juzgado de lo Social n.º 15 de Madrid se sustanció la demanda establecida por los trabajadores de la planta de URALITA de Getafe. La sentencia reconoció indemnizaciones a 23 trabajadores de los cuarenta demandantes por un importe de 1.727.000 euros, así como las acciones emprendidas por las mujeres de trabajadores presentadas por la vía civil (Juzgado de 1.ª Instancia n.º 4 de Madrid).

b) Jurisdicción contencioso-administrativa.

Las sentencias más reseñables en este ámbito son aquellas que condenan a la Administración en su condición de empleador por incumplirlos deberes en materia de seguridad y salud respecto a sus trabajadores o por la responsabilidad *in vigilando* por el mal funcionamiento de sus servicios médicos que no detectaron la patología de un trabajador afectado por asbestosis. Se deben destacar:

- Sentencia de la Sección 5.ª de 30 de mayo de 2012 (Rec. 66/2010) que recae sobre el Ministerio de Educación por los daños sufridos por un trabajador adscrito al Instituto nacional del Carbón.
- Sentencia de la Sección 5.ª de 9 de julio de 2008 (Rec. 285/2007) en la que se declara responsable a la Administración General del Estado (Ministerio de Defensa) en función del reconocimiento a un militar fallecido de que padecía un mesotelioma epitelial maligno como consecuencia de la exposición al amianto utilizados en los buques de la Armada10.
- Sentencia de la Sección 4.ª de 5 de febrero de 2003 (Rec. 581/2001) en la que se condena al Ministerio de Sanidad y Consumo por la muerte de un trabajador que trabajó durante treinta y cinco años en una fábrica de fibrocemento al que no se le facilitó el tratamiento adecuado de su afección de fibrosis pulmonar avanzada.

c) Jurisdicción civil.

Es el segundo ámbito jurisdiccional más utilizado atendiendo al número de demandas que se sustancian por los daños derivados de la exposición al amianto, destacando:

- Tribunal Supremo (Sala de los Civil, Sección 1.ª), Sentencia n.º 67/2007, de 8 de junio (RJ/2007/561).

10 Pitarque, S. y Benavides F. G. (2007). «Amianto y muerte por mesotelioma». *Revista Por Experiencia* n.º 38 octubre 2007 en http://www.porexperiencia.com/ [Consultado en línea: 03/05/2024].

- Tribunal Supremo, Sala 1.ª, Sentencia de 8 de noviembre de 1990, demanda de reclamación de daños y perjuicios sufrido por una trabajadora afectada por fibrosis pulmonar difusa causada por inhalación de cristales de sílice y de amianto. El Juzgado de Instrucción n.º 4 de Sevilla desestimó la demanda. La Audiencia Provincial confirma la Sentencia, pero el Tribunal Superior de Justicia de Andalucía revoca la sentencia. El Tribunal Supremo rechaza el recurso de casación por apreciar prescripción.
- Audiencia Provincial de La Coruña, Sección 3.ª, Sentencia de 22 de junio de 2012, en la que la Audiencia declara la incompetencia de jurisdicción para conocer de la responsabilidad civil derivada del fallecimiento de un trabajador por carcinoma atribuible a la exposición natural al amianto.
- Audiencia Provincial de La Coruña, Sección 3.ª, Sentencia de 10 de marzo, relativa a la indemnización por el fallecimiento de un trabajador expuesto al amianto, desestimando el recurso interpuesto contra la Sentencia del Juzgado de Primera Instancia e Instrucción n.º 6 de Ferrol que ordenó a la empresa.
- Audiencia Provincial de Valencia, Sección 11.ª, Sentencia de 27 de abril de 2005, que estima el recurso de apelación contra la sentencia absolutoria dictada por el Juzgado de 1.ª Instancia n.º 3 de Paterna, en el que se absolvió a la empresa demandada de abonar la indemnización por fallecimiento de un trabajador de una fábrica de fibrocemento fallecido por un cáncer de pulmón.
- Audiencia Provincial de Madrid, Sección 10.ª, Sentencia de 20 de junio de 2012, por la que se desestima el recurso que confirma la sentencia del Juzgado n.º 1 de Primera Instancia e Instrucción n.º 88 de Madrid por la que se condenaba a la empresa por responsabilidad extracontractual por el fallecimiento de un trabajador expuesto a los riesgos del amianto.
- Juzgado de 1.ª Instancia n.º 18 de Madrid, Sentencia de 14 de octubre de 2009, en el que se condena a las empresas a indemnizar a los trabajadores expuestos al amianto.

III.- Posición y acervo doctrinal del Tribunal Constitucional en materia de protección de derechos titularidad de personas afectadas por la exposición al amianto por motivos profesionales o personales

Con respecto a la administración de justicia Constitucional en elementos conexos con la protección de los derechos de los trabajadores afectados por patologías derivadas de la exposición al amianto, el Tribunal Constitucional no ha establecido una posición con vinculación directa con las pretensiones expresadas de forma individual o colectiva mediante el correspondiente recurso de amparo. A pesar de no existir una interpretación del Alto Tribunal al respecto y en los términos expresados en la introducción del estudio existen no menos de diez sentencias recaídas en el periodo 1998-2011 que pueden agruparse en torno a cuatro objetos específicos de intervención:

a) Pronunciamientos del Tribunal Constitucional sobre cuestiones procedimentales relativas a si son susceptibles de amparo recursos interpuestos por afectados/as por patologías derivadas del uso o manipulación por razones profesionales o particulares de amianto: SSTC 215/2001, de 29 de octubre[11]; 16/2004, de 23 de febrero[12] y 196/2004, de 15 de noviembre[13].

b) Posicionamiento del Tribunal Constitucional sobre recargos en las prestaciones otorgadas a personas que padecen efectos y patologías vinculadas con la exposición al amianto: SSTC 2018/2006 de 3 de julio[14]; 16/2008, de 31 de enero[15]; 135/2008, de 27 de octubre[16], 192/2009, de 28 de septiembre[17] y 21/2011, de 14 de marzo[18].

---

11 BOE n.º 207, de 30 de noviembre de 2001.

12 BOE n.º 74, de 26 de marzo de 2004.

13 BOE n.º 306, de 21 de diciembre de 2004.

14 BOE n.º 124, de 22 de mayo de 2018.

15 BOE n.º 245, de 10 de octubre de 2008.

16 BOE n.º 281, de 21 de noviembre de 2008.

17 BOE n.º 254, de 21 de octubre de 2009.

18 BOE n.º 86, de 11 de abril de 2011.

c) Sentencia del Tribunal Constitucional que se pronuncia sobre la distribución competencias para atender lo establecido mediante recurso de amparo por los demandantes en materia de daños producidos por la exposición a las fibras de amianto: STC 13/1998, de 22 de enero[19].

d) Sentencia relativa a la legitimación de las centrales sindicales para actuar sobre pretensiones individuales: STC 2015/2001, de 22 de enero[20].

En relación a los pronunciamientos del Tribunal Constitucional sobre cuestiones procedimentales relativas a si son susceptibles de amparo recursos interpuestos por afectados/as por patologías derivadas del uso o manipulación por razones profesionales o particulares de amianto debe destacarse lo expresado en la STC 2015/2001, de 29 de octubre, relativa al recurso de amparo interpuesto por la Unión General de Trabajadores (UGT) de Castilla y León contra el Auto del Juzgado de lo Social núm. 1 de los de Valladolid, de 12 de abril de 1999, dictado en autos núm. 590/98, que estima el recurso de reposición interpuesto por la Mutual Cyclops y Fibrocementos N.T., S.L., dejando sin efecto la providencia de 1 de marzo de 1999 por la que se acordaba tener por parte en el procedimiento de oficio al Comité de Empresa de Fibrocementos y a la Unión Regional de la UGT de Castilla y León.

El recurso de amparo pretendía determinar si se vulneraba el derecho a la tutela judicial efectiva (art. 24 CE) por la denegación de la legitimación del sindicato Unión General de Trabajadores de Castilla y León en el proceso de oficio iniciado por la Dirección General de Trabajo de la Consejería de Industria, Comercio y Turismo de la Junta de Castilla y León por demanda-comunicación de 27 de octubre de 1998, como consecuencia del procedimiento de imposición de sanciones por infracciones en el orden social iniciado previamente sobre cesión ilegal de trabajadores.

Para la correcta resolución del problema planteado, resulta necesario partir de la doctrina constitucional en materia de legitimación procesal de los sindicatos, así como de la idea de que, cuando el derecho a la tutela judicial efectiva del art. 24 CE se impetra para la defensa de un derecho sustan-

19 BOE n.° 47, de 24 de febrero de 1998.

20 BOE n.° 47, de 24 de febrero de 2015.

tivo fundamental (en el presente caso el de la libertad sindical), el canon de constitucionalidad a aplicar es un canon reforzado y se convierte en un control material más exigente (STC 10/2001, de 29 de enero, STC 84/2001, de 26 de marzo); canon reforzado que también resulta exigible cuando nos hallamos ante el derecho de acceso a la jurisdicción (SSTC 37/1995, de 7 de febrero, 84/2001) (FJ 2.º).

En el caso que recoge la STC 215/2001, de 29 de octubre se ha negado legitimación al sindicato recurrente trae causa de un procedimiento administrativo sancionador previo y que, por regla general, en este tipo de procedimientos los intereses afectados son únicamente los de las partes directamente implicadas: empresa y trabajadores. Sin embargo, en el presente supuesto concurren unos elementos específicos que permiten concluir que también resultan afectados intereses colectivos del conjunto de los trabajadores de la empresa y, en consecuencia, intereses económicos y profesionales cuya defensa puede legítimamente corresponder al sindicato recurrente, ya que la infracción objeto de controversia y la eventual sanción tienen por objeto la tutela de un interés colectivo (FJ 4.º).

Negar la legitimación del sindicato en el proceso de oficio sobre la base de que la Sentencia sólo tiene efectos para las partes (trabajadores y empresarios implicados) lleva consigo una interpretación claramente restrictiva del acceso a la jurisdicción que no tiene en cuenta la especial naturaleza del proceso (FJ 5.ª), declarando finalmente que se había vulnerado el derecho a la tutela judicial efectiva sin indefensión (art. 24 CE) de la Unión General de Trabajadores frente a Mutual Cyclops y Fibrocementos N.T., S.L.

Con respecto al recargo en las prestaciones que se reconocen a las personas afectadas por enfermedades y patologías derivadas de la exposición a las fibras de amianto debe destacarse lo expresado por el Tribunal Constitucional en su Sentencia 21/2011, de 14 de marzo relativa al recurso de amparo núm. 2420-2007, promovido por Ingeniería de Cimentaciones, S.A., contra el Auto dictado por la Sala de lo Social del Tribunal Supremo, de fecha 30 de enero de 2007, que inadmitió a trámite el recurso de casación para la unificación de doctrina interpuesto contra la Sentencia de la Sala de lo Social del Tribunal Superior de Justicia de Cataluña, de 7 de diciembre de 2005, que confirmó la del Juzgado de lo Social núm. 24 de los de Barcelona, de 5 de abril de 2004, en autos núm. 1020-2002 sobre recargo de prestaciones por falta de medidas de seguridad.

El recurso de amparo tenía por objeto determinar si las resoluciones judiciales impugnadas habían vulnerado el derecho de la sociedad recurrente a la tutela judicial efectiva (art. 24.1 CE), al haber tomado en consideración una calificación de los hechos probados que estaría en abierta contradicción con lo declarado en resoluciones judiciales previas a las que quedaban vinculadas declarando el Tribunal Constitucional vulnerado el derecho de la recurrente a la tutela judicial efectiva (art. 24.1 CE) por insuficiente motivación.

En lo relativo a la distribución de competencias debe observarse lo expresado por el Tribunal Constitucional en su STC 13/1998, de 22 de enero en relación al conflicto positivo de competencias núm. promovido por el Gobierno de la Comuidad Autónoma de Euskadi, en relación con determinados artículos del Real Decreto 1131/1988, de 30 de septiembre, por el que se aprueba el Reglamento (en adelante, R.E.I.A.) para la ejecución del Real Decreto Legislativo 1302/1986, de 28 de junio, de evaluación de impacto ambiental (en adelante, L.E.I.A.), donde el Tribunal Constitucional vino a declarar que eran conformes al orden constitucional y estatutario de distribución de competencias los preceptos impugnados del Real Decreto 1131/1988, de 30 de septiembre, por el que se aprueba el Reglamento para la ejecución del Real Decreto Legislativo 1302/1986, de 28 de junio, de Evaluación de Impacto Ambiental.

Finalmente y dentro de la acción tangencial del Tribunal Constitucional con respecto a la acción n de la justicia constitucional relativa a la legitimación de las centrales sindicales sobre pretensiones individuales debe destacarse lo dicho en la STC 2015/2011, de 22 de enero, relativo al recurso de inconstitucionalidad promovido por ciento cuatro Diputados del Grupo Parlamentario Socialista y once del Grupo Parlamentario La Izquierda Plural [Izquierda Unida (IU), Iniciativa per Catalunya Verds-Esquerra Unida i Alternativa (ICV-EUiA) y Chunta Aragonesista (CHA)] del Congreso de los Diputados, contra los arts. 4.3, 12.1, 14.1 y 2, 18.3 y 8, 23.1, así como contra la disposición adicional tercera y la disposición final cuarta 2, de la Ley 3/2012, de 6 de julio, de medidas urgentes para la reforma del mercado laboral por vulneración de los arts. 14, 23.2, 24.1, 28.1, 35.1, 37.1 y 103.3, todos ellos de la Constitución.

Los Grupos Parlamentarios recurrentes destacan el papel que dentro del Estado social juegan los interlocutores sociales (art. 7 CE), el derecho a la negociación colectiva (art. 37 CE), la libertad sindical, así como el derecho de huelga (art. 28 CE), que se erigen en un extremo constitucional indisponible para la defensa de los trabajadores, por lo que los efectos de la Ley 3/2012, de 6 de julio, viene a desdeñar la posición de los interlocutores sociales planteándose como una transformación profunda del Derecho del trabajo, situándose fuera del marco de nuestro Estado social y democrático de derecho y de la propia Constitución.

Los recurrentes plantean que lo que queda constitucionalmente prohibido al legislador es «sustituir los elementos centrales del modelo constitucional» por otros distintos. Y añaden, que cuando el legislador actúa de ese modo, la consecuencia es que «el producto normativo nace al mundo del Derecho fuera de las coordenadas constitucionales». Plantean los Grupos Parlamentarios recurrentes que la decisión del legislador de «ignorar de partida nuestro modelo de relaciones laborales, modelo consecuente con la fórmula del Estado Social y democrático de Derecho» no puede sino saldarse con las inconstitucionalidades evidentes que se imputan a los preceptos recurridos.

Si bien, continúan los recurrentes, es posible aceptar la inaplicación de condiciones de trabajo pactadas en convenio cuando tal decisión sea el resultado de un procedimiento negociado de inaplicación, como ocurría en precedentes regulaciones, resulta inadmisible, por traspasar los límites de lo constitucionalmente aceptable, la actual atribución por iniciativa de la dirección de la empresa, de una facultad final resolutoria a la Comisión Consultiva Nacional de Convenios Colectivos.

No cuestionan los recurrentes las fases del procedimiento de inaplicación anteriores a la intervención de la citada Comisión, pues en ellas la decisión se atribuye a las propias partes negociadoras, o bien a otros sujetos colectivos con legitimación para negociar un convenio en el ámbito correspondiente, manteniéndose el precepto, por lo tanto, en la esfera del respeto de la autonomía de negociación. Por el contrario, la última de las fases se pone en marcha por iniciativa de una de las partes (que en la práctica será el empleador) y es un sujeto ajeno a ellas el que podrá acordar unilateralmente la inaplicación de las condiciones pactadas en convenio colectivo, con patente vulneración de su fuerza vinculante. Mantienen los Grupos Parlamentarios que se trataría de un arbitraje obligatorio y público, en tanto la decisión se adopta en el seno de un organismo de tal carácter cuyos acuerdos tienen la naturaleza de actos administrativos, identificable con el arbitraje obligatorio atribuido a la autoridad laboral para dirimir conflictos colectivos en el Real Decreto-ley 17/1977, de 4 de marzo, que fue declarado inconstitucional por STC 11/1981, de 8 de abril, y cuyos razonamientos consideran los Grupos Parlamentarios son aplicables al caso de la Ley 3/2012, de 6 de julio, para apreciar la vulneración de los arts. 37.1 y 28.1 CE.

Los recurrentes mantienen que la norma impugnada viene a consentir una intromisión pública que afecta claramente al contenido esencial de la negociación colectiva (art. 37.1 CE), como también del derecho a la libertad sindical (art. 28.1 CE) desde el momento en que aquélla constituye un instrumento de la acción sindical. A mayor abundamiento, los recurrentes se quejan del margen de discrecionalidad que tienen la Comisión Consultiva Nacional de Convenios Colectivos o el árbitro para tomar la decisión de inaplicación, pues les basta con comprobar la concurrencia de las amplias causas justificativas previstas legalmente. Consideran que tal circunstancia impide al poder judicial un control de la adecuación o no de la medida, lo que conlleva la lesión consiguiente del derecho a la tutela judicial efectiva del art. 24 CE.

Si bien la STC 11/1981 citada admitió el establecimiento de un arbitraje obligatorio en caso de huelga para situaciones extraordinarias o excepcionales[21], en el caso de autos no concurriría un escenario de excepcionalidad o situación extraordinaria en la regulación del procedimiento de arbitraje obligatorio previsto para la inaplicación del convenio colectivo. Plantean que no puede establecerse comparación entre la competencia asignada a la Comisión Consultiva Nacional de Convenios Colectivos en el precepto impugnado con la que en el pasado ostentó para resolver discrepancias entre las partes a los efectos de cerrar el largo proceso de derogación de las ordenanzas laborales, en tanto que en este último caso la actuación de la Comisión no afectaba a la fuerza vinculante de los convenios colectivos.

21 Dando su conformidad al arbitraje obligatorio previsto en el párrafo segundo del art. 10 del Real Decreto-ley 17/1977, de 4 de marzo.

En segundo lugar, impugnan el apartado primero del art. 12 de la Ley 3/2012, por el que se modifica el art. 41 LET relativo a las modificaciones sustanciales de las condiciones de trabajo, y en el que se reconoce, en sus apartados 4 y 5, la facultad del empleador de acordar unilateralmente la modificación de condiciones de trabajo pactadas en acuerdos o pactos colectivos extraestaturarios. Sostienen los recurrentes que tal precepto vulnera el reconocimiento constitucional de la fuerza vinculante de los convenios colectivos (art. 37.1 CE), la libertad sindical (art. 28.1 CE), y el derecho a la tutela judicial efectiva (art. 24.1 CE).

A juicio de los recurrentes, en este caso el incumplimiento de lo pactado en acuerdos colectivos es mucho más directo que en el supuesto analizado con anterioridad, dado que la decisión de alterar lo pactado colectivamente ni siquiera depende del control de un tercero (arbitraje), sino que es el propio empleador quien lo decide libremente de forma unilateral, con el simple requisito previo de sometimiento a un periodo de consultas con los representantes de los trabajadores, que aunque resulta preceptivo, no es vinculante. Con esta regulación, que afecta a los acuerdos colectivos no regulados en el título III del texto refundido de la Ley del estatuto de los trabajadores se vulnera la garantía del *pacta sunt servanda* colectivo del art. 37.1 CE y del derecho a la libertad sindical (art. 28.1 CE). A este respecto, se indica que la Constitución garantiza la fuerza vinculante de todos los convenios colectivos, tanto de los estatutarios como de los extraestatutarios, sin que quepa que el legislador ordinario saque de esa garantia a determinados pactos colectivos.

Tomando como punto de partida la doctrina constitucional que establece la vinculación existente entre los derechos de negociación colectiva y libertad sindical, la aplicación del precepto legal cuestionado lleva a dos resultados. El primero, la posibilidad de inaplicación de un convenio colectivo sectorial en el ámbito de una empresa, en materias tan específicas de la negociación colectiva como las que se mencionan en el precepto legal. Esta inaplicación sería el resultado de la negociación, en cualquier momento de la vigencia del convenio sectorial, de un convenio de empresa, que, de acuerdo con la Ley, puede suscribirse entre el empresario y el comité de empresa o los delegados de personal, es decir, por representantes no sindicales. Y esto mismo ocurre, en segundo lugar, con la posible inaplicación en virtud de un acuerdo a nivel de empresa, de las reglas y criterios sobre estructura de la negociación colectiva y prioridad de unidades de negociación que hayan sido adoptados en los acuerdos sobre ordenación de la estructura de la negociación colectiva concluidos por las organizaciones empresariales y sindicales.

Por indicación constitucional la negociación colectiva posee un espacio regulativo propio que no puede ser ahogado ni suprimido por completo por parte de la normativa estatal y que el derecho a la negociación colectiva reconocido constitucionalmente debe necesariamente incluir la libre decisión de negociar sobre las materias que las propias partes estimen oportunas. En este sentido, la norma impugnada carecía de justificación, dado que las cláusulas convencionales sobre jubilación pueden responder a la confluencia de diversos derechos subjetivos e intereses legítimos: el derecho al trabajo, el desarrollo de una política de empleo que atienda a las demandas del conjunto de la población, la promoción de condiciones favorables para una distribución más equitativa de la renta, el equilibrio del régimen público de Seguridad Social y la eficiencia económica de las empresas, elementos todos ellos que deben ser ponderados, desde criterios de proporcionalidad, por la negociación colectiva. La norma, además, estaría prohibiendo a la negociación colectiva lo que puede ser decidido unilateralmente por el empresario en el marco de un despido por causas económicas, o acordado con los trabajadores por un simple acuerdo de empresa durante el período de consultas de los citados despidos económicos.

Finalmente, la norma impugnada venía a vulnerar en palabras de los recurrentes tanto el art. 37 CE como el art. 14 CE, en cuanto que limitaría injustificadamente la actividad sindical en una materia, sobre la que se permite al empresario adoptar medidas unilaterales, como la reestructuración del empleo por la vía de los despidos colectivos.

Tal y como expresa la STC 2015/2001 en su FJ 1.º la Constitución confiere al Estado competencias exclusivas tanto en materia de legislación laboral (art. 149.1.7 CE), como para la regulación de las condiciones básicas que garanticen la igualdad de todos los ciudadanos en el ejercicio de los derechos constitucionales (art. 149.1.1 CE), correspondiéndole, pues, la tarea de ordenar los principios y criterios con arreglo a los cuales se ha de regir la materia laboral, desde una concepción del conjunto de sus relaciones como «un» sistema, pero sin estar condicionado cómo debe llevarla a cabo. Tales preceptos hay que ponerlos en relación con el art. 35.2 CE, que encomienda al legislador estatal la regulación de «un» estatuto de los trabajadores, así como con el art. 53.1 CE, que remite a la ley la regulación de los derechos y libertades laborales reconocidos en el capítulo II de su título I.

Debe observarse la especial posición que dentro de nuestro sistema de relaciones laborales ocupa el «sindicato». La Constitución le ha consagrado como un elemento clave dentro de la configuración de nuestro Estado como un «Estado social y democrático de Derecho» (art. 1.1 CE), al incluir su reconocimiento en el art. 7 del título preliminar, que prevé que «los sindicatos de trabajadores y las asociaciones empresariales contribuyen a la defensa y promoción de los intereses económicos y sociales que le son propios». Su especial ubicación en el texto fundamental realza la consideración del «sindicato» como uno de los soportes institucionales básicos de la sociedad para la defensa, protección y promoción de los intereses colectivos de los trabajadores. Así lo ha entendido, además, este Tribunal en numerosas ocasiones en las que no ha dudado en considerar a los «sindicatos», no sólo como «piezas económicas y sociales indispensables para la defensa y promoción» de los intereses de los trabajadores (STC 70/1982, de 29 de noviembre, FJ 5), sino, lo que es más importante, como «organismos básicos del sistema político» (STC 11/1981, de 8 de abril, FJ 11), como «formaciones sociales con relevancia constitucional» (STC 18/1984, de 7 de febrero, FJ 3), y, en definitiva, como una «institución esencial del sistema constitucional español» (STC 101/1996, de 11 de junio, FJ 3).

Conviene señalar también que la determinación del contenido de la relación laboral, junto con la regulación mínima del legislador, «se deja a la responsabilidad de la autonomía colectiva de las partes sociales», esto es, «a la autonomía de los trabajadores y empresarios mediante el ejercicio del derecho a la negociación colectiva que proclama el art. 37.1 CE» (STC 119/2002, de 20 de mayo, FJ 6), siendo tal tipo de negociación «un valor constitucionalmente protegido» (SSTC 39/1986, de 31 de marzo, FJ 6 y 184/1991, de 30 de septiembre, FJ 6). Ese derecho «presupone, por esencia y conceptualmente, la prevalencia de la autonomía de la voluntad colectiva sobre la voluntad individual» (SSTC 105/1992, de 1 de julio, FJ 6; y 225/2001, de 26 de noviembre, FJ 4), siendo los convenios colectivos fruto de su ejercicio, «fuentes de regulación de las condiciones de trabajo» a las que constitucionalmente se reconocen fuerza vinculante (STC 151/1994, de 23 de mayo, FJ 2). La negociación colectiva no sólo contribuye, entonces, «a la mejora de las condiciones de trabajo y de vida de los trabajadores», sino que se erige en un «instrumento esencial para la ordenación de las relaciones de trabajo» (STC 208/1993, de 28 de junio, FJ 4).

El Tribunal Constitucional reitera en la STC 2015/2001 el papel que desempeña el sindicato como defensor de los derechos e intereses de los trabajadores, también lo es el que ocupa la negociación colectiva de condiciones de trabajo dentro de la acción sindical, «puesto que resulta inimaginable que sin ella se logre desarrollar eficazmente las finalidades recogidas en el art. 7 CE» (STC 225/2001, de 26 de noviembre, FJ 5), de manera que «cuando existe un elemento de sindicalidad, esto es, cuando la negociación colectiva es expresión de la acción sindical» (STC 118/2012, de 4 de junio, FJ 4), pasa a formar parte del contenido esencial de aquella libertad (SSTC 134/1994, de 9 de mayo, FJ 4; 222/2005, de 12 de septiembre, FJ 3; y 118/2012, de 4 de junio, FJ 4). En efecto, «entre los rasgos que, tanto histórica como legalmente, caracterizan al sindicato, figura muy destacadamente su esencial vinculación con la acción sindical que se plasma en el ejercicio del derecho de huelga (art. 28.2 CE), en la negociación colectiva (art. 37.1 CE) y en la adopción de medidas de conflicto colectivo (art. 37.2 CE) » (STC 152/2008, de 17 de noviembre, FJ 4).

La Constitución, al institucionalizar los derechos colectivos laborales (huelga, negociación colectiva y conflictos colectivos), no los ha reservado «en exclusiva a los sindicatos» (SSTC 134/1994, de 9 de mayo, FJ 4; y 95/1996, de 29 de mayo, FJ 3), pues ha eludido «la consagración de un monopolio» sindical en esta materia, para partir de un «amplio reconocimiento» de los titulares de aquéllos derechos colectivos «de forma que si el derecho de huelga se atribuye a los trabajadores (art. 28.2), el de conflictos lo es a los trabajadores y empresarios (art. 37.2) y el de negociación a los representantes de éstos (art. 37.1) » (STC 118/1983, de 13 de diciembre, FJ 4). De esta manera, a diferencia de las previsiones contenidas en los arts. 7 CE (que institucionaliza al sindicato como un organismo esencial de nuestro sistema constitucional) y 28.1 CE (que consagra al sindicato como el instrumento básico del ejercicio del derecho fundamental a la libertad sindical), el constituyente no refirió, en su art. 37.1 CE, la negociación colectiva como un derecho perteneciente exclusivamente al ámbito de la acción sindical. Antes al contrario, lo recondujo más genéricamente a los «representantes de los trabajadores», con la clara intención de ampliar el elenco de los legitimados para la determinación de las condiciones de la relación laboral, depositando ese derecho, en consecuencia, no sólo en el sindicato, sino en cualquier sujeto u organización representativa de los trabajadores (como los delegados de personal y los comités de empresa), cuyo fundamento constitucional último no se encuentra en el art. 7 CE, como sucede con los representantes sindicales, sino en los arts. 9.2 y 129.2 CE (SSTC 98/1985, de 29 de julio, FJ 3; y 208/1989, de 14 de diciembre, FJ 3).

El ejercicio del derecho a la negociación colectiva (art. 37.1 CE) le ha sido atribuido también por la Constitución al sindicato, protagonista principal en la defensa de los intereses de los trabajadores (art. 7 CE) a través del ejercicio de la libertad sindical (art. 28.1 CE), no se ha hecho de forma exclusiva ni en modo que descarte a otros posibles representantes de los trabajadores, de manera que no cabe sino concluir que la negociación colectiva está «atribuida constitucionalmente a los sindicatos y a otras representaciones colectivas de los trabajadores» (STC 208/1993, de 28 de junio, FJ 4).

Con base en lo anterior, la Constitución otorga la garantía del derecho a la negociación colectiva laboral (art. 37.1 CE), por lo que el Tribunal Constitucional a la hora de imponer su sentencia se enfrentaba a «un derecho esencialmente de configuración legal» (STC 85/2001, de 26 de marzo, FJ 5), siendo la ley la que ha de concretar y desarrollar, tanto su contenido como los presupuestos para su ejercicio (STC 208/1993, de 28 de junio, FJ 3). En «la configuración legal del ejercicio del derecho a negociar» (STC 224/2000, de 2 de octubre, FJ 4), el legislador goza de un amplio margen de libertad para delimitar, como derecho necesario, aspectos de la estructura, contenido, alcance y límites de la negociación colectiva, en razón de la superior posición que ocupa la ley en la jerarquía normativa.

La Constitución de 1978 no diseña un modelo cerrado de relaciones laborales, ni más concretamente, de negociación colectiva, correspondiéndole al legislador estatal, en el ejercicio de las funciones que la propia Constitución le confiere, configurar el que considere más idóneo en cada momento (STC 11/1981, de 8 de abril, FJ 7), eligiendo entre las distintas alternativas posibles la que estime más adecuada, no solo para alcanzar los objetivos que aquélla le impone, sino también para adoptar las medidas precisas que garanticen su realización. De todo ello se deduce la habilitación al legislador estatal para realizar su conceptuación jurídica en cada momento, entre diferentes alternativas, en atención a las circunstancias económicas subyacentes y a las necesidades sociales a las que se pretenda dar cobertura. El constituyente no quiso definir el modelo de relaciones laborales aplicable, ni tampoco restringir la acción del legislador más allá de los límites explícitos que le ha impuesto, dejándole un importante ámbito de posibilidades para configurar el citado modelo y para articular cada institución que lo integre, no sólo como un instrumento de su desarrollo, sino también como un vehículo a través del cual alcanzar los fines que la Constitución le impone [en el mismo sentido, aunque con relación a la definición del modelo de sistema tributario aplicable, STC 19/2012, de 15 de febrero, FJ 3 c).

Cada una de las normas que han incidido n el modelo de relaciones laborales en el periodo de estudio objeto de la presente comunicación representa una opción legislativa diferente como un instrumento al servicio de una concreta política económica y social del Gobierno y Parlamento de cada momento, respecto de la cual no es suficiente la mera discrepancia política para destruir su presunción de constitucionalidad (STC 19/2012, de 15 de febrero, FJ 3). El Tribunal Constitucional considera que no le compete enjuiciar si las soluciones adoptadas en la Ley impugnada son las más correctas técnicamente, o si constituye la más oportuna de entre las distintas alternativas posibles para la consecución de los fines pretendidos, sino únicamente si se ajustan a los mandatos, reglas y principios que la Constitución impone, por lo que «[n]o resulta ocioso reiterar que toda opción legislativa, por discutible que para algunos pueda ser, resulta admisible desde el punto de vista constitucional siempre que respete las reglas que la Constitución establece» (STC 20/2013, de 31 de enero, FJ 3), lo que llevó a no interferir y por tanto vino a desestimar el recurso de inconstitucionalidad.

IV.- Conclusiones: Omisión de la justicia constitucional frente al «desastre lento» del amianto

A partir del análisis realizado cabe concluir que la legislación compensadora española ha proporcionado durante los últimos cincuenta años reconocimiento médico-legal como enfermedades profesionales (EP) a diversas dolencias causadas por la exposición al amianto o asbesto. La aprobación en 2006 del el Real Decreto 1299/20063, por el que se estableció el Cuadro de Enfermedades Profesionales vigente en la actualidad permite el reconocimiento de 141 enfermedades en línea con lo recogido en la lista europea de EP incluida en la Recomendación de la Comisión Europea de 19 de septiembre de 2003.

A pesar de la existencia de la voluntad de las distintas Administraciones, actualmente carecemos de estimaciones adecuadas sobre el número de trabajadores y población general afectada por las fibras de amianto, con que se traduce en el consiguiente infrareconocimiento del origen profesional de estas enfermedades en nuestro país.

La primera consecuencia de ello es la privación a las víctimas de sus derechos en términos de prestaciones y de reconocimiento social. La segunda es la socialización de los costes de la enfermedad que son transferidos desde las empresas responsables de las exposiciones laborales causantes de la misma a la ciudadanía general y a los Servicios de Salud. La tercera consecuencia es la dificultad que entraña para el desarrollo de programas de prevención de riesgos por parte de las empresas y las autoridades laborales.

La solución individual, mediante demandas individuales sustanciadas en vía judicial presenta serias deficiencias y limitaciones (alta litigiosidad, disparidad de trato, complejidad del proceso y exigencia de culpa). Los afectados por la exposición al amianto son un colectivo uniformemente afectado, donde el origen de su enfermedad radica en la exposición a las fibras de amianto.

La reparación de los daños a personas por exposición al amianto se ha abordado mediante dos mecanismos básicos; por un lado, los mecanismos de indemnización colectiva y por otro la litigiosidad derivada de las reclamaciones colectivas. Atendiendo a lo manifestado en las distintas jurisdicciones. En este escenario cabe reconocer un activo papel de la jurisdicción civil con tres sentencias y un auto emanados de Audiencias Provinciales y una actividad marginal de la jurisdicción penal no existiendo pronunciamiento ni de la Sala Tercera del Tribunal Supremo, ni de los Tribunales Superiores de Justicia, debiendo apelar a la existen de tres sentencias y un Auto de Audiencias Provinciales. A ello debe sumarse la incomparecencia de la justicia constitucional con respecto al impacto sobre la salud y la protección de lo establecido en el art. 43 CE existiendo dentro del acervo jurisprudencial de nuestro Tribunal Constitucional referencias indirectas que a través de diez sentencias se pronuncian sobre cuestiones formales, relativas a la distribución de competencias o sobre la legitimación de las centrales sindicales en relación a peticiones individuales.

Compartiendo que el ámbito de la justicia constitucional no es, a priori, el ámbito natural para establecer la vía del reconocimiento del origen profesional de las enfermedades y patologías derivadas de la exposición al amianto se hace necesaria una reflexión acerca del despliegue que artículos como el 43 CE, así como los anclajes del derecho a la salud con los arts. 9.2, 41, 49, 50, 51.1 CE en lo sustantivo y con los arts. 148.1, 149.1.16. C en los aspectos formales.

"CORPORATE CRIME AND THE CONNECTION BETWEEN SCIENCE AND INDUSTRY: CREATING DOUBT AND SPREADING ASBESTOS HARM"

Marília de Nardin Budó[22]

Universidad Federal de Santa Catarina
University of Birmingham

I.- Introduction

Asbestos is a mineral easily separated into fibers. It is flexible, incombustible, indestructible, and cheap, and has been widely mined and used as a raw material in industry. Different types of this mineral are found in nature: serpentine, a mineral of which the white asbestos, chrysotile, is the most common, and amphibole, which includes the blue crocidolite and the brown amosite (Mendes, 2001). All asbestos types have been banned from 60 countries because of its hazardous effects on human health. However, a theory elaborated in the 1980s supported that chrysotile asbestos is less harmful than amphiboles. The differentiation thesis is still delaying the ban in most parts of the world (McCullogh; Tweedale, 2008).

---

22 Ph.D., Full professor (tenured) at the Federal University of Santa Catarina, Florianópolis-SC, Brazil. Visiting Researcher at the University of Birmingham, UK. This study was financed in part by the Coordination for the Improvement of Higher Education Personnel, Ministry of Education of Brazil (CAPES/MEC) Finance Code 001. E-mail: marilia.db@ufsc.br.

The World Health Organization calculates that at least 107,000 people die every year in the world because of asbestos related diseases (ARD). Furuya et al. (2018) claim offer another number: 255,000 deaths a year. This communication presents the results of a research on scientific discourse on asbestos harms to understand the role played by science in hiding the wounds and deaths caused by corporations. I analyze the disputes for truth on asbestos-related diseases in medical journals through grounded theory (from 1990 to 2017). The objective is to understand the strategies used by scientists funded by asbestos companies to minimize asbestos harms, and at the same time build some credibility about their own discourses hiding the conflicts of interests (CoI). It also seeks to comprehend how scientists represent the consequences of research misconducts (RM).

The criminological study of social harm (Hillyard; Tombs, 2004), liability (Altopiedi, 2011), and victimization related to the productive dynamics of science may be framed in the broad field of the crimes of the powerful, and specifically in the definition of occupational crime and corporate crime (Faria, 2018; Friedrichs, 2010; Budó, 2016). The background of this study is critical and green criminology to analyze a case of crimes of the powerful (Natali, 2015; Barak, 2015).

II.- Method

The research corpus is composed of documents found through the search tool PubMed, using the expressions "chrysotile" AND "amphibole hypothesis" OR "chrysotile biopersistence." From the 80 results, I selected only those which had comments, letters to the editor, corrigenda or errata, resulting in 23 texts (articles and comments), two errata and one corrigenda, organized in six cases. Each case brings a set of texts related to each other. They start with one or more articles that generate the other linked texts, which can be only errata by the publisher and/ or by the authors (cases 2 and 5), or annotations/ comments by other scientists regarding the specific theme discussed in the original paper (cases 1, 3, 4 and 6). The methodology of analysis is grounded theory, under a constructionist approach (Charmaz, 2006).

III.- Results

What is a dispute for truth? *Who* is disputing? *How* is the truth disputed? *What are the consequences* of the disputes for truth? The documents analyzed through grounded theory generated three main conceptual categories: *the relationship between scientists and companies*; *the nature of the scientific controversies,* and *the consequences of research misconducts*. Each of the conceptual categories were divided into many types or models and they are shortly presented below.

The first category reveals a struggle from the research papers' authors to appear as credible sources of truth about asbestos exposure risks. The relationship with the industry, and then, the acknowledgment of a conflict of interest can reduce this credibility. The independent scientist, as one who can dispute for truth, is both an ambiguous and disputed concept. There seem to be an "author-type" to which many subtle strategies can be used to approach or avoid distancing, even if it is necessary to abuse journals' CoI policies. In the analysis I found out that conflicted scientists adopt a range of strategies to hide these links. Some of them are: a) *detaching the conflict timeline from the article timeline*, by revealing the CoI after the publication of the article and only if somebody sends a letter to the editor questioning it; b) *using different titles for the relationships disclosed,* which gives the connotation of degrees of conflicted interests, presented (Consulting expert for chrysotile industry, a specific company; expert witness in litigation for a specific company or for workers; representative of the company); c) *disconnecting the relationships disclosed from the specific published research*, where even in recognizing the receiving of money from industry, the author claims that it did not influence the specific paper; d) *flexibilising the nature of the payments received*, that can be understood as more or less binding to the company's/organization's interests, presented below in ascending order: research grant, payments for the specific paper, payments for conducing the entire research.

The second category, *the nature of the scientific controversies* shows how scientific controversy itself is also an object of dispute. Disputing the existence and the nature of controversy presupposes that science is the product of questioning, doubting, and, at the same time, realizing historicity and the absence of neutrality. Simultaneously, to admit that some theories are consensual in a determined field permits new problems of research to emerge, making science move forward. In the subject of the health risks of asbestos, it is possible to read a dialectical use of the meanings of consensus and controversy.

Some of the consensuses from which all texts started were: 1) the mineralogic, toxicologic, and epidemiologic differentiation between amphiboles and serpentines, and 2) the causation of all types of ARD by amphiboles asbestos. However, the consensuses finish at this point. The use each scientist or group will make of these assumptions will vary, depending on time and scope of the pieces. *Denying further controversies* seems to be a shared strategy between many of the actors. The first strategy of the pro-asbestos scientists is to consider the studies from the 1950's which revealed asbestos harms out-of-date. The use of the word *chrysotile* instead of *asbestos* is a strategy to avoid dealing with the heavy load of scandal and fear associated with it. It could also be seen as a strategy of denial, since *detaching the word asbestos from the object is a procedure for reframing it with another meaning*. If chrysotile is a "completely different mineral," then the words *controversy* and *risk* cannot be linked to it. This idea is connected to another strategy which comes from *the use of a sense of temporality and historicity to deny controversy and risk*. For doing it another strategy is to *describe articles that associate chrysotile to risk with verbs conjugated in the past tense*.

On the one side, controversy is denied by the idea that studies linking health risks and controversy to asbestos are out of date; on the other side, controversy is denied when industry-funded authors support theses of safe controlled use of chrysotile through misleading references and methodologies. In this context, when abusing the basic principles, guidelines and rules, controversy promotes a breach of power, and constructs a space of anomy. When anything is science, then nothing is science. The controversy appears as an object of denunciation.

In the third category, *"Consequences of research misconducts"*, the authors represent RM harm and victimization, directly or indirectly, intentional, or unintentional. First, *research papers can influence political decisions around the world based on bad science*, for example, by separating standards for the different forms of asbestos and the assumption of a possible safe controlled use of chrysotile.

In both temporalities *there are also victims constructed in the discourses*. In general, vulnerable people are characterized: from global South workers to an expanded account of victims encompassing the past, present and future beyond the walls of the factories or mines. The relationship between science and political decisions in the global sphere appear with the idea of an international division of the labor, in the sense that it is easy for corporations and chrysotile institutes from the global North to influence the decisions in the South. When talking about the impact on political decisions of banning asbestos, the actors are representing consequences of projecting harm to the future, which are more linked to political decisions in the global South. When talking about judicial decisions that can be made inside litigation for injured workers, they are representing consequences of denying harm produced in the past, and the victims are described more often as workers from the global North (Castleman, 1995).

Together with the human victims, another victim of this process appears to be science itself: the chrysotile lobby undermines the very integrity of science and environmental health practice. Simultaneously, there is a recognition that the impacts of lawsuits in science also provide good results because the sworn truth has allowed lawyers and campaigners pro-asbestos ban to discover the nefarious ties between science and industry.

IV.- Conclusions

The results show that authors use strategies to achieve credibility: avoiding acknowledging industry funding; constructing a specific meaning for the controversy about asbestos risks; and reflecting about the consequences of research misconducts. The ways of thinking about asbestos risks and harms are migrating through the international division of scientific labor, from global North to global South, both to spread harm and to avoid liability of powerful agents.

THE ETERNIT CASE

Yvonne Waterman
European Asbestos Forum

Before anything else, I think it was such a huge compliment and kindness from Marilia to speak for me in English, because I don't speak a word of Spanish, so thank you so much Marilia, that was unusually kind of you.

Talking about the price of independent scientists like David Bernstein, he cost 3,000 a day just so you know. I suggested giving indeed an impromptu presentation relating to the Eternit case and interestingly, I attended the verdicts last year in Novara. I was there in person on behalf of my Foundation, the European Asbestos Foundation, which actually is a bit of a funny name, because it's a really global setup. I wanted to bear witness on behalf of the Foundation what was happening with the victims and witnessing the Italian Justice, and honoring it by being present there. And it was a very emotional day, I have to say it was particularly a very long day because the jury was out a long time, but eventually when the jury came back they handed a paper to the judge, this was the actual verdict and he read it out loud. It contained hundreds of names, first and last names of the victims, and you could really feel that the judge had trouble not to cry when he was reading out the list of the victims on whose behalf he was giving the verdict. Imagine, in my whole life as a jurist and a former lawyer, I have never seen a judge cry, and this judge was that close to it. He told the whole court, a huge audience, that Schmidheiny effectively was a criminal. He was indicted of a number of crimes, there was a jail sentence, there was a huge compensation, there was a financial punishment; and you think to some extent that there would be joy in the room, that people would say we have won, it's David against Goliath and we, as little David, have won Goliath, Schmidheiny himself.

This was not the case, and it was not I think, because the people who were there in the room, in the court, did not think Schmidheiny would go to jail, because we all know that he will never see the inside of a jail in his lifetime. So that's off the table, and there was no joy because of the big compensation numbers that were named, because all those people, they knew that they were highly unlikely ever to see a single cent of it. They have been litigating for something like 15 years now and so far nobody has received a cent from Schmidheiny. Nearly everybody else wasn't to use many of their warranties, even when they left the courthouse and went to their homes, and the reason for this was very clear, no verdicts could ever bring their loved ones back. The people who have mesothelioma themselves could not be cured by any verdicts, the people who knew that they have a great likelihood of developing asbestos cancers in the future. No verdicts can cure them, no verdicts can take care of their families once they are gone, and this was a very depressive atmosphere even though factually they had won.

It was a very strange contradiction, and one that made a deep impression on me, so even though the court case was won in the first instance, it still felt like a great loss. Now one of the people that where there, who is also an Italian journalist, and she is called Silvana Mossano wrote an open letter to Schmidheiny only last Friday, and she suggested a means of remedy, a sort of restorative justice.

It's a fairly long letter and I will read some parts out of it to give you only the main gist, and then I'll ask Silvana if she gives me permission, even though it's an open letter I'll still ask permission, to share the actual document with you. But I trust that she won't mind that I share a few of her words so and she starts:

> "Herr Stephan Schmidheiny, guten Tag. Herr Stephan Schmidheiny, good morning. I am using what little knowledge I retain from my schooldays and address you in your mother tongue because words are, or can be, a first approach, expression of being willing to

meet. I believe in the power of words as a powerful tool for dialogue. I am writing you this open letter, Herr Schmidheiny, because I hope we can start a dialogue. Indeed, to offer *you* the opportunity for dialogue."

And then I'll skip a considerable bit and go on:

"Fifteen years have passed since the beginning of the Eternit 1 maxi-trial, for wilful disaster, which saw Herr Schmidheiny as the defendant, and which ended with a long sentence, confirmed on appeal, and then swept away by the Court of Cassation on a technicality (the statute of limitations). Then another trail was held for the murder of hundreds of people, this one known as Eternit Bis, in June of 2023, ended with a guilty verdict. Now there will be an appeal, then another Cassation. In the meantime, however, other victims have been added to that long list. This means there could be an Eternit ter, and quater. In the meantime, others fall ill, and suffer, and die, and all of us, really all of us, you know, live with the fear when affected by an insidious cough or a trivial backache or a sneaky exhaustion."

But I'll just stop here and tell you that one of the expert witnesses in this last court case in June last year, a doctor, testified that every day in the town of Navara somebody is diagnosed with mesothelioma, and somebody is buried because of mesothelioma, and I'll remind you again for every mesothelioma victim that are six to eight asbestos lung cancers. And that's not even mentioning all the other cancers, so this is to this day the impacts and I'll continue with her letter:

"And, in the end, who wins? I am horrified of the question. Because the only answer – for me, for my people, for people all over the world who suffer from mesothelioma, but also for you, yes, for you too – is this: you will only win if you are healthy"

And then, she goes further into the disease. I´ll skip a bit and she says:

"We must find a way. And, so far, we have not found it. Even though many – scientists, researchers, doctors – have tried and continue tirelessly to try, by trial and error, by intuition. Everyone does a small, precious, and conscientious part, hoping that one day, the little pieces will fit together. But days go by, and other people develop the disease, suffer, die. Do you know what that means, Herr Schmidheiny? That, while they are engaged in a wonderful project of life, of work, of love for their family and friends, of travel, of discoveries, of breathtaking sunrises and sunsets, of snow-capped cloisters and amazing swells they get bludgeoned to death. A sharp blow."

I'll skip a bit again, forgive me, just for the sake of time, and she ask Schmidheiny:

"Can you bear this burden until the end of your days? Better still, can you bear to pass this burden on to your heirs? Yet there is an alternative. It is called restorative justice. This is my personal appeal. Hear me out, please. There has always been the possibility of coming out of one's defensive stronghold and proposing – with humility, intelligence, and courage – a restorative solution. It was not necessary to enshrine it in law. Now, in addition, this possibility is formally introduced as an organic discipline: it provides for the parties – in this case, your interlocutors are those representing the victim community – to meet and, with the help of a mediator, try and pursue a substantive and therapeutic peace."

And then again she goes on:

"We have all seen, in the case of covid, that by investing and concentrating more resources in research, the result arrived promptly. Lives were saved, Mr Schmidheiny? Thousands of lives, of all ages: yours, mine, those of our children and grandchildren. Why not also try this scourge that is mesothelioma? People do not die of mesothelioma just in Casale Monferrato, but all over the world. You are certainly not responsible for all the asbestos deaths in the world, but you can be responsible for their survival and recovery. You will object: 'But what do I gain by accepting this challenge if, in any case, the trials against me continue?' What do you gain for yourself, Mr Schmidheiny? You gain your conscience, your name and that of your descendants, your image that you care about, you gain in dignity. I am convinced that in late life, when our physical strength wanes, the ability to probe

> one's consciousness more broadly and more deeply increases, you redefine priorities. A commitment of honor, Herr Schmidheiny: make a commitment of honor with a wounded community that wants to heal. Now is the time: promote research (through a pharmaceutical company) and ethical management until the shared goal is achieved: finding the right 'medicine'. You, as an entrepreneur, lead this activity."

I'll skip a little bit and she says:

> "It takes courage to take up the challenge. Now, not later. Lead the way, and others around the world and in other areas will follow. One day you may be remembered for this. I renew my appeal to you on 'Asbestos Victims' Day' because then your voice will reach you louder. My voice along with other voices will travel to every corner of the earth. Even if I were left alone, I will continue to insist, not naive, but tenacious and confident, leaving no stone unturned. Think about it now, do it now. Auf wiedersehen, Herr Schmidheiny. Goodbye. Silvana Mossano".

Silvana is asking Schmidheiny to invest thoroughly in finding a cure for asbestos cancer and, bear in mind, Schmidheiny is a multi-billionaire, I imagine that it would be peanuts to him, but he so far over the decades has refused to do so. He has accepted accolades, honorable accolades and doctorships from universities and the like, but he has never invested a single penny a single euro cent finding a cure. And now Silvana Mossano last Friday asked him; would you please consider doing this and guiding this with all your money and spending some of it in helping us to find a cure, because the only wealth you have is your health?

I would like to invite you, and also the panel to speak your mind and consider this. How do you feel about this? Do you think that he would accept, do you perhaps think that this could be something that a public prosecutor could offer as a means of restorative justice, rather than going to jail, for instance or as a plea bargain?

Anything you like to say on this topic, I'm very curious to hear.

L'ESPOSIZIONE PROFESSIONALE (E NON) AD AMIANTO NELLE NUOVE REGOLE DELLA DIRETTIVA (UE) 2023/2668

Stefania Buoso

1. Premessa

Nel contesto della transizione verde, le ristrutturazioni per l'adeguamento degli edifici ad impatto climatico zero presentano criticità e lati oscuri dovuti alla ri-espansione del rischio da amianto di cui, come noto, è fatto divieto di produzione e utilizzazione nell'Unione europea. Anche la modernizzazione ecologica presenta, invero, conseguenze negative che la direttiva Ue 2023/2668 mira ad affrontare in chiave preventiva e di aggiornamento delle regole sull'esposizione ad asbesto in punto di valori limite, adempimenti preliminari alle attività, adozione delle misure prevenzionistiche appropriate. In quanto sostanza cancerogena priva di soglia, l'intervento regolativo si basa sulla definizione «di un rapporto esposizione/rischio» che consenta di «stabilire un valore limite di esposizione professionale tenendo conto di un livello accettabile di eccesso di rischio» (cfr. considerando 7); la migliore protezione dei lavoratori passa, difatti, dall'abbassamento del livello di esposizione: risultano allora significativi sia l'ammontare dei valori limite sia la metodologia di misurazione.

Nella direttiva recente il rischio professionale è affrontato con una prospettiva più ampia, in accordo alle questioni relative all'esposizione secondaria (in particolare di genere) e passiva.

Rileva, quindi, l'analisi sintetica dell'apparato degli strumenti di tutela anticipatoria e degli obblighi datoriali volto a garantire «un livello coerente di protezione contro i rischi connessi con l'esposizione professionale all'amianto» (cfr. considerando 1).

La direttiva (Ue) 2023/2668 modifica la direttiva 2009/148/CE sulla protezione dei lavoratori contro i rischi connessi con un'esposizione all'amianto durante il lavoro e si colloca nell'ambito delle iniziative promosse dal Quadro strategico dell'UE in materia di salute e sicurezza sul luogo di lavoro 2021-2027, volte a dare attuazione al Green Deal europeo e alla strategia dell'Ue in materia di sostanze chimiche sostenibili, nell'ottica di favorire sia la transizione verde che di rafforzare la prevenzione delle malattie professionali. Sulla stessa linea si colloca, anche, la recentissima direttiva Ue 2024/869 di revisione dei valori limite per piombo e composti inorganici e dissociati che modifica le direttive 98/24/CE sugli agenti chimici e 2004/37/CE sugli agenti cancerogeni, mutageni e reprotossici.

2. Tratti innovativi sul piano della classificazione dell'esposizione

Nel domandarsi quali siano i caratteri innovativi della direttiva (UE) 2023/2668 occorre distinguere tra la parte dei *considerando* iniziali e quella relativa al corpo regolativo in senso stretto.

Tra i considerando la direttiva conferisce uno specifico spazio definitorio alle due categorie di esposizione che, di fatto, attestano il carattere ubiquitario del rischio da amianto: l'esposizione passiva riguarda «i lavoratori che operano vicino a una persona che lavora con materiali contenenti amianto o in locali in cui si sta verificando il deterioramento di materiali contenenti amianto». D'altro canto, l'esposizione secondaria riguarda le persone che, di fatto, coabitano con lavoratori esposti professionalmente (letteralmente «le persone (...) esposte alle fibre di amianto che i lavoratori esposti professionalmente portano a casa soprattutto attraverso i loro indumenti e i loro capelli»): questi ultimi si trovano, difatti, a reiterare fuori dal luogo di lavoro la presenza di amianto attraverso i capelli o gli indumenti (si veda, in particolare, il considerando 5).

Ebbene, la direttiva più recente distingue e definisce, per la prima volta in modo esplicito, esposizione professionale e non professionale, anche descrivendo i caratteri tipologici delle sotto-categorie della esposizione passiva e di quella secondaria. La più blanda partizione tra esposizione diretta e indiretta ad asbesto si arricchisce, in altre parole, di una più precisa rappresentazione definitoria.

È bene rilevare che non si trova traccia letterale nel *corpus* della direttiva di detti riferimenti ovvero di misure espressamente deputate a incidere sulle «nuove» partizioni tipologiche di esposizione; si può, tuttavia, sostenere che il rafforzamento delle misure preventive e protettive attinenti all'esposizione professionale sia idoneo a concorrere a incidere sulla eliminazione e riduzione, anche, dell'esposizione passiva e secondaria. Quest'ultima, in particolare, pur essendo un'esposizione ambientale e non professionale troverebbe il suo fondamento causale nella prossimità ad un soggetto esposto professionalmente. Dunque, un punto interessante e inedito sul piano definitorio, sebbene in definitiva da ricondurre causalmente all'esposizione professionale.

Al *considerando* 5 viene, altresì, precisato – con riguardo all'esposizione passiva ad amianto – che la lettura coordinata della direttiva quadro 89/391/CEE e 2009/148/CE, già stabilivano l'obbligo per i datori di lavoro di valutare tutti i rischi riguardanti la salute e la sicurezza e individuare anche quelli potenziali derivanti dall'esposizione passiva, mettendo in atto misure preventive e protettive.

Invece, l'esposizione secondaria ad amianto o ai materiali contenenti amianto è governata mediante gli strumenti di cui alla nuova direttiva Ue 2023/2668, per evitare tale esposizione. Le donne vengono dichiarate particolarmente a rischio, soprattutto con riguardo all'esposizione secondaria.

3. Le principali linee di intervento sul piano tecnico operativo

Accostandosi alle direttive del 2009 e del 2023 il lavoro d'analisi su integrazioni e sostituzioni di disposizioni tra la versione più datata e quella recente è impegnativo perché la numerazione degli articoli resta quella precedente e si tratta, pertanto, di ricavare – dalle modifiche intervenute in una sorta di taglia e cuci regolativo – i tratti salienti sul piano dell'orientamento finalistico e delle misure operative implementate. Si effettuerà, qui, una selezione dei contenuti più significativi e ritenuti più rilevanti.

Nella prospettiva del rafforzamento del programma prevenzionistico, l'art. 3 par. 2 della direttiva 2009/148/CE è modificato nel senso di «dare priorità alla rimozione dell'amianto o dei materiali contenenti amianto rispetto alle altre forme di manipolazione», in aggiunta alla confermata valutazione del rischio «in modo da stabilire la natura e il grado di esposizione dei lavoratori alla polvere proveniente dall'amianto o di materiali contenenti amianto». Si tratta, in altre parole, di un apprezzabile rafforzamento della prevenzione, prioritariamente a carattere primario.

Si porrà peculiare attenzione agli articoli oggetto di sostituzione integrale o di nuovo inserimento, per i risvolti sistematici della loro modifica: si tratta degli articoli 6, 8 e 15 rispettivamente riguardanti la riduzione al minimo «e in ogni caso al più basso valore tecnicamente possibile» dell'esposizione dei lavoratori alla polvere d'amianto, le nuove specifiche quantificazioni dei valori limite, l'attività da svolgere «prima dell'inizio dei lavori» per le imprese che intendono effettuare lavori di demolizione o rimozione dell'amianto. Sono da menzionare anche i nuovi articoli 21 e 22 bis relativi rispettivamente alla tenuta di registri da parte degli Stati membri dei casi di malattie asbesto correlate e alla nuova tempistica di valutazione dell'ulteriore abbassamento dei valori limite.

Gli articoli 6 e 8 sono strettamente connessi tra loro perché raccordano il piano teleologico con quello più strettamente tecnico-operativo e delle misure da porre in essere per il conseguimento della riduzione dell'esposizione al più basso valore tecnicamente possibile (così anche il considerando 20). Si tratta di un riferimento esplicito al principio della massima sicurezza tecnologicamente fattibile idoneo a orientare le condotte datoriali al contenimento dell'esposizione al di sotto dei valori limite stabiliti.

Ciò si verifica mediante una serie di condotte datoriali obbligatorie che trovano precisazione nel testo dell'art.6: la limitazione del numero dei lavoratori esposti al più basso possibile, nel concepimento dei processi lavorativi in modo da evitare di produrre polvere di amianto o, comunque, nell'adozione di misure di eliminazione, l'aspirazione alla fonte, la sedimentazione delle fibre d'amianto sospese nell'aria; queste ultime tre misure volte ad evitare emissioni di polvere non erano in precedenza contemplate. Oltre a questo, il riferimento è, anche, alla sottoposizione dei lavoratori ad adeguata procedura di decontaminazione, negli ambienti chiusi della garanzia di un'adeguata protezione, nell'efficace pulizia dei locali e delle attrezzature per il trattamento dell'amianto, nel trasporto in imballaggi chiusi dei materiali idonei a rilasciare polvere di amianto, nel raccoglimento e nella rimozione dal luogo di lavoro dei residui.

A questo si aggiunge la riduzione da 0,1 a 0,01 di fibre d'amianto per cm cubo fino al 20 dicembre 2029 con la garanzia, da parte del datore di lavoro, del rispetto di almeno uno dei valori limite indicati al nuovo par. 2 dell'art. 8, in un tempo di esposizione di 8 ore; l'aggiornamento del valore limite prevede, in sostanza, una riduzione di 10 volte rispetto al precedente. Rilevante è, peraltro, anche la dimensione delle fibre: un punto sul quale incide il completamento della transizione tecnologica verso la microscopia elettrica; si legge, invero, al considerando 14 che «al fine di garantire un approccio equilibrato, sarebbe opportuno fissare valori limite diversi a seconda della dimensione della fibra presa in considerazione (...), segnatamente fibre di larghezza compresa tra 0,2 e 3 micrometri, nonché, una volta completata la transizione tecnologica verso la microscopia elettronica, fibre di larghezza inferiore a 0,2 micrometri». L'obiettivo è, in altre parole, quello di raggiungere risultati di misurazione delle fibre di minori dimensioni sempre più accurati.

Il nuovo articolo 15, poi, stabilisce che le imprese che intendono effettuare lavori di demolizione o rimozione dell'amianto devono ottenere, prima dell'inizio dei lavori, «un'autorizzazione dall'autorità competente anche fornendo «i certificati attestanti il completamento della formazione conformemente all'art. 14» e al nuovo allegato 1 bis. Quest'ultimo (elaborato integralmente *ex novo*), al punto 5, sottolinea il valore del processo di acquisizione di conoscenze e competenze per i lavoratori esposti di fatto o potenzialmente a polvere di amianto o materiali contenenti amianto in particolare mediante una formazione teorica e pratica incentrata, tra le altre cose, sulle proprietà e gli effetti sulla salute dell'amianto, sui tipi di prodotti o materiali che possono contenerne, sulle operazioni che possono comportare esposizione, sulle prassi di lavoro sicure, i controlli, i dispositivi di protezione e le loro funzioni e utilizzi, le procedure di emergenza e di decontaminazione oltreché la necessità di sorveglianza medica.

Tra le attività preliminari di nuovo conio si segnalano quelle attinenti la notifica all'autorità competente dell'inizio lavori per manutenzione, rimozione, smaltimento dell'amianto e trattamento dei rifiuti nonché bonifica delle aree interessate, la stessa deve contenere una descrizione sintetica di ubicazione del cantiere, del tipo e quantitativi di amianto utilizzati, dei procedimenti applicati, del numero di lavoratori interessati, della data d'inizio dei lavori e durata, delle misure adottate insieme al prospetto dei dispositivi di protezione utilizzati (cfr. art. 4 par. 3 co. 2). Si tratta di disposizioni da leggere congiuntamente a quelle del nuovo co. 1 dell'art. 11 sulla individuazione della presenza di amianto in locali costruiti prima dell'entrata in vigore del divieto negli Stati membri. Per i datori di lavoro è prevista l'obbligo di adozione di «ogni misura necessaria volta a individuare la presenza di materiali a potenziale contenuto di amianto», chiedendo «informazioni ai proprietari dei locali, ad altri datori di lavoro» o ottenendole da altre fonti quali «registri pertinenti»; in assenza di questo è previsto l'esame da parte di un operatore qualificato.

4. Considerazioni finali

La revisione della Direttiva amianto – che dovrà essere oggetto di recepimento negli ordinamenti nazionali entro il 21 dicembre 2025 – arricchisce e aggiorna, pertanto, l'apparato delle regole europee di armonizzazione relative all'esposizione occupazionale ad asbesto che è, ancora, in Europa responsabile del 78 % dei tumori di origine professionale (secondo i dati Eurostat).

L'adeguamento della disciplina alle più aggiornate e attuali conoscenze scientifiche pare, conclusivamente, uno dei tratti più significativi, da segnalare per i risvolti sul corretto compimento del processo di eliminazione e riduzione del rischio. L'ulteriore abbassamento dei valori limite – da considerare anche in rapporto alla metodica di misurazione microscopica delle fibre di asbesto – è ritenuto, nell'art. 22 bis, da valutare, nella sua fattibilità, da parte della Commissione europea entro il 31 dicembre 2028 sulla base della disponibilità di prove scientifiche, sviluppi tecnici oltreché del rapporto tra i nuovi metodi analitici e il valore numerico del valore limite.

Si tratta, dunque, di una disciplina di armonizzazione che aggiunge nuovi e importanti tasselli all'approccio della «salute in tutte le politiche» anche evidenziando la dimensione trasversale della protezione della salute dei lavoratori dall'esposizione all'amianto (così il considerando 4).

«MESOTELIOMA E RESPONSABILITÀ PER ESPOSIZIONE AD AMIANTO, TRA RESISTENZE GIURISPRUDENZIALI E LETTURE GARANTISTE»

Linda Pincelli

Dottoranda in Diritto penale, Dipartimento di Giurisprudenza di Ferrara

Tra le molteplici problematiche che si affacciano nei processi per malattie professionali causate dalla diffusione di polveri sottili di amianto, specie con riguardo ai mesoteliomi pleurici, persiste quella inerente alla verifica della correlazione tra la riferibilità causale delle morti da mesotelioma alle emissioni di polveri di asbesto che connotano la condotta espositiva, a fronte del succedersi di plurime posizioni di garanzia. Problematica che involge il più ampio tema dell'accertamento del nesso di causa.

Come noto, infatti, al tradizionale assunto della lunga latenza del mesotelioma si sommano le incertezze scientifiche attinenti all'esistenza di un «effetto acceleratore» derivante dalle plurime esposizioni, con conseguente difficoltà di perimetrazione delle parentesi temporali note, rispettivamente, come periodo di induzione e periodo di latenza clinica.

Il tema proposto alla riflessione può essere vagliato attraverso l'analisi dei passaggi salienti della pronuncia della Suprema Corte intervenuta nel noto caso *Fibronit* di Broni, la n. 34341 del 2020, la quale sintetizza i punti nevralgici dell'accertamento della responsabilità dei datori di lavoro per danni cagionati ai propri dipendenti, che abbiano, nello specifico, contratto un mesotelioma quale patologia asbesto-correlata.

In via preliminare, un breve *excursus* sui fatti oggetto della pronuncia. La vicenda di cui si tratta ha origine con il decesso per mesotelioma pleurico di alcuni lavoratori, dipendenti dello stabilimento Fibronit di Broni nel periodo in cui i due imputati, rispettivamente dal 1977 al 1981, l'uno, e dal 1985 al 1987, l'altro, ricoprivano una posizione di garanzia in relazione alle funzioni apicali esercitate.

Con riferimento a tali pregiudizi, venivano contestate agli imputati molteplici ipotesi di omicidio colposo *ex* art. 589, co. 2, c.p. con violazione di norme sulla prevenzione degli infortuni sul lavoro, in particolare per non aver adeguatamente informato i lavoratori circa i pericoli derivanti dall'esposizione all'asbesto, né fornito agli stessi adeguati DPI.

In primo grado, il Tribunale di Pavia aveva riconosciuto la penale responsabilità degli imputati per la quasi totalità delle imputazioni di omicidio colposo.

La Corte d'Appello di Milano aveva poi sostanzialmente confermato gli esiti a cui era pervenuto il giudice di prime cure, ad eccezione di un'ulteriore declaratoria di non doversi procedere per intervenuta prescrizione. Più nel dettaglio, il collegio giudicante adottava la decisione, con riguardo alla patogenesi del mesotelioma, sulla base dei criteri indicati dalla *III Consensus Conference on Malignant Mesothelioma of the Pleura* del 2015, da cui sarebbe possibile evincere, grazie a studi di coorte condotti su determinate popolazioni, l'esistenza di un effetto «acceleratore» a fronte di plurime esposizioni all'amianto, oltre che sui risultati della C.T. richiesta dal P.M., in ossequio alla quale, tenuto conto di un periodo di latenza clinica equivalente, in media, a 10 anni, tutte le esposizioni verificatesi in epoca anteriore al decennio precedente alla manifestazione clinica della malattia sarebbero state causalmente rilevanti.

Avverso la decisione dei giudici distrettuali, i difensori degli imputati proponevano ricorso per Cassazione, lamentando, per quel che qui interessa, due principali ordini di vizi: in primo luogo, l'erroneo percorso argomentativo della Corte volto ad individuare, nell'ambito dell'accertamento della cd. causalità generale, la regola scientifica della durata pari a 10 anni della latenza clinica, sulla quale sussisterebbe, al contrario, incertezza scientifica; in secondo luogo, ulteriore vizio di motivazione in punto di causalità individuale, avendo omesso di verificare, al protrarsi del periodo espositivo, l'effettiva rilevanza causale delle esposizioni all'asbesto riconducibili alle condotte degli imputati.

Il primo profilo di interesse della decisione della Suprema Corte, che funge da presupposto di partenza nell'ambito dell'apprezzamento della bontà delle argomentazioni logico-giuridiche sulla ricostruzione del nesso di causa, riguarda il raggiungimento di una posizione apparentemente definitiva quanto alla natura dose-correlata (o dose-dipendente) del mesotelioma: esisterebbero ormai attendibili e sufficienti studi epidemiologici in grado di testimoniare la relazione tra maggiore esposizione ed aumento del rischio di mesotelioma e, specularmente, tra maggiore esposizione e anticipazione del *dies a quo* di insorgenza della malattia.

L'inquadramento del mesotelioma nella categoria della dose cumulativa rappresenta senz'altro un punto di svolta, per quanto assuma rilevanza solo sul piano della causalità generale, potendosi dire ormai superata l'incertezza scientifica dinanzi alla quale, in passato, in taluni casi permaneva un «ragionevole dubbio» in merito all'efficacia eziologica delle diverse condotte espositive susseguitesi nel tempo, conducendo ad un esito assolutorio, mentre in altri, più discutibilmente, si applicava «analogicamente» la teoria multistadio della comune cancerogenesi polmonare, pur di giungere ad una sentenza di condanna (come avvenuto nell'ambito della notissima vicenda *Quaglierini*).

L'adesione alla teoria della dose-dipendenza, nonché del cd. effetto acceleratore, determina quindi l'individuazione, da parte della Corte, ai fini della selezione delle condotte espositive rilevanti per lo sviluppo della patologia, di due distinti segmenti temporali, rispettivamente la fase induttiva e progressiva, cui si è fatto menzione in apertura. Appartengono alla «induzione» tutte le esposizioni che hanno contribuito all'accelerazione dello sviluppo della malattia, mentre la «progressione», anche nota come periodo di latenza clinica, si caratterizza per l'irrilevanza degli ulteriori eventuali contatti, essendo la cancerogenesi divenuta irreversibile a partire dal cd. *failure time*.

Se i confini temporali anzidetti non rappresentano un elemento di novità, il secondo punto di forza della decisione in questione è senza dubbio costituito dalle argomentazioni in parte motiva sull'accertamento della causalità individuale, consistente nella verifica in concreto dell'effetto acceleratore esplicato dalle condotte espositive attribuite agli imputati, unitamente alla fissazione del *failure time*.

Per fare ciò, si pone come preminente l'obiettivo di selezione di una legge scientifica – «*o quantomeno una consolidata regola di esperienza*» – in grado di collocare temporalmente il *failure time*, vero e proprio punto di non ritorno dell'evoluzione del mesotelioma.

Il rigoroso rispetto dell'accertamento bifasico della causalità inaugurato con la celeberrima sentenza *Franzese* (Cass., Sez. Un., 11 settembre 2002, n. 30328) costringe, quindi, gli Ermellini a fare i conti altresì con gli insegnamenti della sentenza *Cozzini* per la selezione del sapere scientifico (Cass. pen., Sez. IV, 13 settembre 2010, n. 43786). Orbene, quella che dai giudici di merito viene trattata alla stregua di una legge scientifica di copertura, vale a dire l'assunto per cui il tempo medio stimato di 10 anni per la manifestazione del rischio associato all'esposizione consentirebbe di far retroagire di circa un decennio dall'avvenuto decesso il *failure time*, è attentamente vagliata dai giudici di legittimità alla luce dei canoni di validità e attendibilità, anche in considerazione del grado di condivisione nella comunità scientifica.

A tal proposito, si osserva come Tribunale e Corte d'Appello fossero giunti a tale approdo aderendo alle sole dichiarazioni rese dal consulente dell'accusa, che peraltro fissava il predetto principio compiendo un mero calcolo «a ritroso», nonostante, in alcuni passaggi precedenti delle rispettive sentenze, essi avessero esplicitamente dichiarato l'impossibilità, al momento, di identificare le precise dinamiche dell'innesco causale e del «*vero periodo di latenza*» (§7). La collocazione del *failure time* approssimativamente 10 anni prima della diagnosi risulterebbe allora del tutto apodittica, oltre a difettare un confronto rispetto alle teorie con essa contrastanti, quale quella che postula come plausibile una latenza convenzionale – *id est* il periodo intercorrente tra la prima esposizione e la diagnosi – della durata di 40 anni, solo la metà dei quali rientrerebbe nella fase induttiva.

Sicché, in applicazione delle coordinate ermeneutiche tracciate dalla giurisprudenza anteriore, la Corte prende atto che le attuali conoscenze scientifiche sul mesotelioma non consentono di determinare in modo certo la durata della latenza preclinica nel periodo stimato di 10 anni a ritroso dall'evidenza clinica/diagnosi, con conseguente impossibilità di individuare il momento a partire dal quale ogni esposizione alla sostanza cancerogena è irrilevante.

Oltremodo, rileva la Cassazione, i giudici di merito avrebbero dato per scontato che tutte le vittime avessero contratto il mesotelioma pleurico a causa delle polveri disperse nello (o dallo) stabilimento di Broni.

In definitiva, si denuncia un triplice errore nel percorso motivazionale seguito da Tribunale e Corte d'Appello: *in primis*, un cattivo governo del principio generale in tema di nesso causale per cui risulta indispensabile, ai fini dell'accertamento della valenza impeditiva della condotta doverosa rispetto all'evento *hic et nunc* verificatosi, escludere possibili decorsi causali alternativi; *in secundis*, una scorretta applicazione dei criteri enunciati nella sentenza *Cozzini* nella scelta del sapere scientifico utile a individuare la fase induttiva; *in tertiis,* l'omessa verifica del reale effetto acceleratore dispiegato da ciascuna delle condotte espositive contestate agli imputati, onde poterle effettivamente collocare, con univoca certezza, all'interno dell'ampio arco temporale dell'induzione delle singole cancerogenesi.

Indipendentemente dalla soluzione adottata nel caso di specie, l'interesse della pronuncia in commento risiede nel corretto recepimento di principi che da oltre vent'anni si rinvengono nelle pronunce della Quarta Sezione della Cassazione, ma che a lungo hanno faticato a radicarsi in tema di malattie amianto-correlate. Essa ben potrebbe essere adottata quale modello di argomentazione in materia di *toxic cases*, rappresentando il giusto punto di equilibrio tra rispetto dei principi del diritto penale e flessibilizzazione nell'accertamento di un istituto cardine quale il nesso di causa.

Così facendo, si dovrebbe scongiurare il rischio di evidenti difformità tra pronunce talvolta anche coeve, ponendo rimedio ad una situazione di incertezza del sistema ormai divenuta intollerabile.

CLAUSURA DEL CONGRESO

Víctor M. Macías Caro
Universidad Pablo de Olavide

Por mi parte, quiero hacer más una clausura que una que unas conclusiones, porque hay, como no podría ser de otro modo, opiniones distintas y contrastantes. Por ejemplo, está la cuestión de si el desastre del amianto es un ejemplo de macrocriminalidad, o es el resultado de una decisión política y social, en la que uno pone en una balanza lo que el doctor NATALI, que no nos acompaña, llama el flujo de placeres, es decir, el placer de hoy con los posibles riesgos de mañana; o es verdaderamente una forma de macrocriminalidad.

Otra de las cuestiones que creo que sí que ha quedado clara es que el estudio de este fenómeno, por utilizar un término neutral, tiene que hacerse de manera interdisciplinaria, no solo entre distintas ramas del derecho, sino también entre el derecho y la geología, las ciencias naturales, la medicina, la criminología... Pero también comparada. Esto es una cuestión global, y en este sentido hay muchísimas cuestiones, tanto médicas como sociológicas que no están claras. Porque como decía Juan Carlos, ¿por qué muchos de los expuestos no enferman? Eso es una cuestión que médicamente está todavía por resolver, porque es cierto que hay, aunque sean pocos, un 5 % o 10 % de personas que desarrollan un mesotelioma sin haber estado expuestos al menos no por su ocupación o por una exposición doméstica al amianto, sino por exposición ambiental.

Por otra parte, si el amianto es tan ubicuo como lo es, tampoco es descabellado pensar que haya otras muchas enfermedades de las cuales ahora no conocemos las causas que estén relacionadas con la exposición ambiental a ese amianto. ¿Cuáles son los factores que determinan en qué lugares y en qué momento se organizan los afectados las víctimas para reclamar respuestas? ¿Por qué en unos ordenamientos jurídicos se sustancian los mismos o muy parecidos casos en una jurisdicción o en otra. ¿Tiene que ver con el activismo político de los jueces, es el poder de las empresas que es mayor o menor en ordenamiento o en otro, o son factores coyunturales?

Otra cuestión de la que se ha hablado hace cinco minutos es, ¿es el derecho penal verdaderamente el mejor instrumento para dar una respuesta a los casos de amianto y en general a los casos de delincuencia empresarial tóxica? Unos opinan que no, porque si el resultado es una condena, esa condena está basada en el retorcimiento, la violación de los derechos y de los principios fundamentales, en muchos casos, del derecho penal. Y si no hay condena, hay una frustración de la expectativa de las víctimas. Sin embargo, hay otros que opinan, opinamos personalmente, que sí, porque retomando también una de las últimas preguntas que lanzaba a la doctora WATERMAN, ¿qué es la justicia? Es decir, ¿qué significa la justicia en este caso? En este caso, y en cualquiera, yo creo que la justicia es sobre todo verdad, compensación, y no repetición.

La verdad, que quede establecida en los hechos probados, en la sentencia. La compensación, por supuesto, del daño que se ha hecho, pero, yo creo que es muy importante la no repetición. Entonces, ¿tiene un efecto verdaderamente preventivo la justicia restaurativa en la economía, en la delincuencia empresarial o las empresas calculan el coste de esas multas como un coste de empresa y por lo tanto en el precio de sus productos y sus beneficios ya se ha descontado esa multa y, por lo tanto, no tiene ningún efecto preventivo para el futuro porque el futuro potencial delincuente empresarial pensará: «bueno, lo intento en el peor de los casos simplemente tengo menos beneficio, en el mejor de los casos tengo el beneficio completo».

Sin embargo, si la amenaza es de pena de prisión sí que se puede, al menos esa es la opinión mayoritaria, no estará de acuerdo conmigo Marilia, pero la opinión mayoritaria es que la amenaza de la pena de prisión si puede ayudar a la no repetición.

Otra opción son los fondos de compensación sin culpa, como el fondo francés, el fondo belga o el fondo español, que está realizándose. Pero también hemos visto que también tiene otros problemas: ofrecen menos dinero que los de una jurisdicción, a lo mejor incluso pueden suponer si se hace o si se ejecuta mal por parte de los órganos judiciales, puede suponer una paralización de esos procesos, o al menos, del de cómo se cuantifican los daños, porque se puede utilizar el baremo que utiliza ese fondo como el baremo que vayan a utilizar también los órganos jurisdiccionales. En fin, demasiados problemas, demasiadas cuestiones, quizás esta no deba ser la última vez que nos veamos para hablar de este tema. O al menos, no debe ser la última vez que hablemos porque debemos yo creo mantenernos en contacto, y seguir, como decía Marilia, pensando juntos.

Muchas gracias a todos y a todas por estar aquí hasta esta hora. Gracias a Pastora, gracias a Donato. Gracias a los ponentes que han venido aquí y han participado, no solo hablando sino también en el debate. Gracias a los estudiantes, al CIC. Nos ha ayudado la Facultad, el Vicerrectorado, la Universidad de Brescia, la Universidad Milano-Bicocca, el centro Macrocrimes.

Y nos vemos, si todo sale bien, el año que viene en el tercer congreso sobre macrocriminalidad. Queda clausurado el segundo Congreso.

Cód. 05-03

Made in the USA
Monee, IL
17 July 2026

57533417R00116